IF TODAY
WERE
TOMORROW

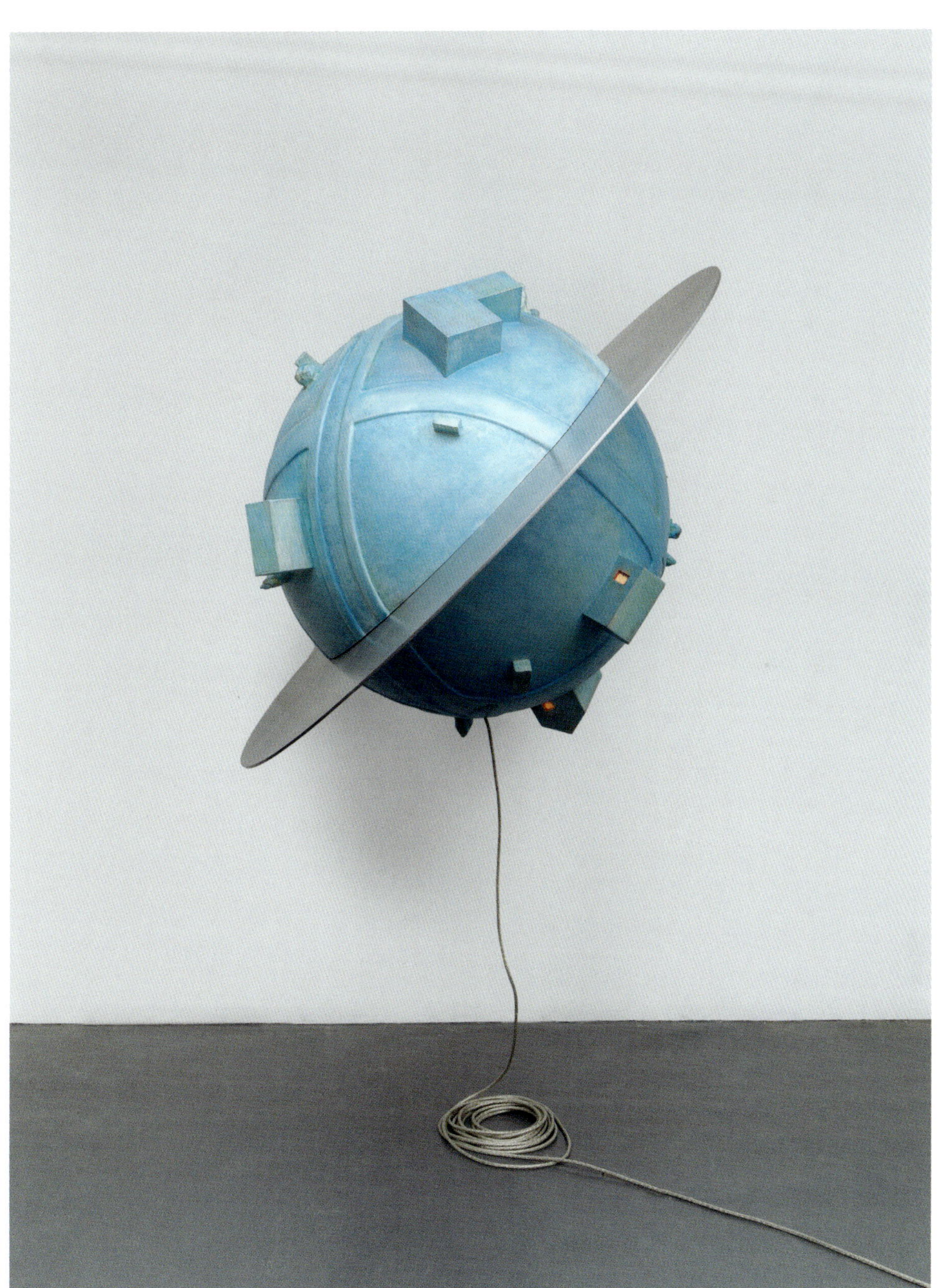

OLIVIA ERLANGER

IF TODAY WERE TOMORROW

EDITOR

PATRICIA RESTREPO

CONTRIBUTORS

LYDIA KALLIPOLITI
CHRIS KRAUS
MARK VON SCHLEGELL

HATJE
CANTZ

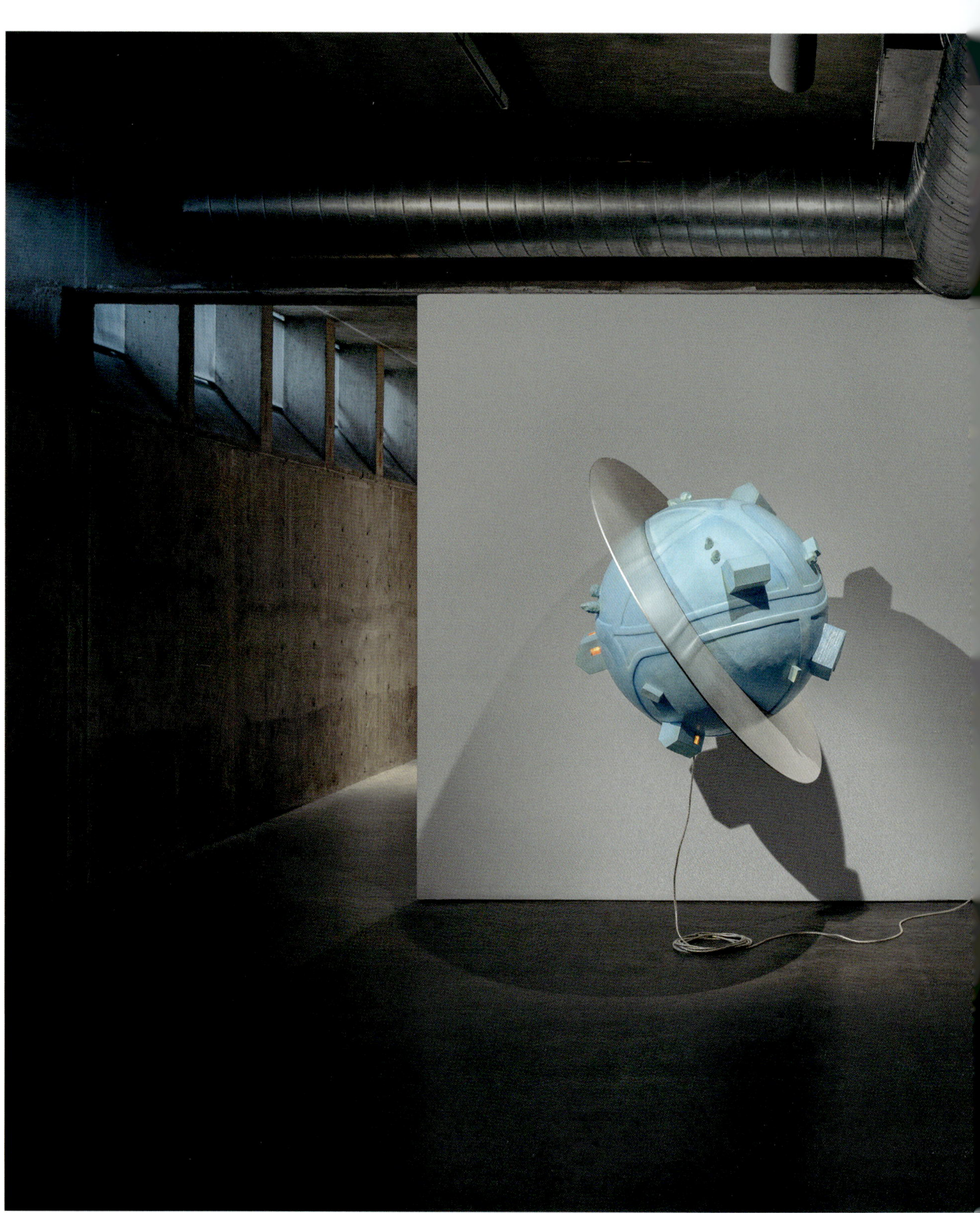

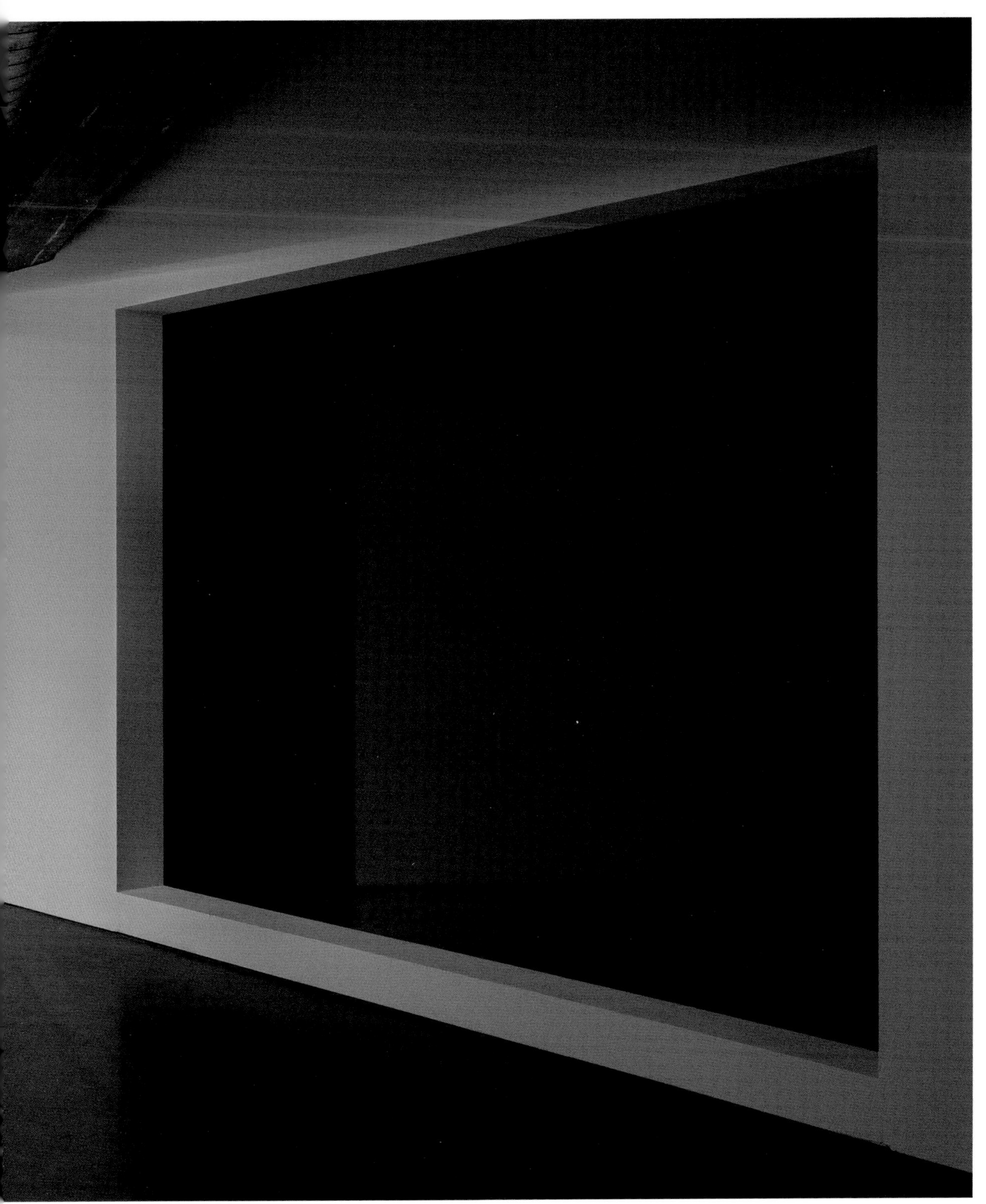

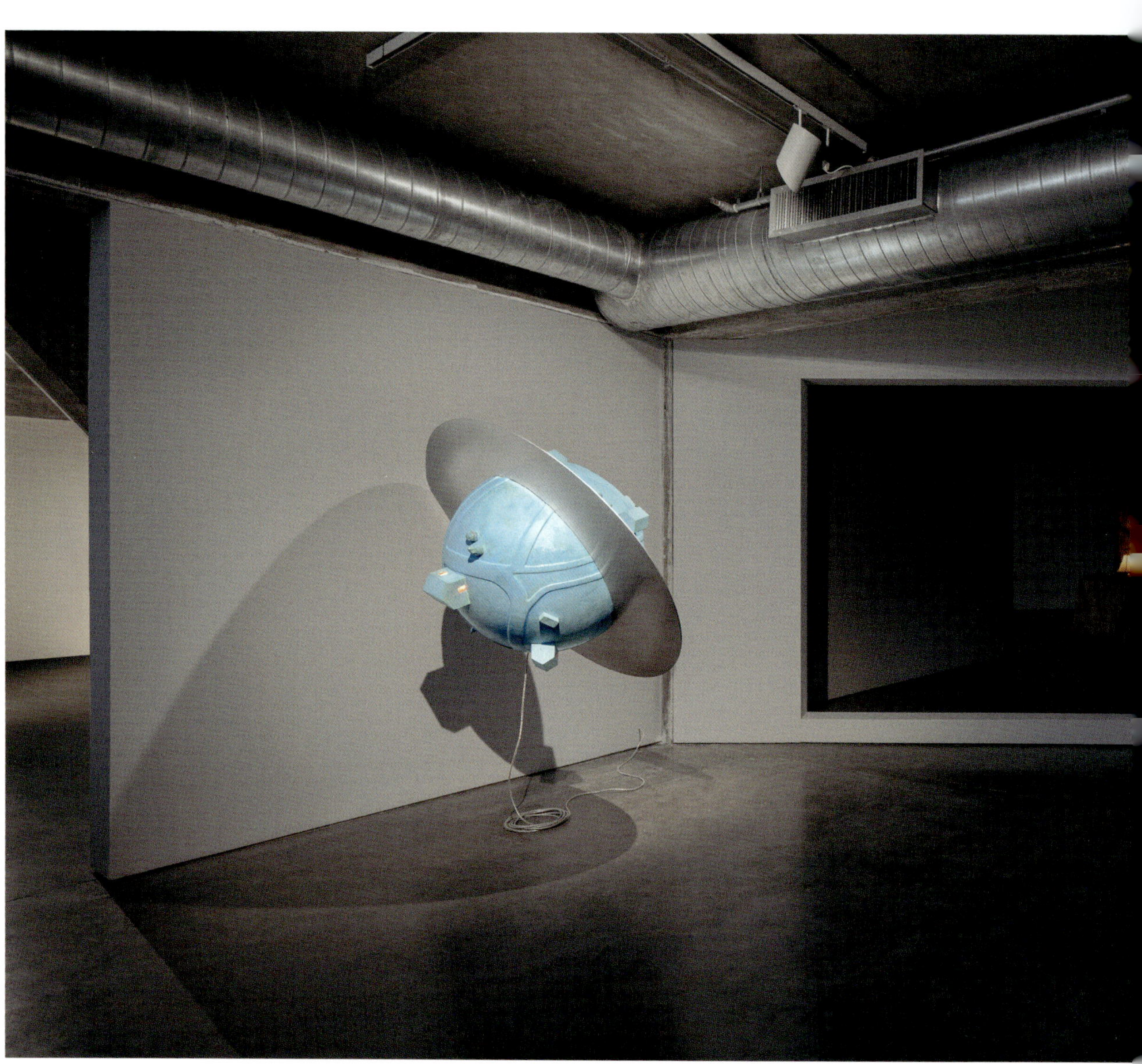

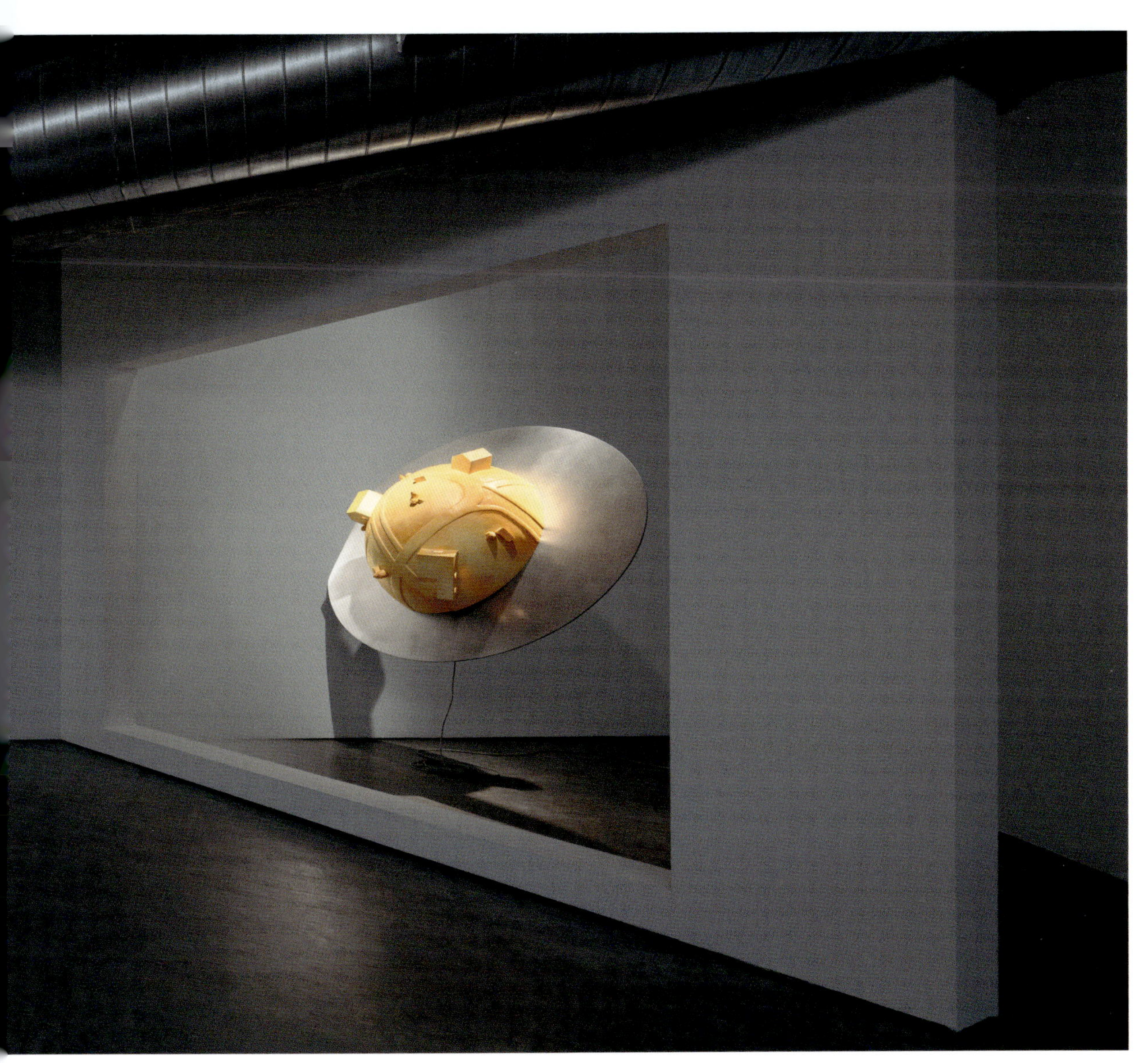

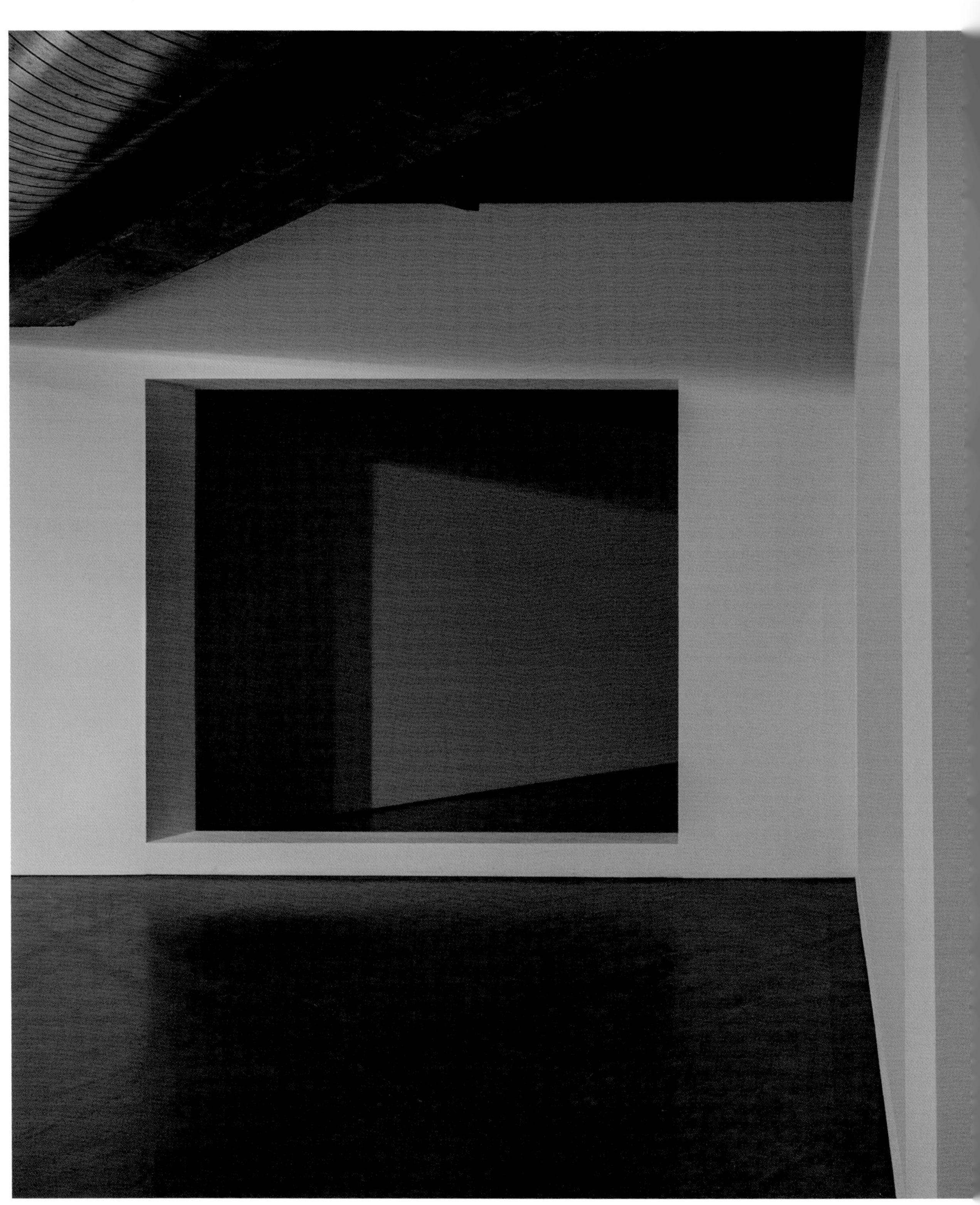

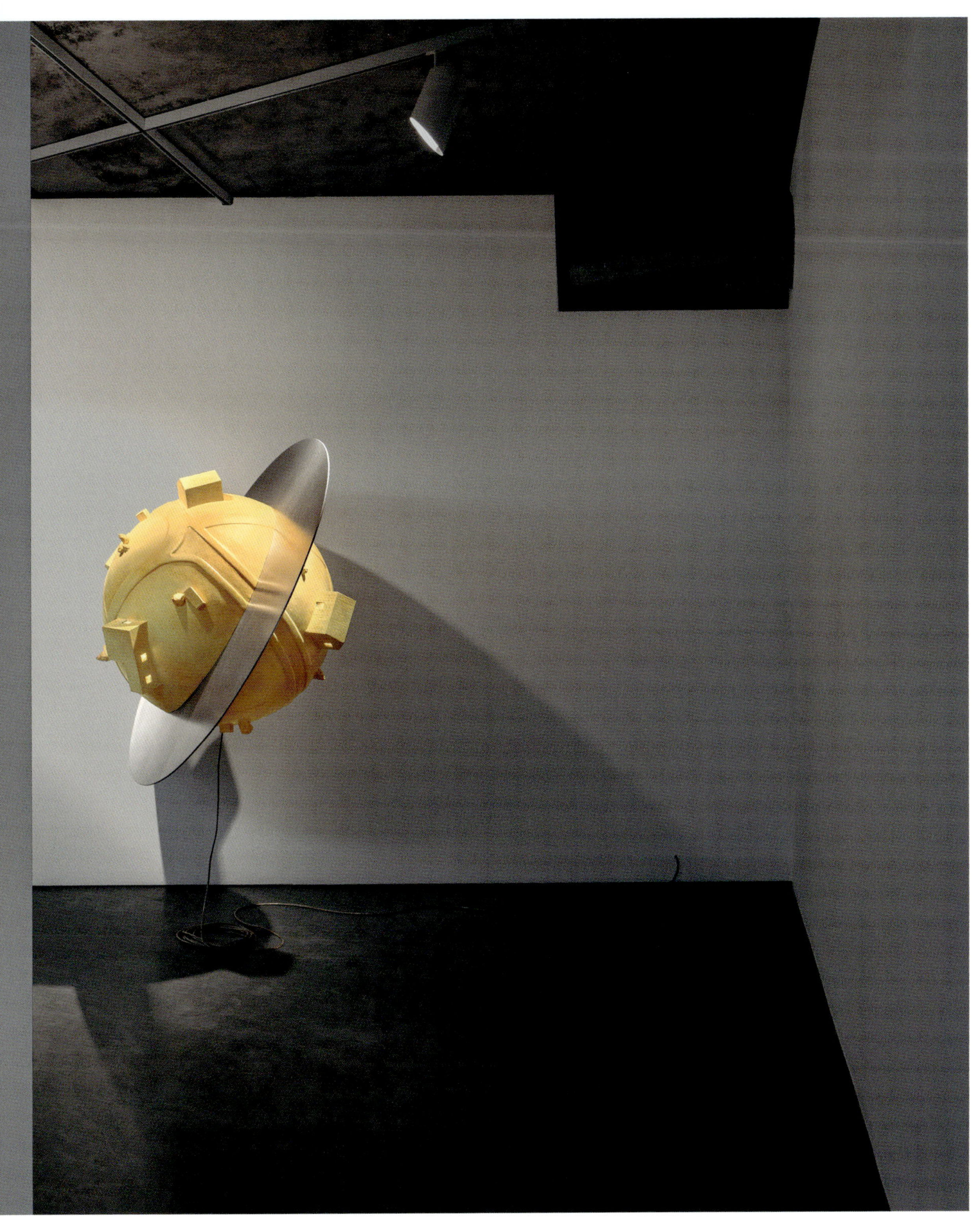

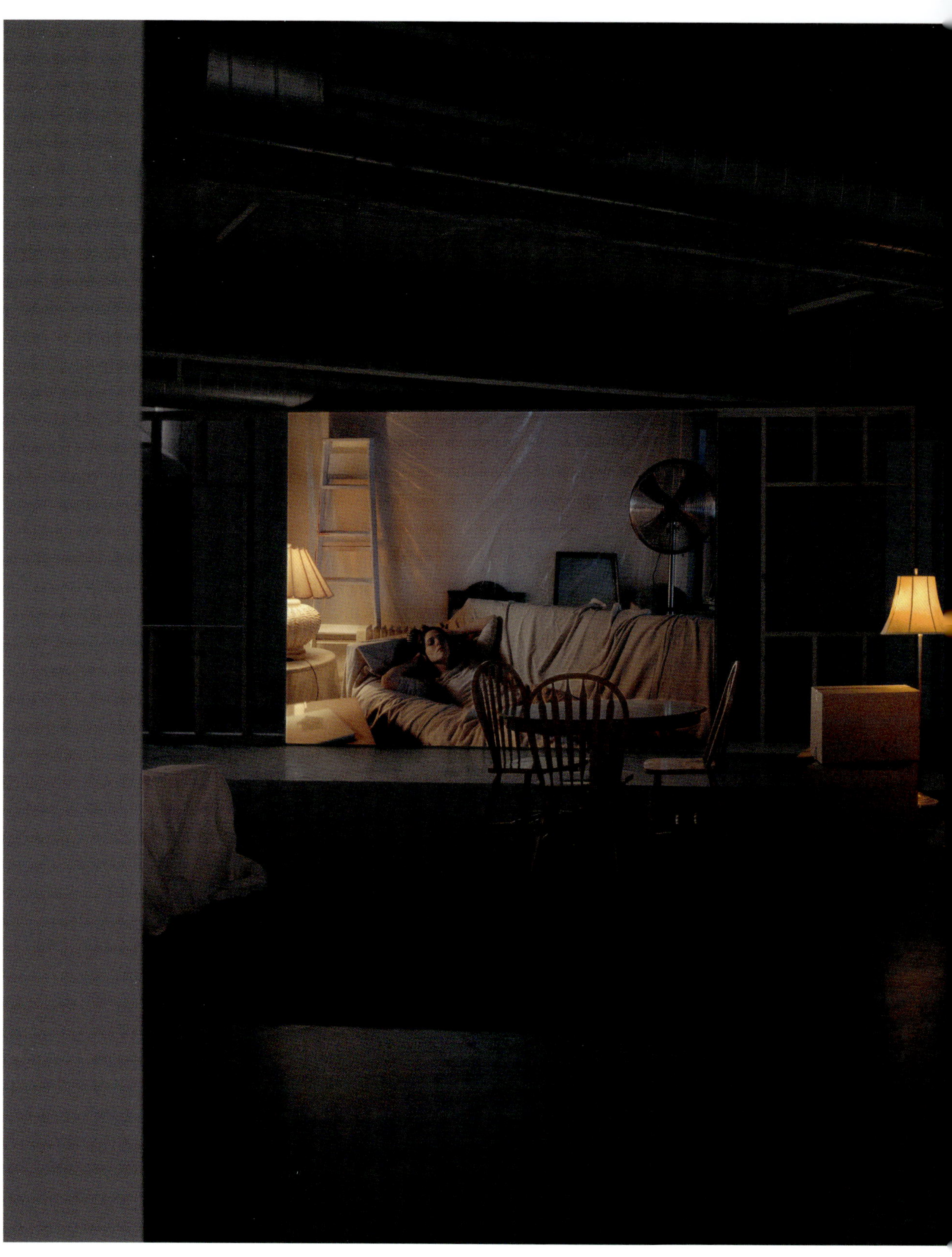

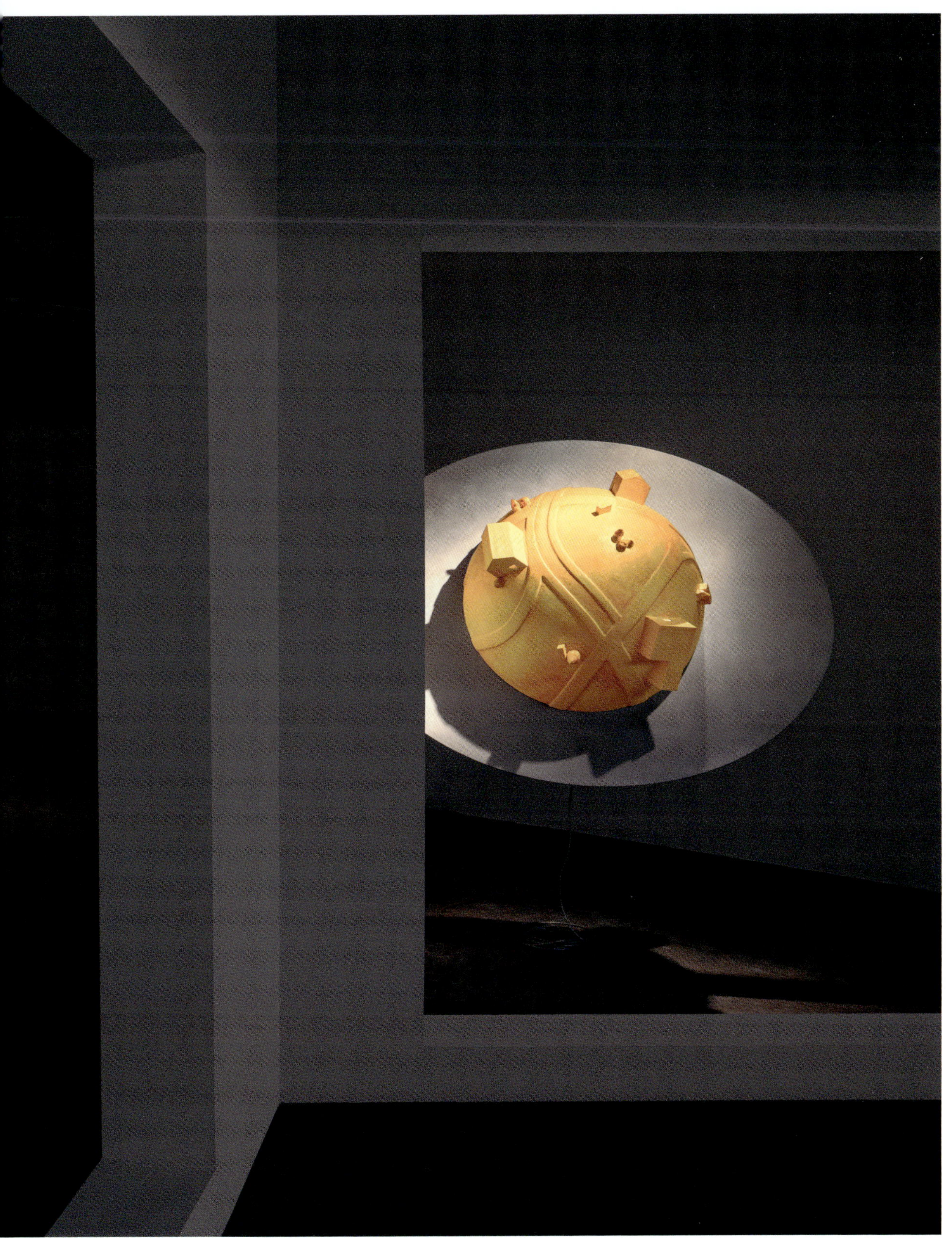

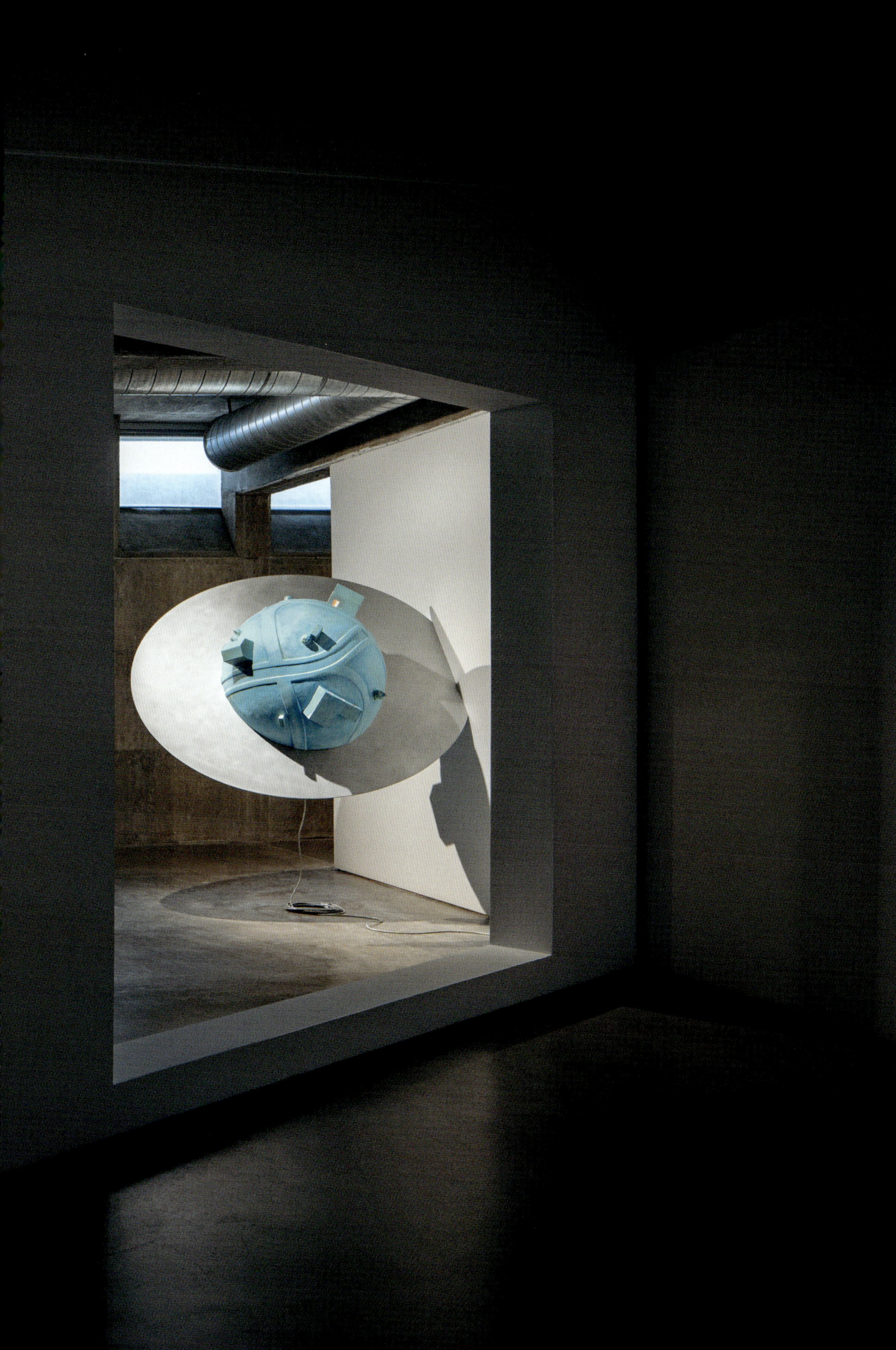

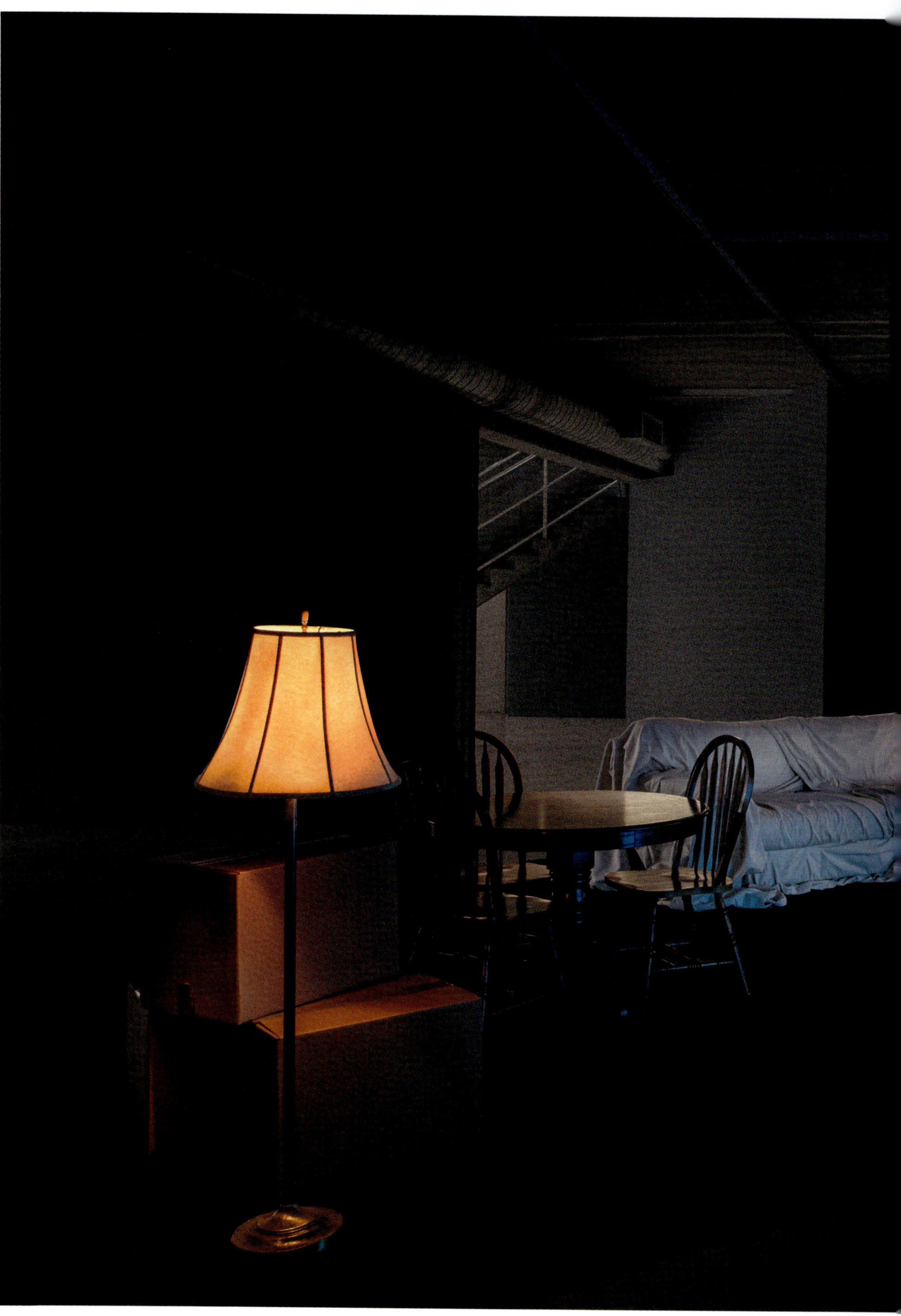

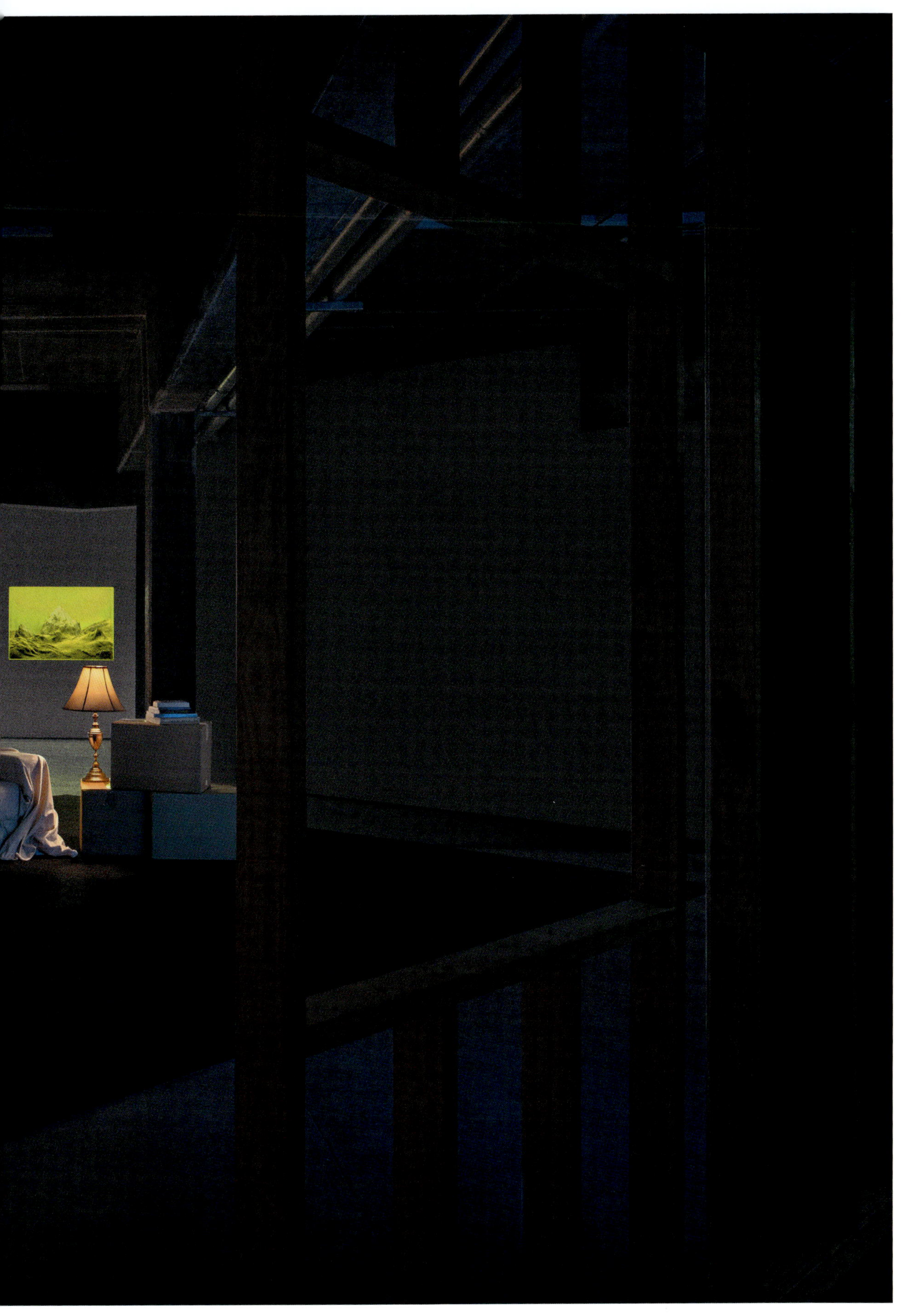

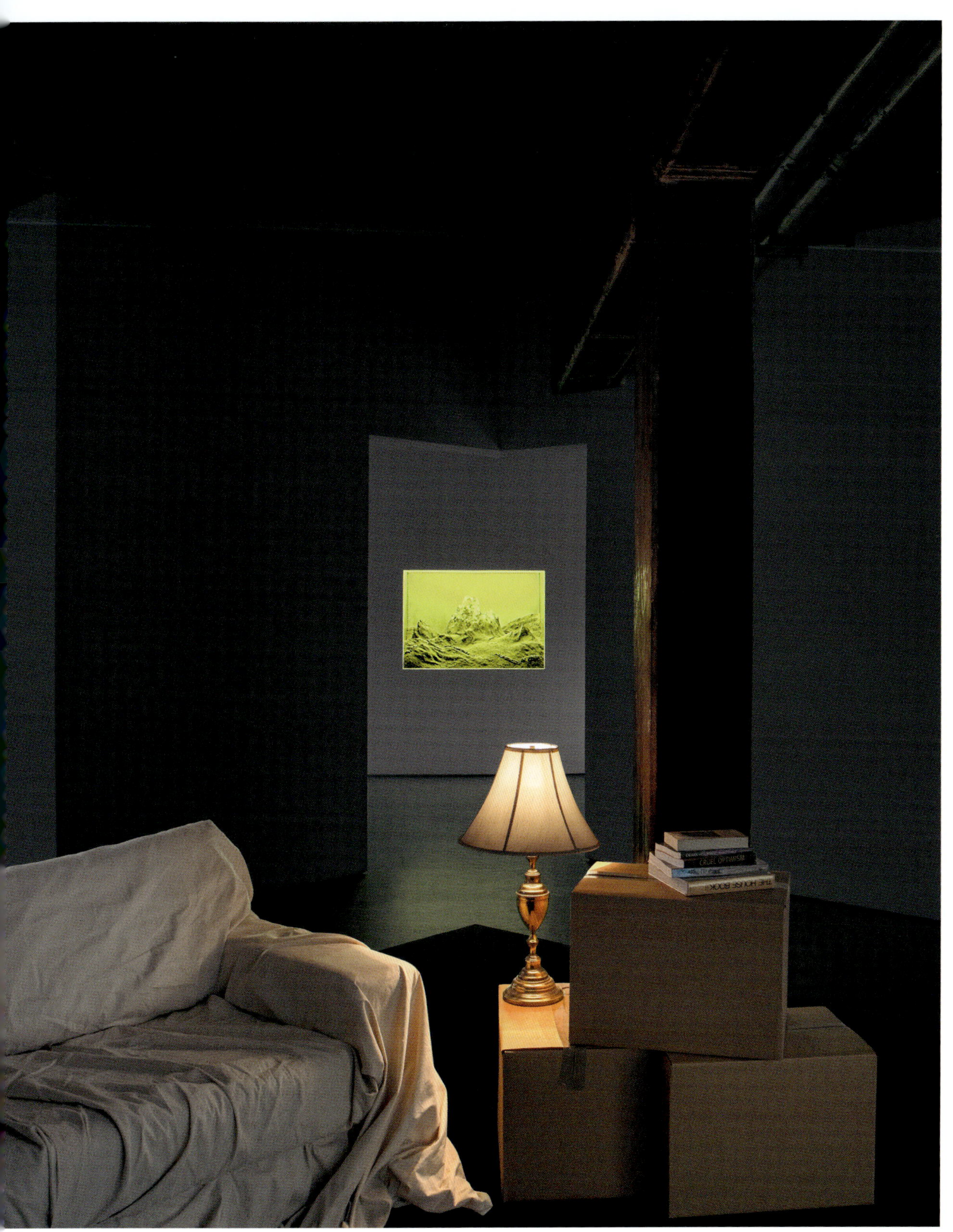

CRUEL OPTIMISM
THE HOUSE BOOK

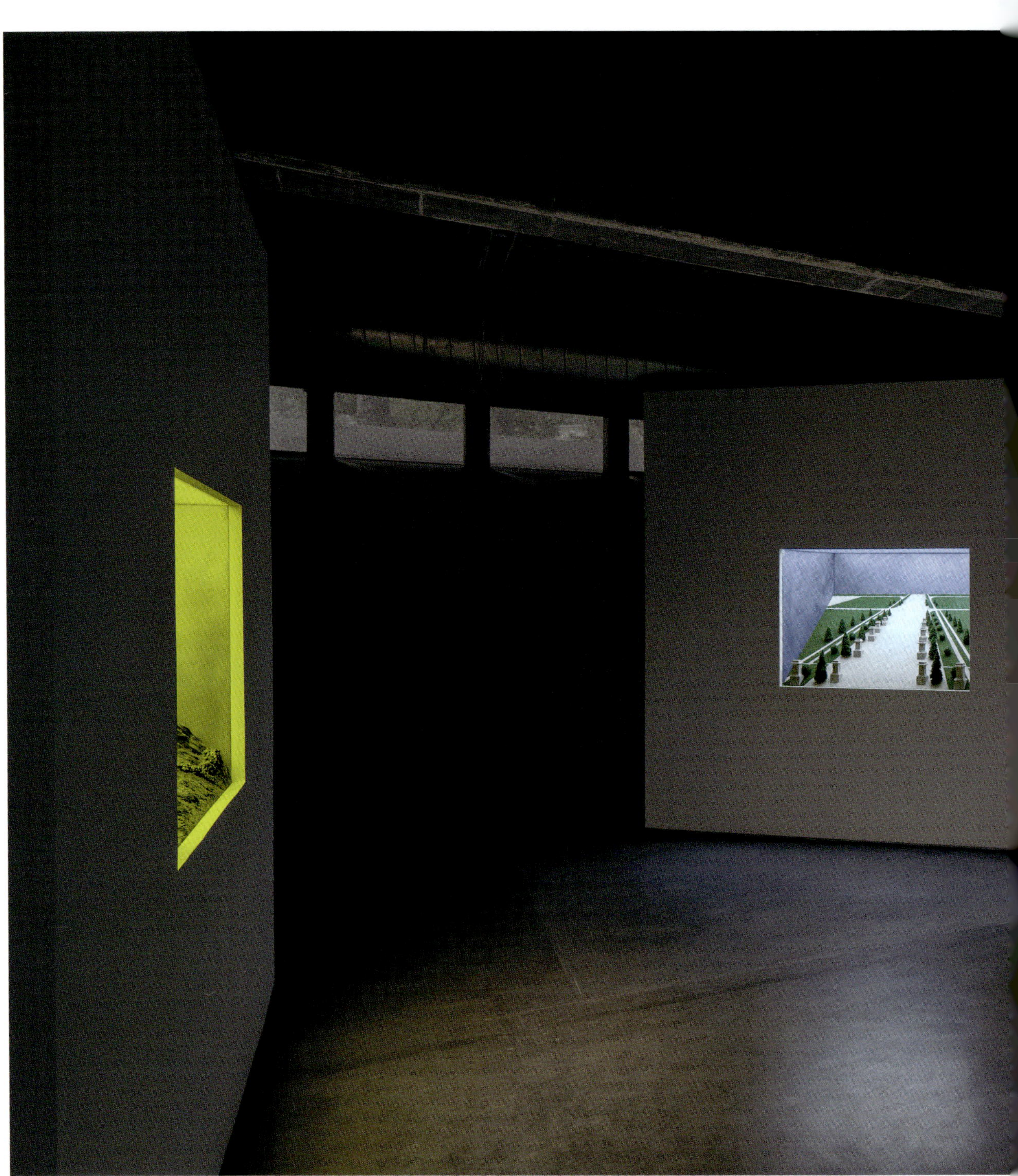

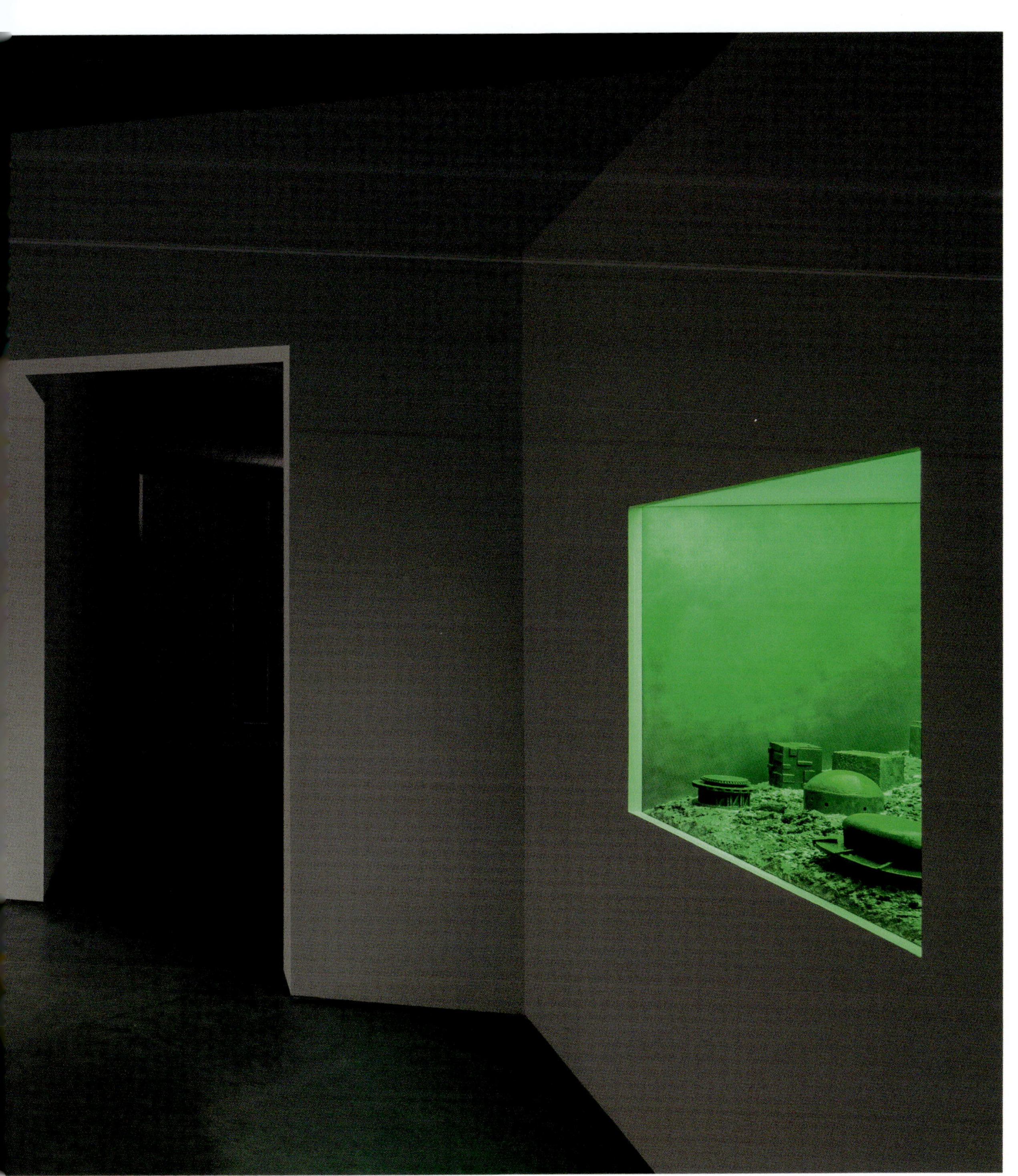

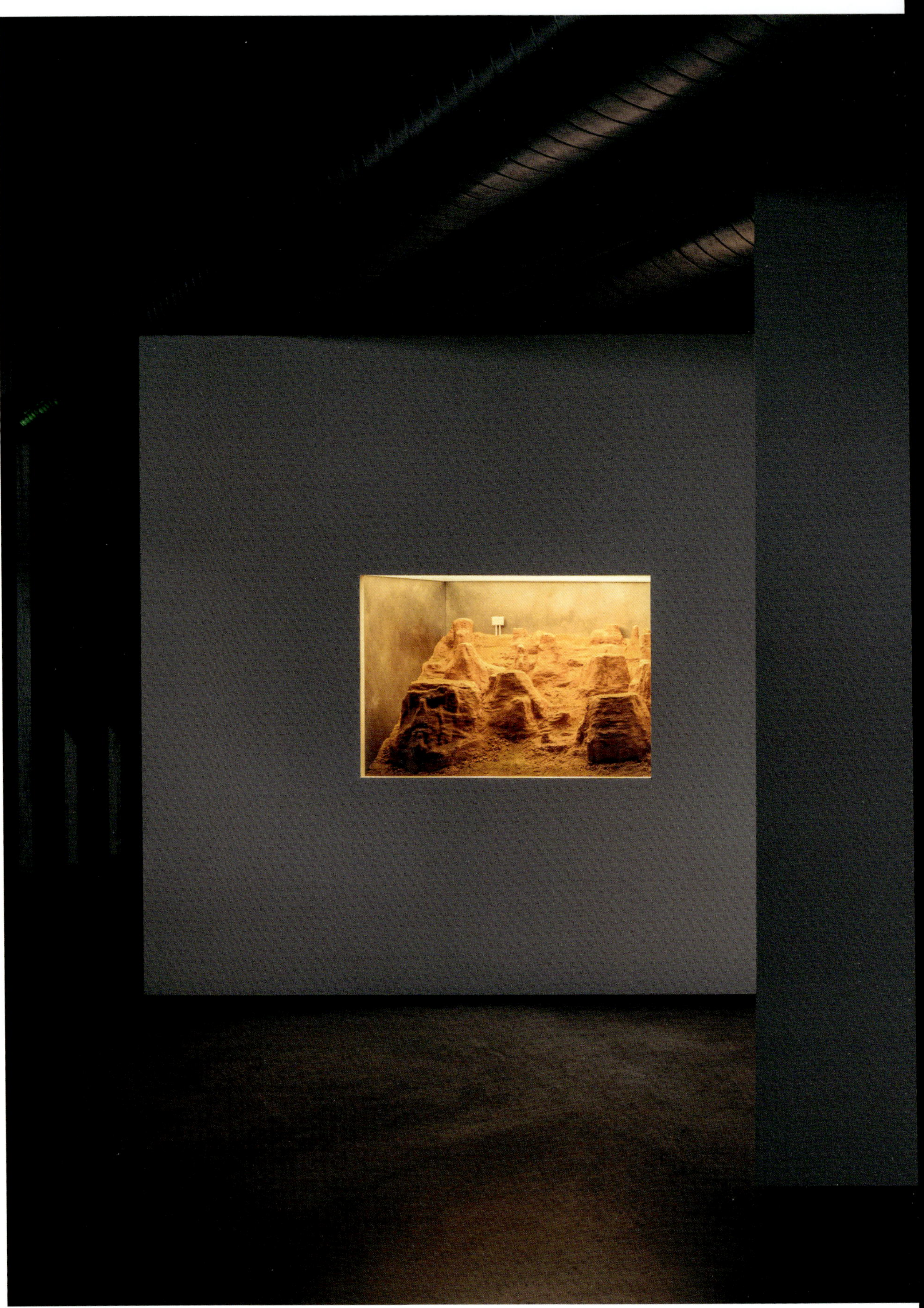

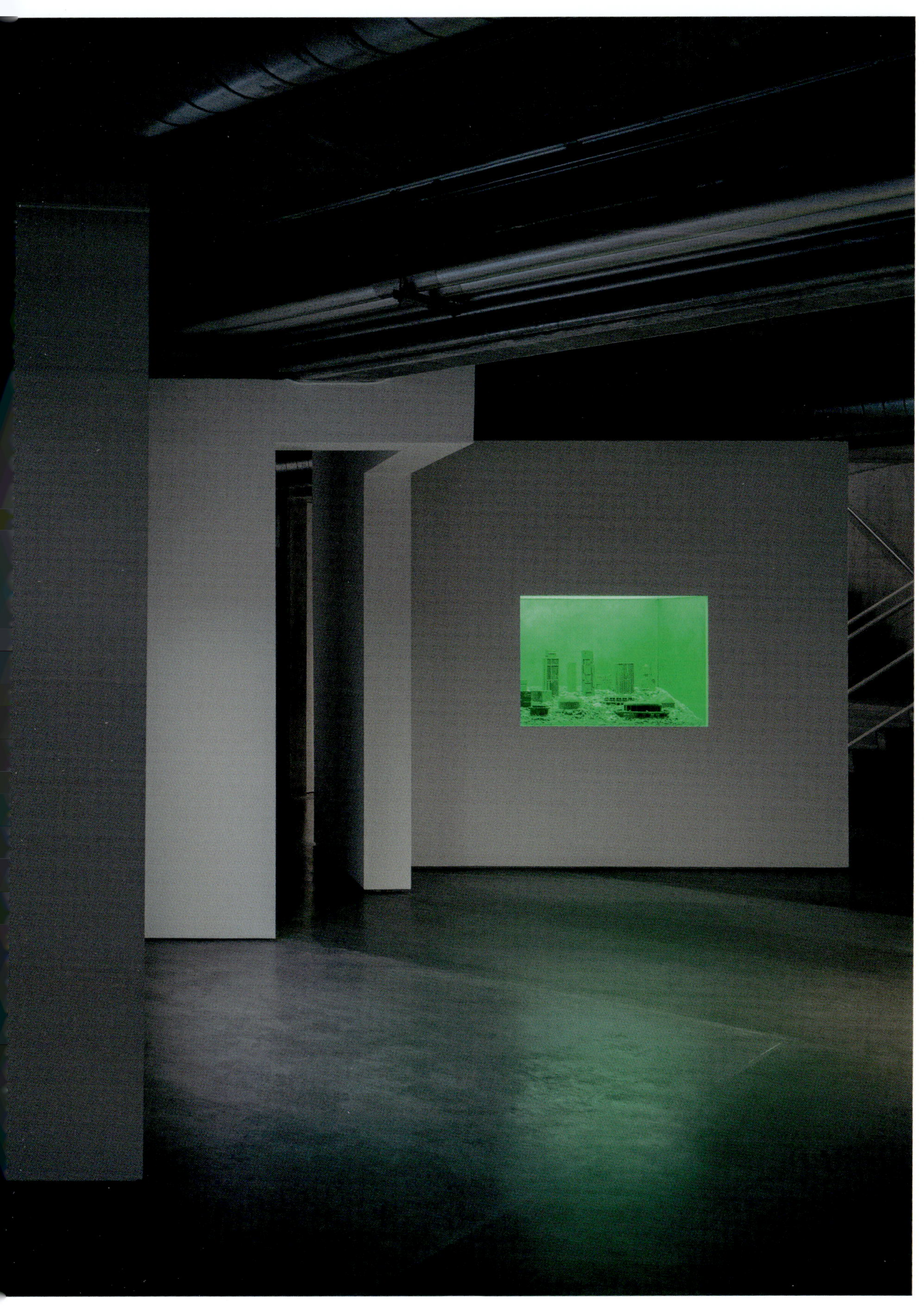

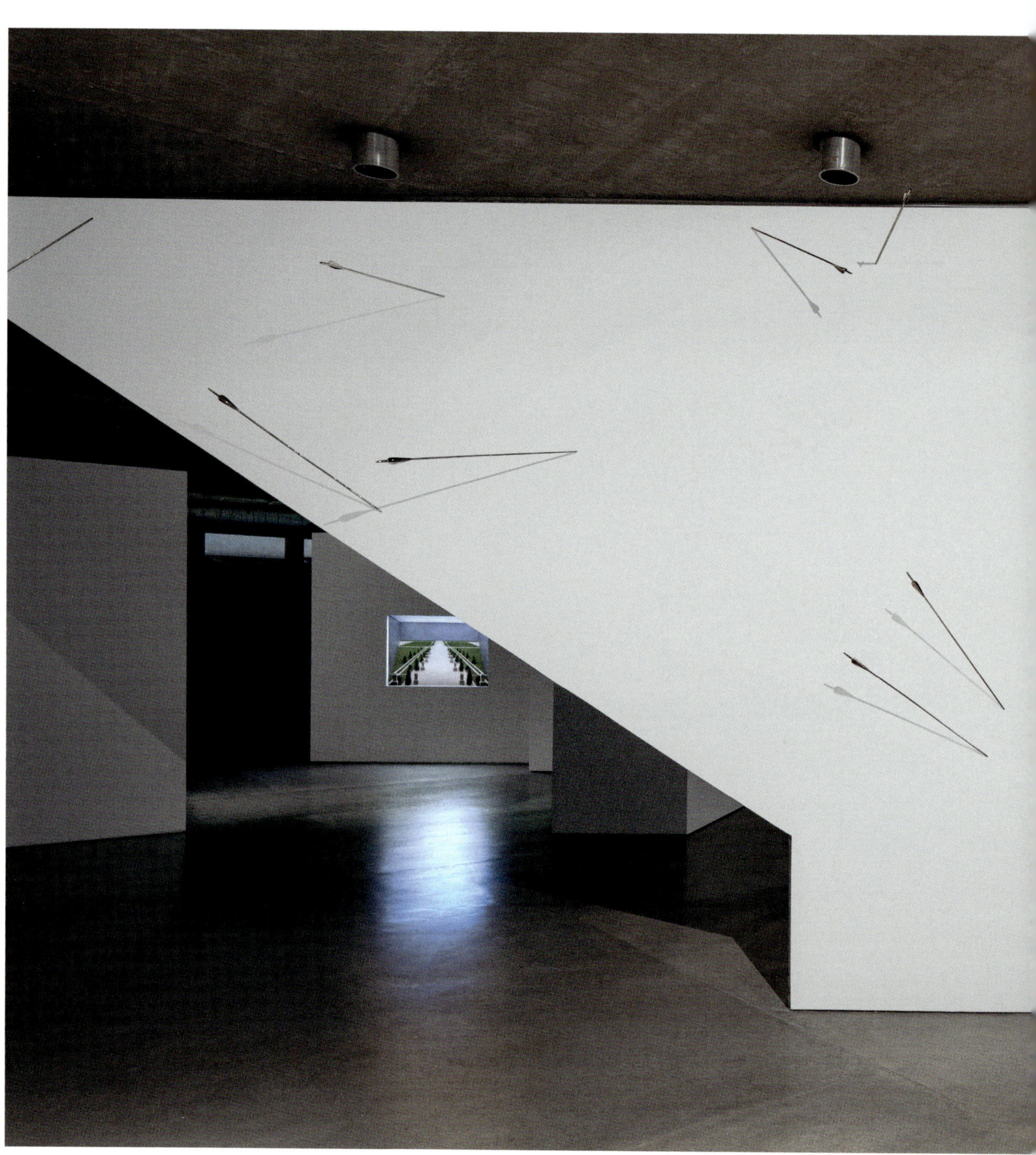

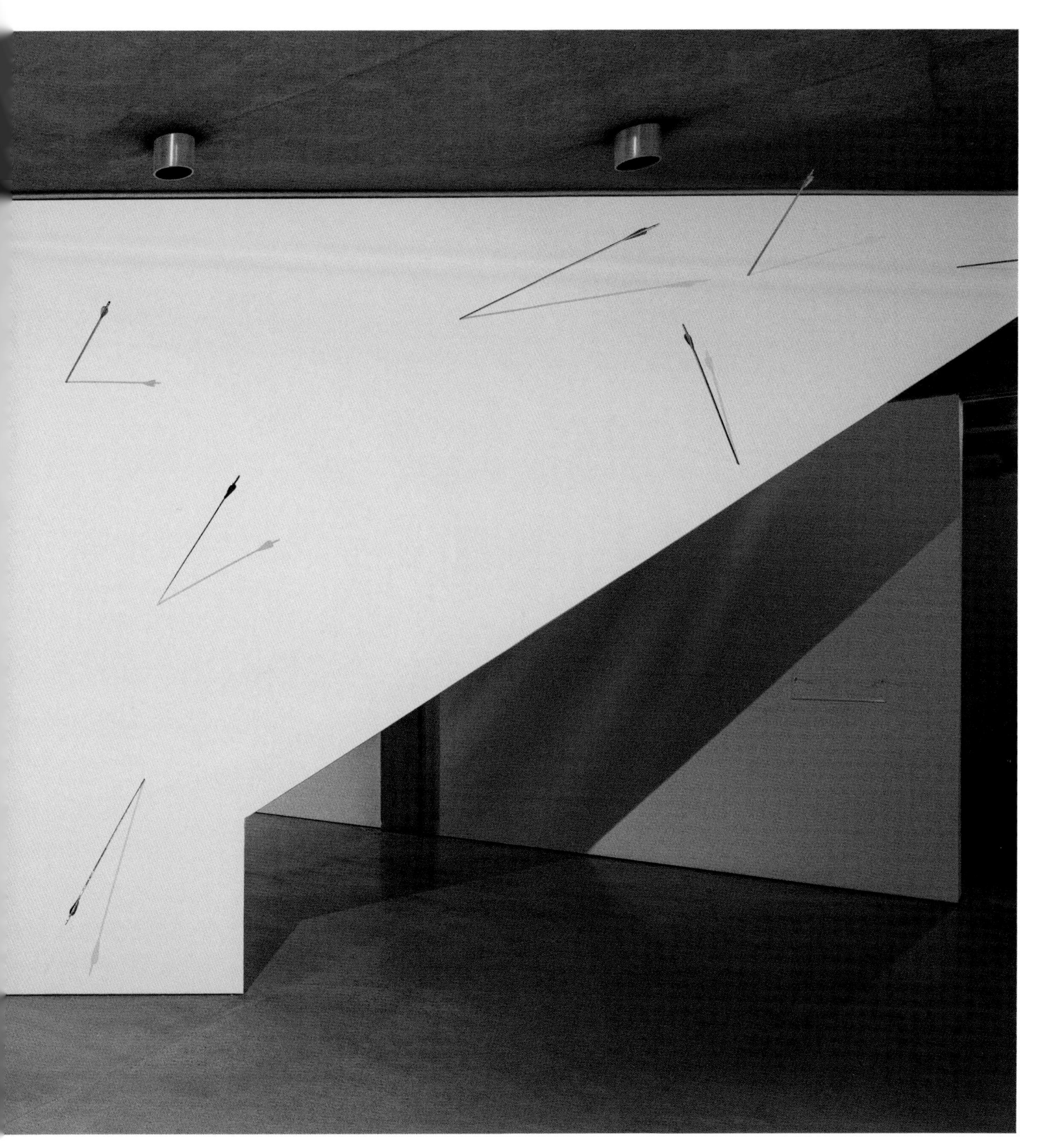

PATRICIA RESTREPO

Every House Is a Haunted House

"Something is here. Not here *per se* but leading elsewhere. It is an energy that pulls me through." Crystal, a psychic, is on a house call investigating disturbances experienced by Sophie, the protagonist of Olivia Erlanger's *Appliance* (2024) who recently relocated into an older home. Throughout the video's seventeen-minute run, we wonder: are the strange noises and visual distortions a product of Sophie's mind, or is an external force involved? Is her house, indeed, haunted? Crystal turns to her tarot cards for insight. Pulling the card of desire, she explains: "You can think of it as a doorway or threshold." Sophie desperately retorts: "A doorway to what?" [**Figure 1**]

The scene cuts from Sophie's dining table to her bedroom, where Crystal peers through an illuminated hole the size of a salad plate in the hardwood floor. The enigmatic scene is frozen on this catalogue's cover.

A doorway to what?

A home is defined by physical boundaries that delineate the interior and exterior of private property. Thresholds, be they doorways or windows, function dialectically as both apertures and mechanisms for closure for the house, itself a "symbol of the human psyche."[1] For French philosopher Gaston Bachelard, the window, a "transitional object," is "the surface that separates the region of the same from the region of the other."[2] "[Windows] often

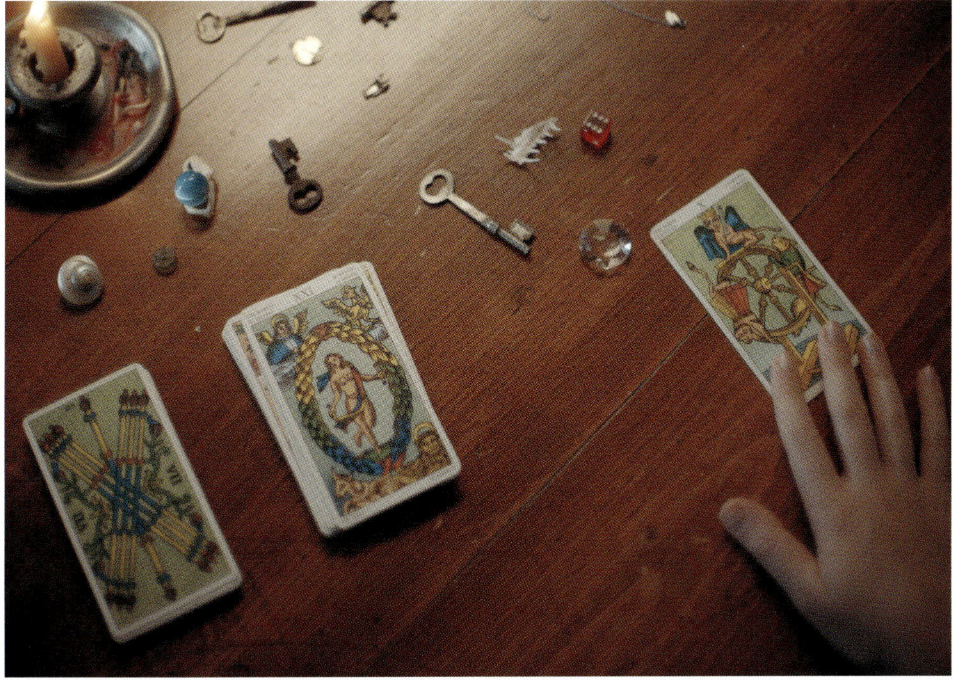

1   Olivia Erlanger, *Appliance* (video still), 2024

appear as a barrier, a border, a place of fracture between the familiar and the foreign; they belong to the public and private spheres simultaneously."[3] These permeable portals protect a domicile's celebrated value, particularly in the suburbs: its ability to be open to guests and exterior views, or invited intruders, and closed to the threats of the outside world like a fortress of old, surrounded by a moat. A house's component passageways, with their shifting yet interrelated functions, parallel philosopher Timothy Morton's musing on the house as a whole: "A shadow play of presence and absence intertwined."[4]

Just as a home only makes sense in the relationship of its voids to its solids, the same logic applies to its counterparts of windows and doors. The classic Taoist text *Tao Te Ching* beholds that, "We chisel out doors and windows; It is precisely in these empty spaces, that we find the usefulness of the room. Therefore, we regard having something as beneficial: But having nothing as useful."[5] The English word "window" has roots in the Old Norse word *vindauga*, or "wind eye," alluding to the time when windows were glass-less openings in walls. This architectural history makes evident that windows do not symbolize solely separation; they allow many modes of communication—light, air, and sound—to enter and to exit.

The symbolism of thresholds has long played a central role in textual, visual, and cinematic works. For painters of the Romantic period in the first half of the nineteenth century, the window often typified unfulfilled longing. Windows and doors play a crucial role in the plot of Emily Brontë's *Wuthering Heights* as the sites of trespassing borders and ensuing violence. Emily Dickinson, a recluse whose chief interactions with the external world were mediated by looking through her provincial home's seventy-five windows, considered windows "a spatial dimension of power."

Interstitial architectural interfaces, the thresholds between "in" and "out," are not only materially built but also socially constructed. Media historian Lynn Spigel details how normative forms of living have been produced over centuries:

> In the years following World War II, … technological utopia was joined by a complementary housing utopia which was for the first time mass produced. Although the 1950s witnessed the most extreme preoccupation with the merging of indoor and outdoor space, this ideal had been part of the model for interior design in the first suburban houses of the latter nineteenth century. In their widely read book of 1869, *The American Woman's Home*, Catherine Beecher and Harriet Beecher Stowe suggested [that…] the merging of indoor and outdoor worlds was a response to the Victorian cult of domesticity—its separation between private/female and public/male domains.[6]

Olivia Erlanger: If Today Were Tomorrow transforms and modernizes today's cult of domesticity. The exhibition operates as an allegorical threshold, perforating and destabilizing the distinctions between interior and exterior, self and non-self, body and home. Erlanger has made decisive cuts, both physically and conceptually, into our understanding of the home, in turn producing a "pregnant void."[7] Her generative holes refute the home as a neutral container. Instead, the artist unearths how such thinking obscures underlying power structures, be they unjust, discriminatory, patriarchal, or polluting, as evidenced by our country's histories of colonization, redlining, gendered design, and excessive waste. As Erlanger positions the house as a quasi-body, the thresholds recurrent in her work also become orifices inviting osmosis and leakage between the conscious and subconscious.

"Thresholes"

If Today Were Tomorrow is Erlanger's debut solo museum exhibition in the United States and also marks the first time that her sculptural, filmic, and installation-based works are showcased in dialogue. She has converted CAMH's subterranean gallery into a sculptural landscape comprising distinct yet interrelated zones: a constellation of arrows piercing the museum's iconic staircase, dioramas of fantastical worlds, cantilevered planets, and a video installation in an exploded set recreation.

Earlier work by Erlanger feeds this most recent corpus. In *Ida* (2019), the artist produced silicone mermaid tails draping out of washing machines, the device's round opening functioning as a threshold for the surreal. Her witty oversized snowglobes, which debuted in *Split-level Paradise* (2020), are marked by large perforations within their contained ecosystems. These openings have allowed the snowglobes' fake snow, typically cheery and latently mobile, to fall to the subspace below, static. This series' fractured and immobilized landscape, or precarious ground, offers an apt analogy for the horrors of our country's 2008 housing market crisis. [Figure 2]

Erlanger's voids link her to the overlooked history of women artists puncturing the land. Rosalind Krauss's groundbreaking 1979 essay "Sculpture in the Expanded Field" begins by investigating Mary Miss's *Perimeters/Pavilions/Decoys* (1978). At the center of a field, *Sunken Courtyard* is a square pit sixteen-feet wide at ground-level. A peek into the hole reveals that the dirt has been cut back beyond the opening, birthing a cavernous space inscribed by a ceiling of both earth and sky. Through this disjuncture, the "viewer becomes aware that the ground s/he has just walked across and presumed to be solid is undermined," Miss states.[8] In an earlier landwork, *Battery Park Landfill* (1973), Miss installed five walls in a wintery Hudson River landfill.

2

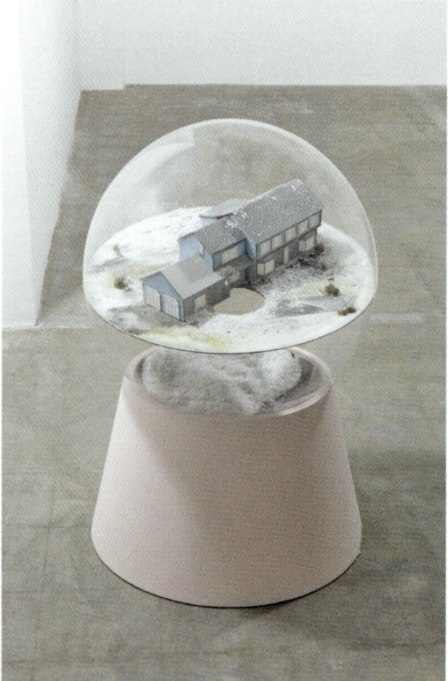

3

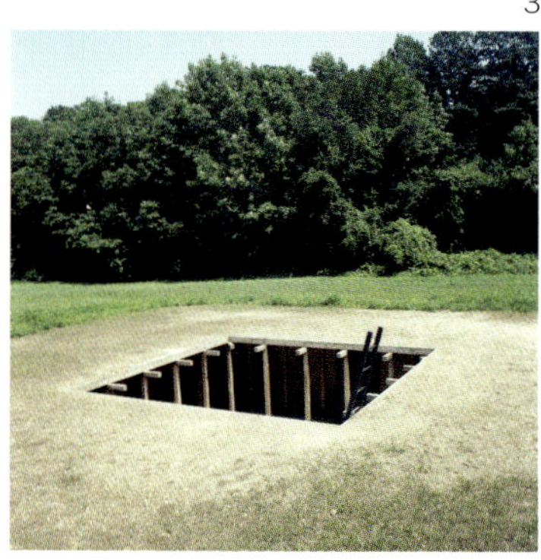

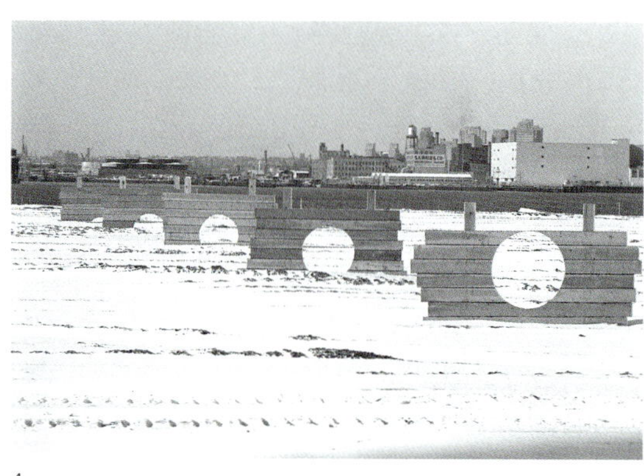

4

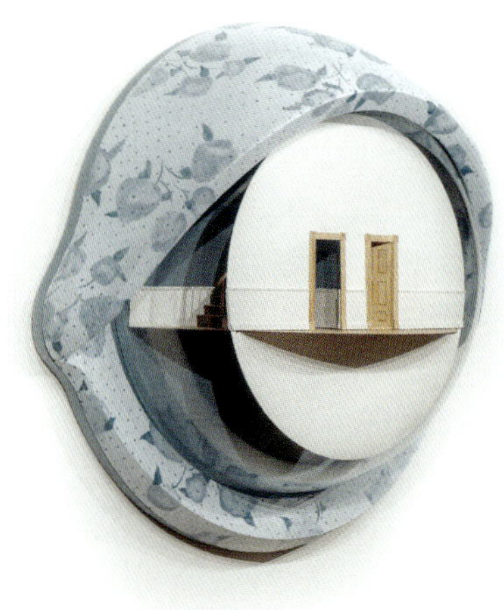

5

2 Olivia Erlanger, *Soft Kiss*, installed in *Split Level Paradise* at Bel Ami, Los Angeles, California, 2020. Plexiglass, architectural model, urethane resin, dibons, lichen, charcoal, wood, acrylic paint, and artificial snow #19, 45 × 30 × 30 in. Courtesy the artist and Bel Ami. Photo: Paul Salveson.

3 Mary Miss, *Perimeters/Pavilions/Decoys*, 1978. Three tower-like structures, two semi-circular mounds, and an underground courtyard, build using vernacular construction techniques and materials situated within a four acre clearing. Nassau County Museum of Art, Roslyn, New York. Courtesy Mary Miss.

4 Mary Miss, *Battery Park Landfill*, 1973. Wood, 5.5 × 12 ft. sections at 50 ft. intervals, temporary installation. Courtesy Mary Miss.

5 Olivia Erlanger, *Act I*, 2022. Basswood, MDF, foam, paint, sconces, LED lights, and battery, 44 × 46 × 18 in. Courtesy the artist and Del Vaz Projects. Photo: Esteban Schimpf.

The planes of wood planks, installed at fifty-foot intervals, held a series of concentric circles descending into the ground. Critic Lucy Lippard wrote: "This piece happens when you get there and stand in front of it. Its identity changes abruptly. … The experience is telescopic. As the modestly sized holes (and the adjacent walls that these holes incorporate into your vision) are perceived, they expand into an immense interior space."[9] [Figures 3, 4]

Evoking scenography, Erlanger's more recent sculptures are wall-bound eyeballs containing layered slices of domestic interior design, a peeling back of mise-en-scène. Over four feet in diameter, *Act I* (2022) is a cross-section of a dollhouse's interior corridor, while her earlier works in this form offer objects and furnishings as disquieting synecdoches in the absence of their users. In these voyeuristic inquiries into homes devoid of their inhabitants, Erlanger rejects anthropocentrism, or the privileging of the human over the nonhuman; such thinking, after all, has enabled ecological crises on our planet. Instead, objects throughout her work—picket fences, outlets, kitchen ovens—are given agency and value rivaling their human counterparts. [Figure 5]

Erlanger's slices of miniaturized architectural spaces complement the "building cuts"[10] made by artist Gordon Matta-Clark from 1971 to 1978, in which he transformed abandoned structures into sculptures by incising holes through layers of floors and walls. Rosalind Krauss wrote that such transformations succeeded "in bringing the building into the consciousness of the viewer in the form of a ghost,"[11] while Anne M. Wagner wonders: "Does some pale shadow hover around these [cut out] corners, conjuring the absent whole? Remember that not all ghosts come when called."[12] Matta-Clark's comment on our futile desire for permanence is palpable in the vertical passageways he cut between floors and ceilings for *Bronx Floors: Thresholes*, "thresholes" one of the artist's signature cheeky spelling variations. [Figure 6]

Beyond material manipulation of space, Matta-Clark wrote about his desire to convert "a building into a state of mind."[13] He recorded this pseudo mantra on a notecard:

A RESPONSE TO COSMETIC DESIGN
COMPLETION THROUGH REMOVAL
COMPLETION THROUGH COLLAPSE
COMPLETION THROUGH EMPTYNESS[14]

Both Matta-Clark and Erlanger address the temporality of the built environment, albeit on vastly different scales—his extrahuman, hers miniaturizing. We might imagine, playfully, Erlanger's interior cross-sections plugging Matta-Clark's building cuts.

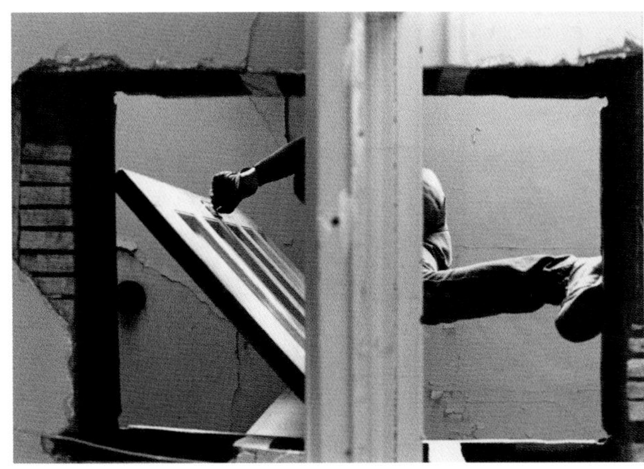

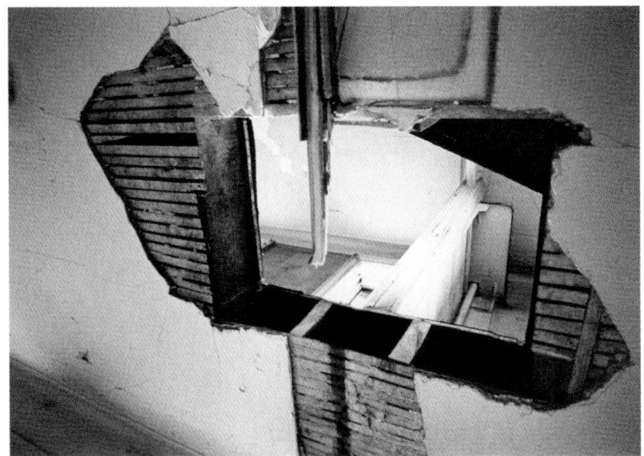

6

6 Gordon Matta-Clark, *Bronx Floors: Thresholes*, 1973.
Black and white photograph, 21.65 × 27.75 in.
©2024 Estate of Gordon Matta-Clark/Artists Rights
Society (ARS), New York. Courtesy David Zwirner.

The two artists also share a concern with the body, despite typically abstaining from its visualization. As is the case with Erlanger's works, "for all its interest in staging the open and transparent, the body still haunts Matta-Clark's sculpture. Not only does it hover there as repression or memory, but it is also summoned by the range of behaviors and optics to which the work lays active claim."[15]

Constellations

Erlanger's act of cutting extends to the sculptures that populate *If Today Were Tomorrow*. *Eros (When Night Was Last Dark)*, a celestial constellation of sixteen elegant stainless steel arrows, pierces CAMH's brutalist staircase. These polished weapons recall the way stars seemingly pierce the night sky as their light punctures darkness, a site ever fewer of us encounter given increasing light pollution and the growing proportion of urban dwellers. Their inability to provide illumination and navigation as once possible is echoed in Timothy Morton's assertion: "Arrows of desire don't point at all."[16]

With *Eros (When Night Was Last Dark)*, Erlanger again finds herself in dialogue with Matta-Clark. In a performance preceding his building cuts, Matta-Clark used a BB gun to shoot out the windows of the gallery hosting his show. With *Window Blow-Out* (1976), as he named it, the artist "meant to aerate architectural hermeticism on several levels, even while throwing formalist precision, along with caution, to the winds."[17]

Erlanger's configuration also brings to mind the gilded night skies pictured by the painter Martin Wong (1946–1999), a "documenter of the constellation of social life."[18] Wong's dense surfaces are populated with symbols drawn from astrological and architectural sources. He searched for novel forms of communication through his work, often imbuing his paintings with numerous languages and modes of speaking, most uniquely American Sign Language and his signature clusters of stars. In contrast to Erlanger's industrially produced constellations, Wong's configurations are gossamer-like webs. Both artists craft depictions of their environments approaching that of stage sets, offering "enthralling fusions of the decorative and real, the documentary and the fantastic."[19] The documentary in Erlanger's case: the constellation reveals what Houston's sky would have looked like on January 26, 1880. The fantastic: her poetic claim that this date was "the last day the sky was dark," as Thomas Edison received the patent for the lightbulb the following day. [Figure 7]

Unlikely Models for the Twenty-First Century

Nestled inside *If Today Were Tomorrow* are Erlanger's four dioramas inset in walls. Entitled *Green Sky*, *Orange Sky*, *Blue Sky*, and *Yellow Sky*, these contained tableaux alternatively could be called "Unlikely Models for the Twenty-First Century" in a riff on the title of Norman Klein's book.[20] Each complex vista offers an uncanny mix of familiar symbols with proposals for potential futures. Here, Erlanger's cuts manifest differently. In *Yellow Sky*, for instance, fragments of dry stacked stone walls seen in the northeastern United States dot a landscape resisting this effort; its erupting mountainous peaks render the attempted division of property futile, a fool's errand. The craggy terrain of *Yellow Sky* recalls Caspar David Friedrich's *Wanderer above the Sea of Fog* (1818), where we see a lone figure's back overlooking a totalizing landscape. [Figure 8]

Despite the recurring physical challenges to contain and control nature, human efforts persist. Our insatiable desire to regulate our surroundings is evident in *Blue Sky*, Erlanger's diorama of a French-style, geometrically organized park. The park's logic is governed by meticulous order, with its manicured lawns, perpendicular paths, and gridded trees. The parkscape references Schloss Nymphenburg, one film location for Alan Renais's French New Wave film *Last Year at Marienbad* (1961). Renais's subtle upheaval of reality is encountered in the park's surreal scenes, where the actors cast shadows while their neighboring trees do not. Like Renais's cinematic approach to "exceed … the drive of cinema to closure,"[21] Erlanger blurs what is real and what is imagined, reflecting the ambiguities about our present and our possibilities. [Figure 9]

Orange Sky, Erlanger's third diorama, renders layers of desert mesas with a lone advertising sign anchoring and piercing the horizon line. This sole signage reveals the power of an "outsider object,"[22] or something seemingly nonsensical in its environment. Disorienting, yet not overwrought, this gesture offers no proximate signs or structures from which contextual meaning can be derived, whereby typically, as artist and writer Dan Graham notes: "For a sign to convey meaning, it must conform to the general code shared by the surrounding signs and distinguish itself from—establish its position relative to—other signs. Each sign depends ultimately for its meaning upon its position in relation to the others."[23]

The dioramas also contend in nuanced ways with the varied manifestations of power and speculation, insofar as land, property, and investments are signifiers we lay claim to own. Erlanger's dioramas explore these "ecosystems of power," as she terms them: speculative real-estate investments in the cityscape, power over nature in the parkscape, delineation of property in the mountainscape, and commercial property in the desertscape.

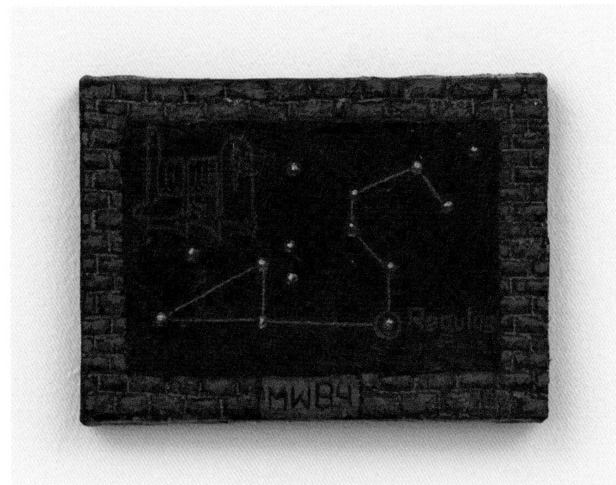

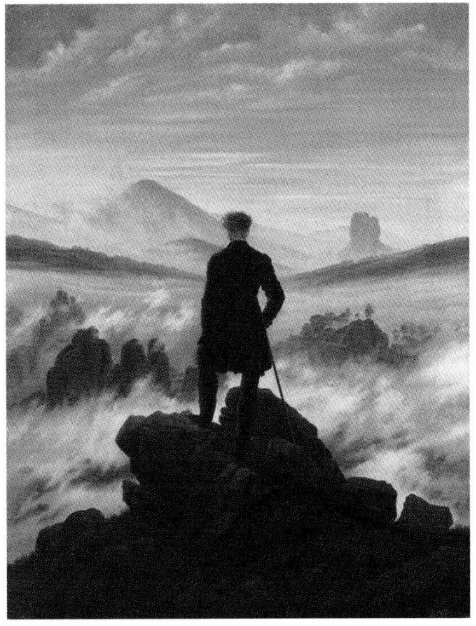

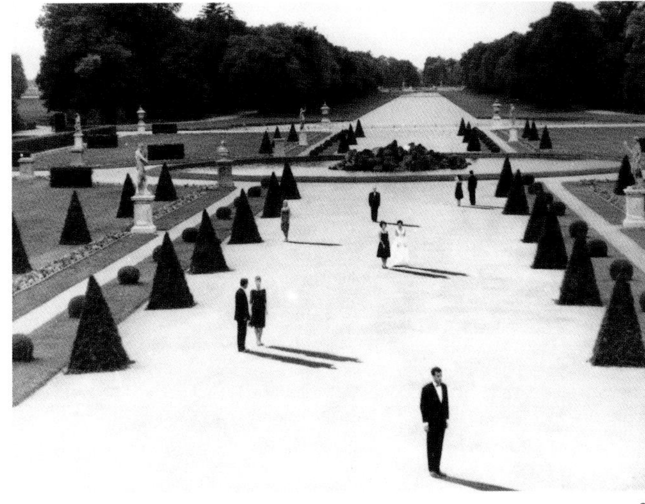

7   Martin Wong, *Leo*, 1984. Acrylic on canvas,
11¼ × 11¼ in. © 2024, Martin Wong Foundation.
Courtesy of the Martin Wong Foundation and
P·P·O·W, New York.
8   Caspar David Friedrich, *Wanderer above the
Sea of Fog*, 1818. Oil on canvas, 37.32 × 29.45 in.
Collection Hamburger Kunsthalle.
9   *Last Year at Marienbad* (film still), 1961.
Directed by Alain Resnais. Photo: TERRA / Album /
Art Resource, NY.

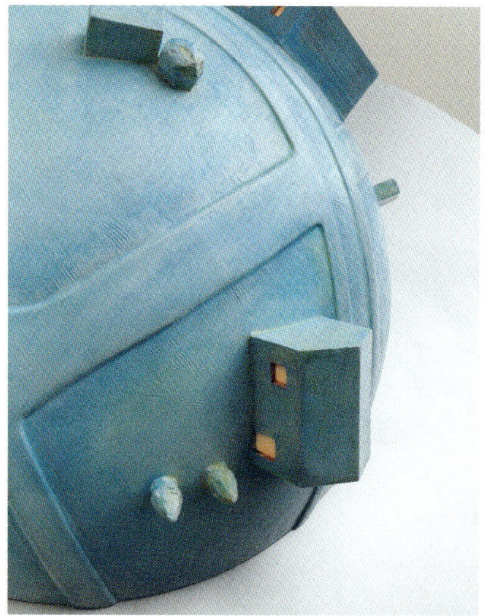

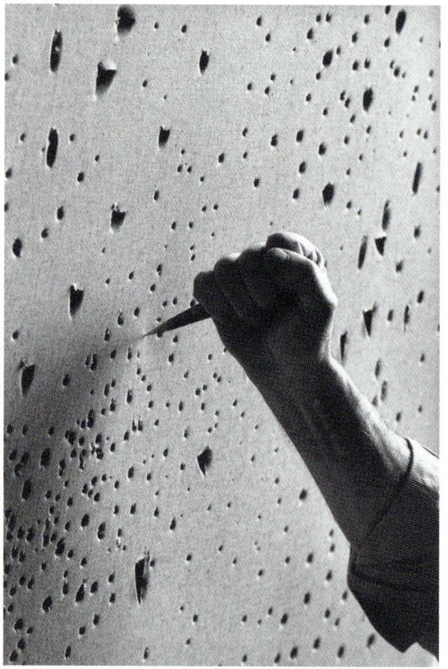

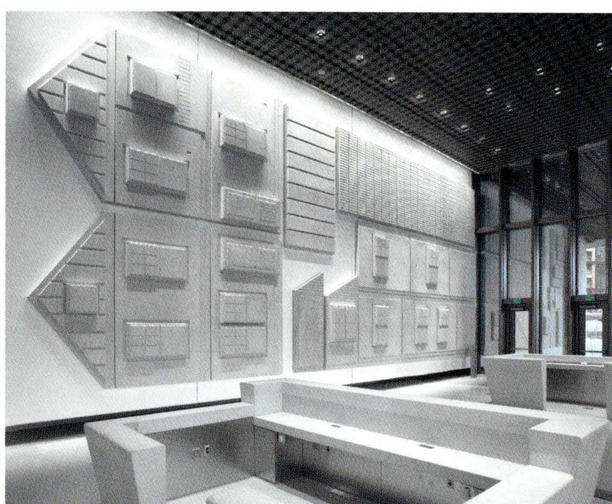

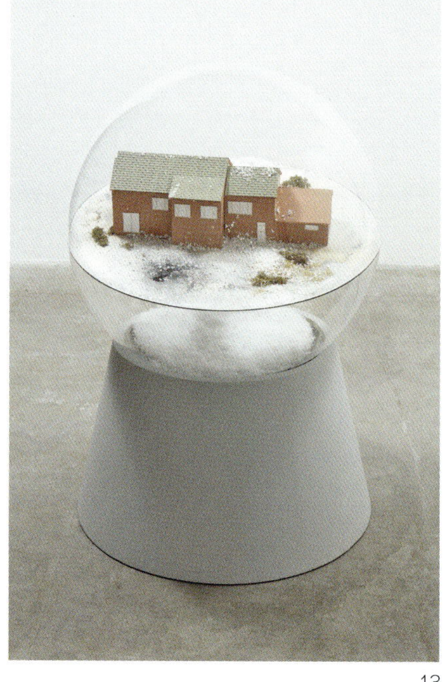

10 Olivia Erlanger, *Antimeridian (detail)*, 2024.
Aquaresin, aluminum, LEDs, drivers, and cord,
dimensions variable. Courtesy the artist and Soft
Opening, London. Photo: Daniel Terna.
11 Rachel Whiteread, *US Embassy (Flat pack house)*,
2013–15. Mixed media, overall: 252.8 × 1035.4 in.
© 2024, Rachel Whiteread. Courtesy the artist,
Luhring Augustine, New York, Galleria Lorcan O'Neill,
Rome, and Gagosian Gallery. Photo: Mike Bruce.

12 Ugo Mulas, Lucio Fontana: *Milan* (detail),
ca. 1963. Silver bromide print, 14.96 × 10.7 in.
© 2005, Ugo Mulas Estate. Courtesy Archivio
Ugo Mulas.
13 Olivia Erlanger, installation view of *Split Level
Paradise* at Bel Ami, Los Angeles, California, 2020.
Courtesy the artist and Bel Ami. Photo:
Paul Salveson.

Matta-Clark similarly subverts the American dream of home ownership in his *Fake Estates* project (1974), in which he purchased microtracts of unbuildable and remote land, his estate thereby having negligible economic value.

The dioramas, from a distance, transcend windows while seemingly reading as digital screens. Erlanger's video *Appliance*, meanwhile, is projected on a large screen within its installation, gesturing toward the video's domestic space with its carpeting, lamps, and couches, creating porosity between the set on screen and the set in the space. Screens are often likened to virtual windows or openings to other worlds, their contained moving image eclipsing time and space. They provide portals to worlds far removed from their environment, far more detached from their surroundings than the physical barrier of a window's glass or the wood of a door. Spigel explores how the earliest domestic screen, the television, has been a site for controlling space. She correlates the growing dissemination of televisions in the 1950s to the mass construction of the suburbs: "Given its ability to bring 'another world surfaces' into the home, it is not surprising that television was often figured as the ultimate expression of progress in utopian statements concerning man's ability to conquer and to domesticate space."[24] Once again, Erlanger transforms and modernizes this domestic trope.

Canned Domestic Cosmos[25]

We again experience the gesture of cutting in Erlanger's pair of illuminated planets, *Antimeridian* and *Prime meridian* (both 2024), enlarged versions of her intimately scaled *Planet Me* (2022). These celestial bodies appear to be floating, subject to their own laws of gravity. Aluminum planetary rings do not merely orbit; the discs violently slice through the surfaces' landscapes, in the process bisecting the globe's arterial roads and disturbing the networks connecting the sites of work, leisure, and home. The works' gashing aluminum—an industrial material associated with the cold, both tactilely and energetically—foil the orbs' skin of sculpted resin, which boasts the artist's hand-tooled marks. [Figure 10]

Uninhabited renderings of the suburban home muster the spirit of Rachel Whiteread's *US Embassy (Flat pack house)* (2013–15), where the cast sections of a 1950s suburban American house are arranged vertically on a wall, thereby stripped of both their interior volume and occupants. While we identify familiar parts of a house, such as staircases, windows, and outlets, their flattened mounting is unsettling. Whiteread's clinical portrayal touches on the social and political forces responsible for packaging notions of home. Recessions in Whiteread's surfaces recall the sculpted suburban surfaces of Erlanger's planets in their poetic play of texture and dynamism. [Figure 11]

Erlanger's disturbances of the picture plane held sacred through much of art history—her cuts, her holes, her piercings, her orifices—can be positioned as feminist inheritors of the poetic perforations of the canvas, or *buchi* (holes), by artist Lucio Fontana. The Argentine–Italian artist is celebrated as the founder of Spatialism, a group dedicated to expanding artworks' spatial presence. To this aim, he remarked, "I do not want to make a painting; I want to open up space, create a new dimension, tie in the cosmos, as it endlessly expands beyond the confining plane of the picture."[26] [Figure 12]

Erlanger's cuts, however, are more than modernist ruptures; they exceed this formal gesture in their transgression, offering fleshed out portals to surreal scenes, both ambiguous and engrossing. These strategies succeed not only on a formal level but also on a conceptual level, ushering in considerations of object agency, precarious ecosystems, gender discrimination, and new domestic arrangements.

In the transhistorical nature of Erlanger's works in this exhibition, suturing the nineteenth century in her arrow constellation to the planets' seeming contemporaneity, as well as the unspecified futurity in her dioramas, Erlanger also produces holes in the material of time. In *The Politics of the Very Worst*, Paul Virilio considered the impact that events will have on Earth since we operate presently on "one-world time."[27] According to Virilio, the historical three dimensions: past, present, and future have been replaced by "the hyper-concentration of time into 'real time' [that] reduces all trajectories to nothing."[28] An accident, as a result, affects the entire planet. For Virilio, "globalization doesn't make the planet bigger, it signals the beginning of 'the great confinement.' Soon, Virilio suggests, we are going to experience the end of the world—not the apocalyptic end, but the world as finite. … This extermination of world-space is a cataclysmic event. For the first time, history has hit a cosmological limit."[29] Erlanger's dioramas grapple with such elastic notions of time.

Cut!

We do encounter an embodied presence in Erlanger's first narrative film investigating the psychology of interior spaces. *Appliance*, premiering in *If Today Were Tomorrow*, is a short video following the protagonist Sophie, who has been living in her new house for a week. In her isolation, she begins to hear strange noises emanating from her appliances. She also experiences visual distortions, such as an outlet seemingly integrated into her cheek.

Lydia Kallipoliti, a contributor to this catalogue, opens her 2022 text *Soft Machines: Cellular Synthetic Environment* with: "Horror, as Virginia Woolf once suggested in 'The Cinema,' is all in all the anticipation of formlessness:

constant change and indeterminacy."[30] Woolf, meanwhile, begins her short story *A Haunted House* with a reference to thresholds: "Whatever hour you woke there was a door shutting."[31] Woolf's tale straddles the edge of reality and subconsciousness, offering a passage into an unknown world. A slate of eerie events unfolds in the home of the narrator, who, like Erlanger's protagonist Sophie, is alone at night during these encounters. Woolf's narrator is convinced the house has a pulse, but is this sensation simply her own heartbeat? Both *Appliance* and *A Haunted House* offer the relatable experience in which we are able to hear every nightly noise the house conjures, in turn crafting unnerving sources.

Beyond human actors, domestic objects, and architectural fragments steer much of the progression in *Appliance*. Design writer Sarah Archer jokes: "In 1986, I was promised a future where I could talk to my house. I don't mean conversing with Alexa, the deferential Amazon-invented digital butler who glibly lurks inside blue-lit Bluetooth speakers. I'm imagining a home where every inanimate object talks back to you."[32] Archer's nostalgia for "yesterday's future"[33] references the fantastical, campy habitat Paul Reubens created as the set for his series *Pee-wee's Playhouse* (1986–90). Erlanger offers a much more ambiguous array of communicative household devices, from Sophie's vocal oven to shattering light bulbs. Their disquieting speech guides the destabilizing narrative, one in which the house talks back.[34] The video's sound design—utilizing on-set recordings of domestic devices—also gives power and voice to the seemingly inert.

Just as Erlanger extends the modernist gesture to prick a surface open, so too does she extend the contours of horror. A classic trope of the horror genre includes encounters experienced within or through domestic thresholds. Consider Fritz Lang's 1947 film noir *Secret Beyond the Door*, where portrayals of an impossibly oversized door allude to oversized secrets and the trappings of its occupants' hidden obsessions.

Similarly, in his 1954 film *Rear Window*, Alfred Hitchcock masterfully deploys dual strategies of cut shots and filming through thresholds to manipulate our sense of reality and the reliability of the film's protagonist, L. B. Jeffries. A photographer with a broken leg, Jeffries passes time in his Greenwich Village apartment by observing his neighbors through his window, ultimately convinced that he has witnessed a murder. Quick cross-cut shots are used repeatedly to confirm that what we are watching is exactly what Jeffries is seeing, enabling us to adopt his point-of-view. Hitchcock required all activity be filmed from Jeffries's vantage point, a mandate that created immense technical and set design challenges. The large courtyard of the film's massive composite set consisted of thirty-one apartments with some apartment buildings five-stories high, one of the largest sets ever built at Paramount. *Rear Window* even boasted seventy thresholds, chiefly windows, recalling Erlanger's play with perspective and scenographic treatment in her sculptural work.

Throughout *Appliance*, passable portals are significant; we often watch the video's tense action through the interstitial spaces of Sophie's home. Sophie is rattled when she finds her front door ajar in the morning, leaving her vulnerable to trespassers with no clear opening agent. We observe her through stratified door openings as she completes her nightly routine of cleansing her face, brushing her teeth, and injecting herself with hormones. Erlanger's layered lenses remind us of the artifice of her artistic framing. There also are more surreal and disquieting domestic thresholds, such as the cabinet enclosing the sink producing sludgy water, the door to the babbling oven, the drain to the kitchen sink through which spoiled milk is poured, and the curtain behind which a shower seems to turn on by its own volition. These non-human orifices offer psychological analogies for cuts to interiority, to the porosity between home and body. [Figure 14]

Let's return to the mystifying hole in the floor of Sophie's bedroom, which over the course of the video serves as an unexpected beacon of light, as well as a passthrough for a gloved hand flailing as Sophie sleeps. What else might be accessible through this portal, or alternatively hidden beyond the house's various thresholds: the outlet's cover, the oven's front flap, the refrigerator's doors? As James Attlee observes about the hidden portions

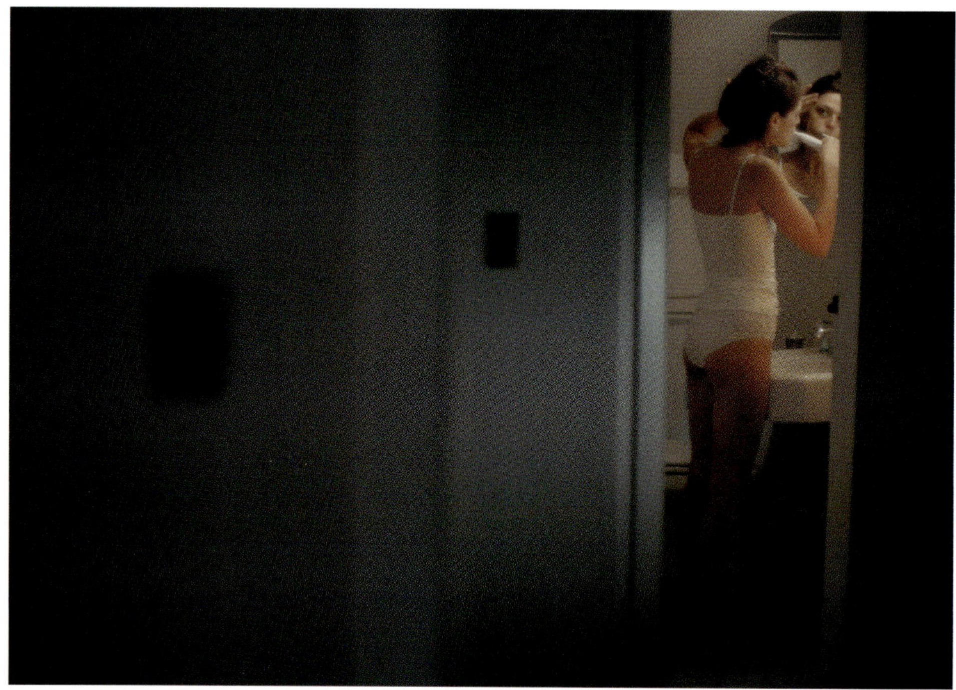

14 Olivia Erlanger, *Appliance* (video still), 2024

of a metropolis: "In carefully controlled modern urban environments, the unseen regions underground can be taken to represent the subconscious, from which, on occasion, spill out the repressed memories and unlawful impulses."[35] Matta-Clark's writings on his holes also are apropos here: "A simple cut or series of cuts, act as a powerful drawing device able to redefine spatial situations and structural components. What is invisibly at play behind a wall or floor, once exposed, becomes an active participant in a spatial drawing of the building's inner life."[36] Through *Appliance*'s portals and physical passages, Erlanger similarly reveals the speculative and uncanny inner lives of her protagonist's domicile.

Erlanger's flirtation with the horror genre exceeds alienating openings. As she expands our understanding of the home to encompass more than a physical structure, so too does she stretch the possibilities of the horrifying and haunting. When exploring architectural histories, Timothy Morton quipped: "Every house is a haunted house."[37] This reality has been particularly true for women in the United States throughout the twentieth century. Architectural theoretician Beatriz Colomina reminds us how gender is inscribed in spaces, rebuking the notion that home design can be gender neutral.

Not only can spaces be haunted, but so too are bodies. "*Appliance* questions where real body horror lies," Erlanger asserts. Body horror is rendered anew in her video, where its most graphic part, depending on your phobias, occurs when Sophie injects herself with her hormone treatment in her pursuit of fertility. Her bruised abdomen keeps the score of her efforts. These microscopic holes, or crafted orifices, into the hopeful maternal figure remind us that bodies are not as static and self-contained as we might believe. Julietta Singh relays: "While the skin is a visual sign of the body's exterior limit, the physicist Karen Barad emphasizes how in fact bodies extend into space well beyond the skin. Molecularly we spread into the 'outside' world, mingling with it in ways that are not apparent to us. Our bodies are porous, as Nancy Tuana reminds us when she calls into question 'the boundaries between our flesh and the flesh of the world.' These feminist formulations of the body insist on our vital engagements with the outside world, complicating any easy binary demarcations of 'inside' and 'outside.'"[38] Another contributor to this catalogue, writer Chris Kraus, similarly stripped down singular subjectivity in her genre-defying book *Aliens and Anorexia*: "If the 'I' is the only thing we truly own, we must destroy it. Use the 'I' to break down the 'I,'"[39] Kraus writes, quoting the philosopher Simone Weil.

The contours of horror transcend physical bodily horror in the hands of Erlanger, whose practice also explores the horrors of economic, gender, and ecological conditions. As Sophie is convinced her appliances are embodied and speaking, Erlanger states: "Appliances are associated with aspirational anxieties tied to the commodification of home and domestic labor, making them the perfect antagonists for a haunting."[40] In the beginning of the video, Sophie shares her initial excitement over the fixtures in her home, particularly the brand new appliances in her kitchen, her "favorite part of the house." Yet her appliances are not decorative and alluring as they seem; they are non-compliant and subversive in their haunting effect.

Aliens

Before we get too carried away in search of passing through holes, we would be remiss to overlook the closing function of a threshold. Might we consider Erlanger's practice similar to the efforts of an oyster, with dual and merging functions of opening and closing in its filtrating labor? Her ability to cut and break—a landscape, a gallery wall, a hardwood floor, the picture plane, our quotidian perspective—is countered by her impulse to enclose. Erlanger's sculptures of snowglobes and eyelids, for instance, mine our search for safety in the form of physical bubbles, most often realized within the confines of the home. [Figure 13] This drive to enclose evokes Todd Haynes's film *Safe* (1995), in which a suburban housewife, increasingly ailed by environmental conditions, isolates herself within a desert community of similarly afflicted individuals.

The artist's inset dioramas, meanwhile, recall displays we encounter in natural history museums, where encased scenes are historicized. Yet the artist's proposals contained within the dioramas are not part of our collective history, instead presenting speculative modes of futurity, which are nonetheless offered as if fated. Erlanger's act of framing, creating a contrived threshold between the natural world and the built environment, messies their relationship. Emily Dickinson observed, "Nature is a haunted house; art, a house that wishes to be haunted."[41]

The distance imposed by Erlanger's enclosed worlds, observable but not accessible, makes evident their artificiality. Critic Sabrina Tarasoff writes: "Goethe's protagonist in *The Laocoön* … at some point gives the good advice that opening and closing your eyes rapidly will amount to a kind of cinematic effect. Lids making reality more real, as artifice. I think of each blink as a cut, a decision."[42] Erlanger's miniature worlds crack open their scenes as having been produced. The development of the window, after all, was crucial to the emergence of the genre of landscape painting; windows framed the landscape as a separate sphere, both organized and apart from the zone of living. By only offering a fragment of the outside world, Anne Cauquelin argues the "window puts the wild at a distance,"[43] thereby manufacturing the graspable invention of the landscape, itself not outside the realm of the human made.

As Beatriz Colomina writes: "Shelter, separation from the outside, is provided by the window's ability to turn the threatening world outside the house into a reassuring picture."[44]

Modalities of control and fantasy in Erlanger's imagescapes echo cultural critic Norman Klein's observation: "We live in an age of globalized localism—everything seems wired into the master computer system yet everything is also simultaneously an enclave—a fantasy narrative that is supposed to feel intimate but actually leaves no clear boundary between private and public events … [These] spheres of globalized localism unveil the close relationship between artifice and functionality."[45] In Erlanger's uncanny facsimiles of our environment, the artist questioned, "If fantasy is a form of escapism, what happens when life becomes stranger than fiction?" With her, we psychically and physically cross this threshold.

Bachelard finds the window as a site of existential reflection; both in and out are clearly identifiable simultaneously, the window a reflection on alienation. Evident estrangement was unpacked by playwright Bertolt Brecht in his writings on the "alienation" or "distancing effect" in the dramatic arts, advocating for jarring reminders of performance's artificiality. Television as a meta-space for surveillance and external looking was explored in "The Window," a self-reflexive episode of the science fiction series *Tales of Tomorrow* from 1952. The show is interspersed with intruder footage, or an "alien image,"[46] when a non-sequitur domestic scene filmed through a house window is broadcasted, only to cut back to a confused television crew at the studio. The "interfering" surveillance footage returns with the woman inside plotting to murder her husband. After the deed is done, the wife looks outside her windows and admits to her accomplice that she has had the eerie sensation of having been watched through the night.

The alien can transcend the allegorical. As Sophie unpacks and moves about her home, she tunes into Congress's 2023 UFO hearings, the diegetic sound becoming a secondary soundtrack for Erlanger's video. Mark von Schlegell, another contributor to this catalogue, crafts otherworldly settings in texts including *Sundogz* (2015), a tale of shape-shifting set on the moons of the planet Uranus. "Fiction can be this art object that doesn't show us anything new about reality, but draws out everything fake,"[47] von Schlegell shared, while in his 2009 book *Realometer*, he quotes literary critic Northrop Frye: "Life has no shape; literature has." Art's alienating strategies can liquify otherwise petrified thought-loops.

Erlanger's contained universes draw on her investigations into self-reliant architectural systems, informed particularly by the scholarship of Lydia Kallipoliti. In her text *The Architecture of Closed Worlds Or, What Is the Power of Shit?*, Kallipoliti explores closed environments, which she defines as: "a self-sustaining physical environment demarcated from its surroundings by a boundary that does not allow for the transfer of matter or energy,"[48] offering case studies of synthetic habitats including office buildings, EPCOT, space capsules, and the House of the Future. "Unlike an open system, which is part of an exterior world and linked to its surroundings, a closed system … implies an architecture of containment and detachment."[49] Roland Barthes mused on our desire "to shrink [the world], to populate it, to reduce it to a known and enclosed space"[50] in order to condense it to a manageable territory, enabling those contained within to be organized and supervised. As these environments often are intended to simulate our planet on a utopian smaller scale, Kallipoliti questions: "When the Earth is miniaturized in an artificial closed ecosystem, do scaling and simulation change the relationship between systems and subsystems?"[51]

Inevitably, no matter the budget or extent or control exercised over the attempts at self-sustaining structures, efforts were impeded by unexciting challenges, such as skin cells skewing systems. Erlanger wrestles with Kallipoliti's conclusion that it is challenging to create microworlds without replicating the referent world's problems. So, then, is our human attempt to close merely a moot maneuver? Even more suspect, is it dangerous? After all, the history of the suburbs spawned from efforts to withdraw into safety are linked to systems of power imbalance and multifaceted discrimination, resulting in inequities such as food deserts and withholding of financial services to urban pockets with residents of color. Erlanger probes these issues, thereby bringing them to the fore.

open-end[52]

Erlanger's work finds itself in a simpatico space in CAMH's 1972 Gunnar Birkerts's structure. Former director Sebastian "Lefty" Adler mandated the building be "flexible enough so that it can function inside and out as an artistic medium in which artists can create imaginative works."[53] Adler understood architecture as not a monument but a "transformer station" for the flow of creative energy.

Erlanger's portals render *If Today Were Tomorrow* a window, its utility the perforation between interior and exterior. Windows are recurrent within this exhibition—windows framing her inset dioramas, windows playing a central role in *Appliance*, windows within the exhibition offering vistas onto physically neighboring yet energetically distant spaces, and windows a source of illumination from the homes rising from her cantilevered planets. These thresholds are echoed in Erlanger's exhibition design, which the artist conceived as a totalizing sculptural landscape. She has moved from, to borrow phrasing from Henri Lefebvre, the production of things in space to the production of space.[54] Erlanger has architectured CAMH's space as never before seen, enlisting the aid of accordion walls displaying her dioramas. A corner of these folding walls has been removed, the missing nexus instead serving as a passthrough, recalling the excised corners of Matta-Clark's *Four Corners*. Erlanger's planets are visible across CAMH's gallery through large picture windows, one of which also functions as a navigable ingress. Sitting at the set's dining table watching *Appliance*, a turn of head offers an otherworldly vista of the planetary structures through the window.

What do Erlanger's dual and dialectical modes of opening and shutting bring to the fore? She punctures what sculptor Richard Nonas termed architecture's "hard shell,"[55] or resistance to change, perhaps "destabilizing the experience of the interior (as place and metaphor): the gesture both cleaves and restores what is a charged and isolated social sphere."[56] In turn, Erlanger shows how spaces condition American dreams and disappointments. Her work exists in a state that isn't entirely resolved, instead creating possible openings to new meaning through new relations. The logic this work proposes is both unsettling and familiar, haunting and comforting. It sits on the threshold of inside and outside, reality and fantasy, presented and hidden. Erlanger extends hospitality to the alien, the unknown.

1   Amy Arbus, *No Place Like Home* (New York: Doubleday, 1986).

2   Gaston Bachelard, *The Poetics of Space*, trans. Maria Jolas (Boston: Beacon Press, 1994), p. 222.

3   Karolina Katsika, "The Window: Openings and Perspectives 23–24 January 2015 Besançon, France," Call for Papers, English UPenn, May 3, 2014.

4   Timothy Morton, "Timothy Morton: _Haunted Houses_," lecture at Southern California Institute of Architecture (SCI-Arc), March 14, 2016.

5   Lao-tzu, *Te-Tao Ching*, trans. Robert G. Henricks (New York: The Modern Library, 1993), chapter 11.

6   Lynn Spigel, "Installing the Television Set: Popular Discourses on Television and Domestic Space, 1948–1955," in *Private Screenings*, ed. Lynn Spigel and Denise Mann (Minneapolis, Minnesota: University of Minnesota Press, 1992), pp. 7–8.

7   Gordon Matta-Clark, interview by Liza Bear, "Gordon Matta-Clark……..," *Avalanche* (December 1974), p. 36.

8   "1977–1978: Perimeters/Pavilions/Decoys," *Mary Miss*, http://marymiss.com/projects/perimeterspavilionsdecoys (accessed March 5, 2024).

9   Lucy Lippard, "Mary Miss: An Extremely Clear Situation," *Art in America* (March–April 1974), p. 76.

10   Pamela M. Lee, "On the Holes of History: Gordon Matta-Clark's Work in Paris," *October* 85 (1988), p. 65.

11   Krauss, "Notes on the Index, Part 2," in *The Originality of the Avant Garde*, quoted in Anne M. Wagner, "Splitting and Doubling: Architecture and the Body of Sculpture," *Grey Room* 14 (Winter 2004), p. 38.

12   Wagner, "Splitting and Doubling," p. 38.

13   James Attlee, "Towards Anarchitecture: Gordon Matta-Clark and Le Corbusier," *Tate Papers*, no. 7 (Spring 2007).

14   Gordon Matta-Clark, "A Response to Cosmetic Design / Completion through Removal / Completion through Collapse / Completion in Emptiness," 1970–1978, black felt-tip pen on card, Collection Centre Canadien d'Architecture / Canadian Centre for Architecture, Montréal Don de la succession Gordon Matta-Clark / Gift of Estate of Gordon Matta-Clark.

15   Wagner, "Splitting and Doubling," p. 30.

16   Timothy Morton, *Hell: In Search of a Christian Ecology* (New York: Columbia University Press, 2024), advanced preview.

17   Wagner, "Splitting and Doubling," p. 28.

18   As referenced in a description of Martin Wong's work for his exhibition *Exit Art* at P.P.O.W. in 1988, quoted in "P.P.O.W.," *ArtNet*, https://www.artnet.fr/galeries/ppow-gallery/1981-2021/ (accessed March 1, 2024).

19 Roberta Smith, "Martin Wong Is Dead at 53; A Painter of Poetic Realism," *New York Times*, August 18, 1999.

20 Full book title *Unlikely Models for the City in the Twenty-First Century*.

21 Term borrowed from Patricia White, "Female Spectator, Lesbian Spectre: *The Haunting*," in *Women in Film Noir*, ed. E. Ann Kaplan (London: British Film Institute, 2019), p. 147.

22 For Scale and Sarah Archer, "Pee Wee and the Human Condition," Substack, August 7, 2023.

23 Dan Graham, "Art in Relation to Architecture," *Artforum* 17 (February 1979), p. 22.

24 Lynn Spigel, *Make Room for TV: Television and the Family Ideal in Postwar America* (Chicago, IL: University of Chicago Press, 1992), p. 102.

25 Term in Lydia Kallipoliti, *The Architecture of Closed Worlds, Or What Is the Power of Shit* (Zurich: Lars Müller Publishers, 2018), p. 13.

26 Quoted from a 1965 symposium cited in Gyorgy Kepes, "Art and Ecological Conciousness," in *The Universitas Project: Solutions for a Post-Technologica Society* (New York: Museum of Modern Art, 2006), p. 154.

27 Publisher comments for Paul Virilio, *Politics of the Very Worst: An Interview with Philippe Petit*, ed. Sylvère Lotringer, trans. Michael Cavaliere (Cambridge MA: MIT Press, 1999).

28 Ibid.

29 Ibid.

30 Lydia Kallipoliti, "Soft Machines: Cellular Synthetic Environments," in *Radical Pedagogies* ed. Beatriz Colomina, Ignacio G. Galán, Anna-María Meister, and Evangelos Kotsioriss (Cambridge MA: MIT Press, 2022), p. 340.

31 Virginia Woolf, *Haunted House and Other Short Stories* (San Diego, CA: Harcourt, Brace, and Company, 1944), p. 3.

32 For Scale and Sarah Archer, "Pee Wee and the Human Condition," Substack, August 7, 2023.

33 From the title of Lynn Spigel, "Yesterday's Future, Tomorrow's Home," *Emergences: Journal for the Study of Media & Composite Cultures* 11, no. 1 (July 1, 2010).

34 For Scale and Sarah Archer, "Pee Wee and the Human Condition," Substack, August 7, 2021.

35 James Attlee, "Towards Anarchitecture," *Tate Papers*, no. 7 (Spring 2007).

36 Gordon Matta-Clark, *Gordon Matta-Clark: An Archival Sourcebook* (Berkeley, CA: University of California Press, 2022), p. 261.

37 Timothy Morton, "Timothy Morton: _Haunted Houses_," lecture at Southern California Institute of Architecture (SCI-Arc), March 14, 2016.

38 Julietta Singh, *No Archive Will Restore You* (Montreal: 3 Ecologies Books / Immediations, 2018), p. 30.

39 Chris Kraus, *Aliens and Anorexia* (Los Angeles: Semiotext(e), 2000), p. 27.

40 Email with Patricia Restrepo on March 14, 2024.

41 Emily Dickinson, *The Letters of Emily Dickinson* II, ed. Thomas H. Johnson (Cambridge, MA: Harvard University Press, 1965), p. 330.

42 Sabrina Tarasoff, "Vera Lutz, Patty Martori, Valentina Triet 'Love House' at FELIX GAUDLITZ, Vienna," *Mousse Magazine*, November 3, 2024.

43 Anne Cauquelin, *L'Invention du Paysage* (Paris: Presses Universitaires de France, 2013), p. 105.

44 Beatriz Colomina, *Privacy and Publicity: Modern Architecture as Mass Media* (Cambridge, MA: MIT Press, 1996), p. 7.

45 Norman M. Klein, "Imaginary Space: Building the Impossible, The Need for New Directions in Mass Culture Studies," *Nevada Historical Society Quarterly* 36, no. 4 (Winter 1993), p. 278.

46 Lynn Spigel, "Installing the Television Set: Popular Discourses on Television and Domestic Space, 1948–1955," in *Private Screenings*, ed. Lynn Spigel and Denise Mann (Minneapolis: University of Minnesota Press, 1992), p. 26.

47 Erika Landström, "Mark von Schlegell," *BOMB Magazine* (August 4, 2015), https://bombmagazine.org/articles/2015/08/04/mark-von-schlegell/ (accessed March 15, 2024).

48 Lydia Kallipoliti, curatorial statement for exhibition *Closed Worlds* at Storefront for Art & Architecture, New York, 2016.

49 Kallipoliti, *The Architecture of Closed Worlds*, p. 15.

50 Roland Barthes, *Mythologies* (New York: The Noonday Day Press, 1957), p. 66.

51 Kallipoliti, *The Architecture of Closed Worlds*, p. 176.

52 *open-end* was the title Marlene Dumas chose for her 2022 solo presentation at Palazzo Grassi in Venice.

53 Jay Jacobs, "A COMMITMENT TO THE FUTURE: Adler of the CAM," *The Art Gallery Magazine* (May 1970), p. 22.

54 Henri Lefebvre, *The Production of Space* (Hoboken, NJ: Wiley, 1992), p. 357

55 Richard Nonas, letter to IVAM, August 1992, reprinted in Maria Casanova and Gordon Matta-Clark, *Gordon Matta-Clark* (Valencia: IVAM Centre Julio González, 1993), p. 374.

56 Anne M. Wagner, "Splitting and Doubling: Architecture and the Body of Sculpture," *Grey Room 14* (Winter 2004), p. 36.

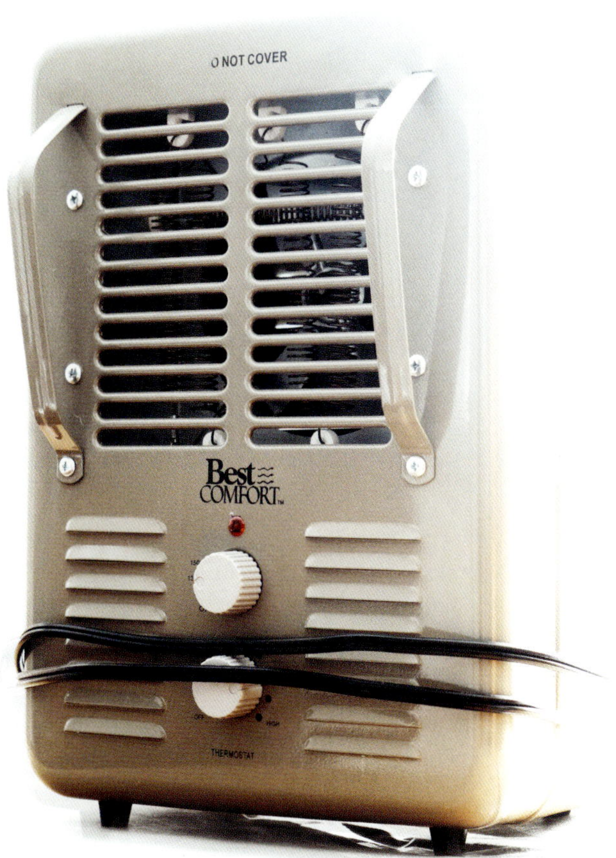
O NOT COVER
Best
COMFORT
THERMOSTAT

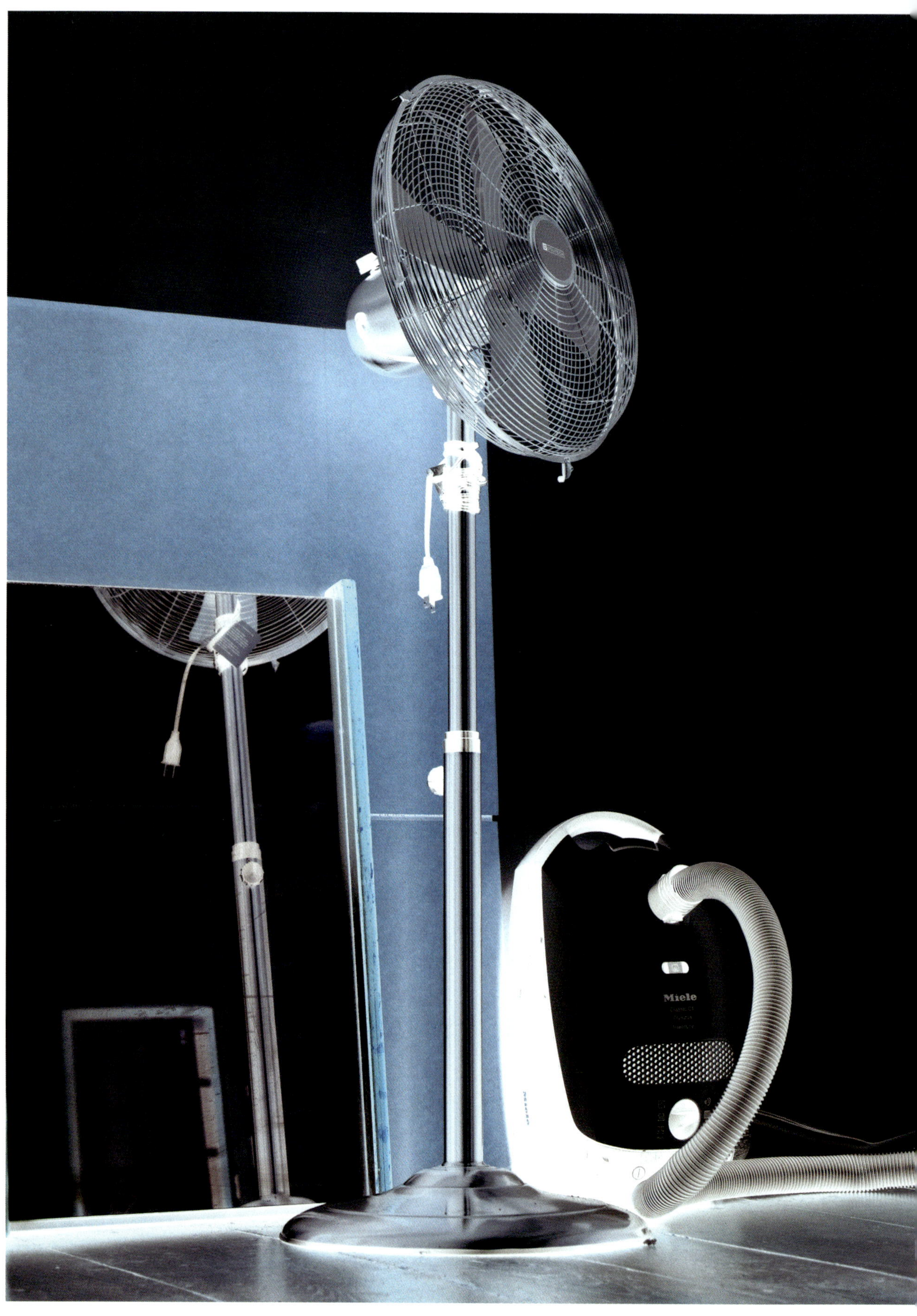

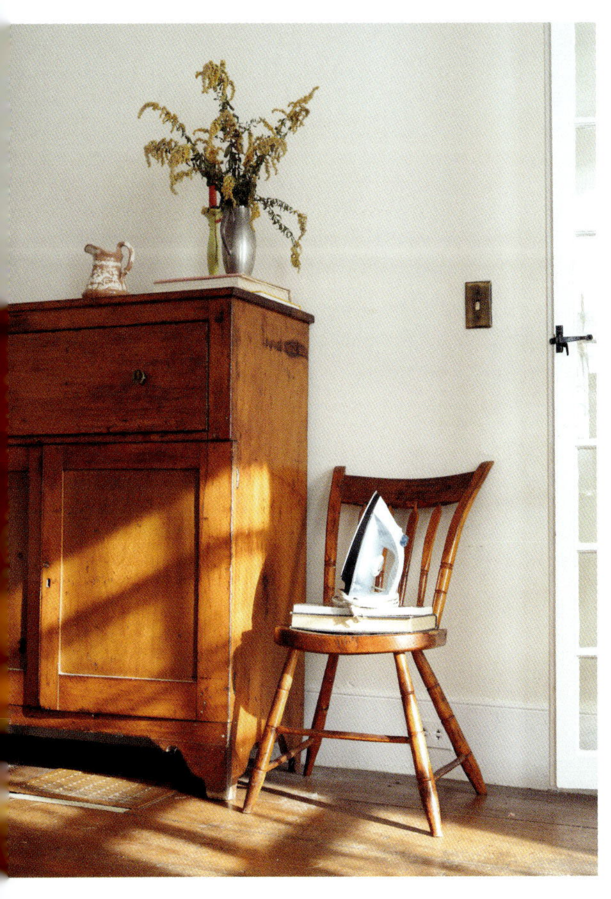

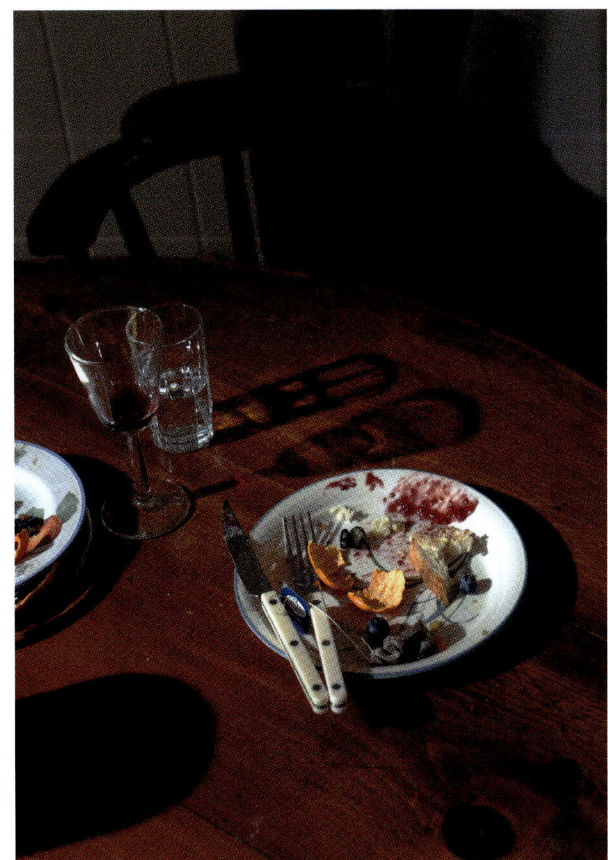

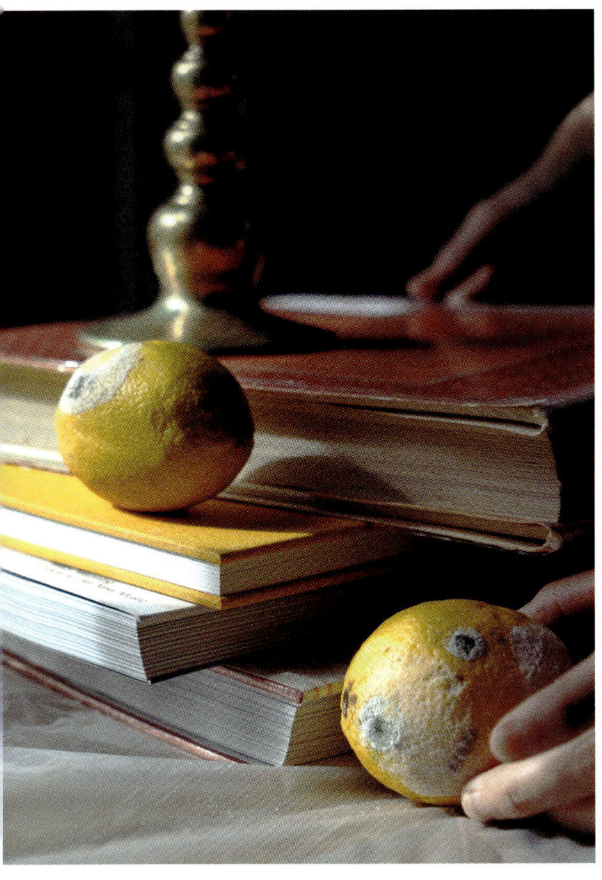

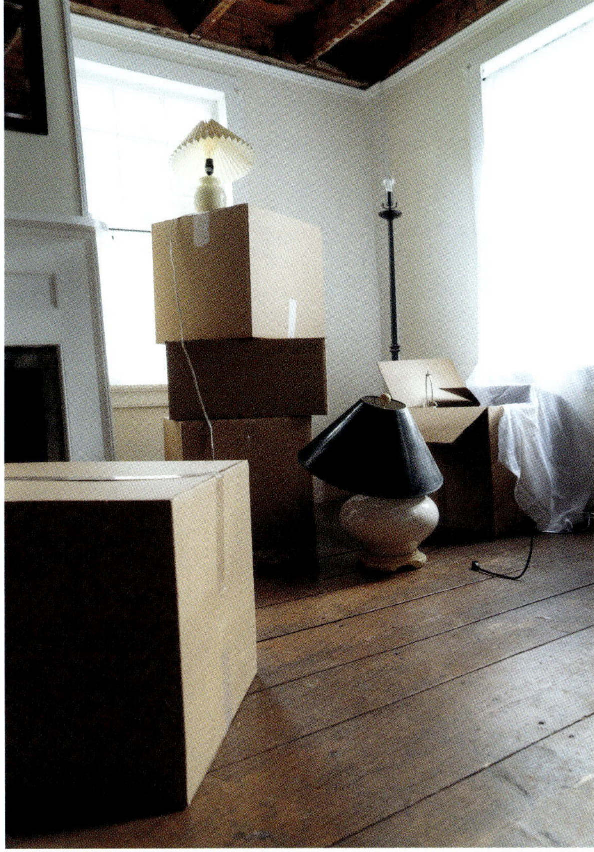

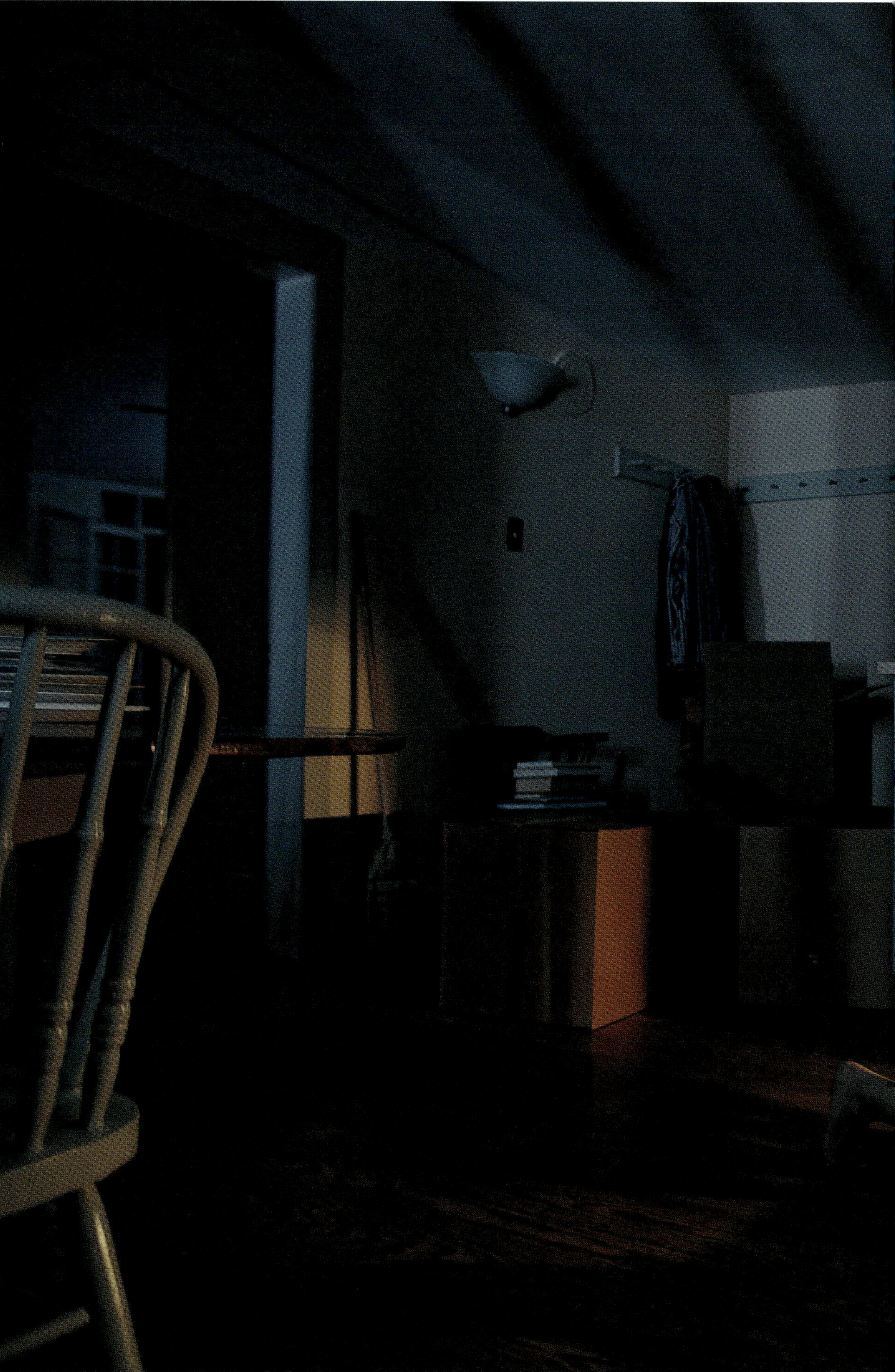

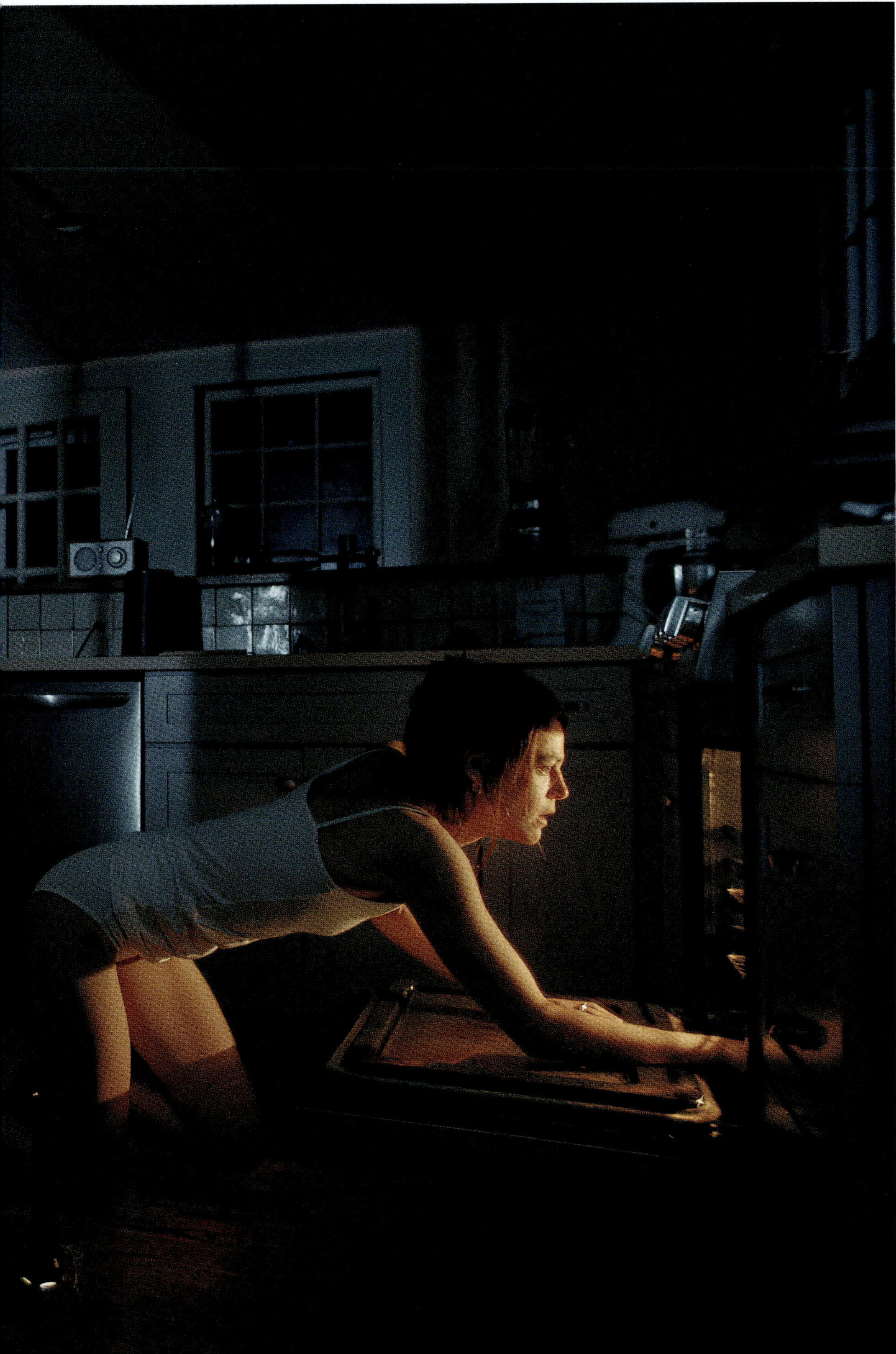

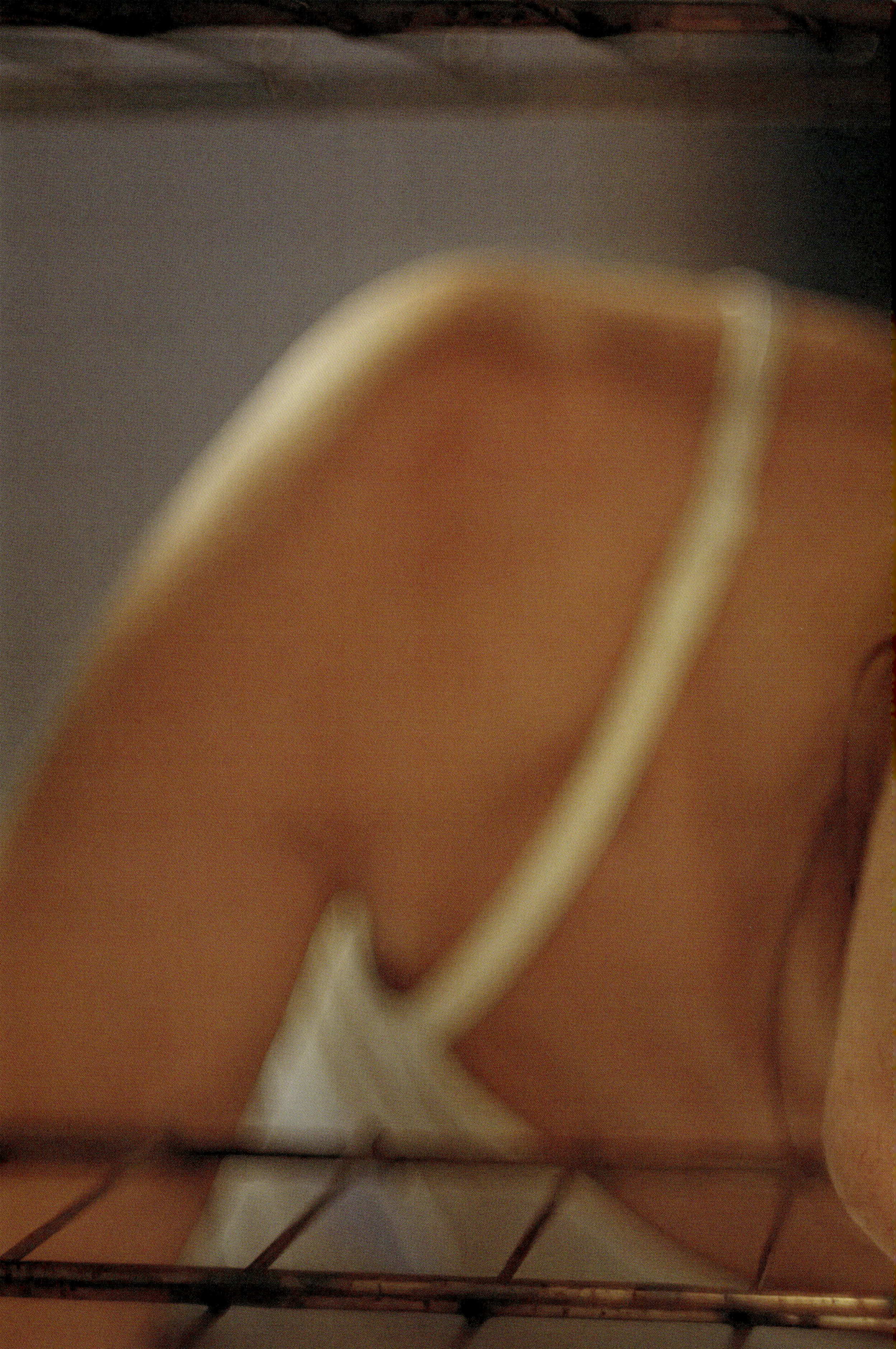

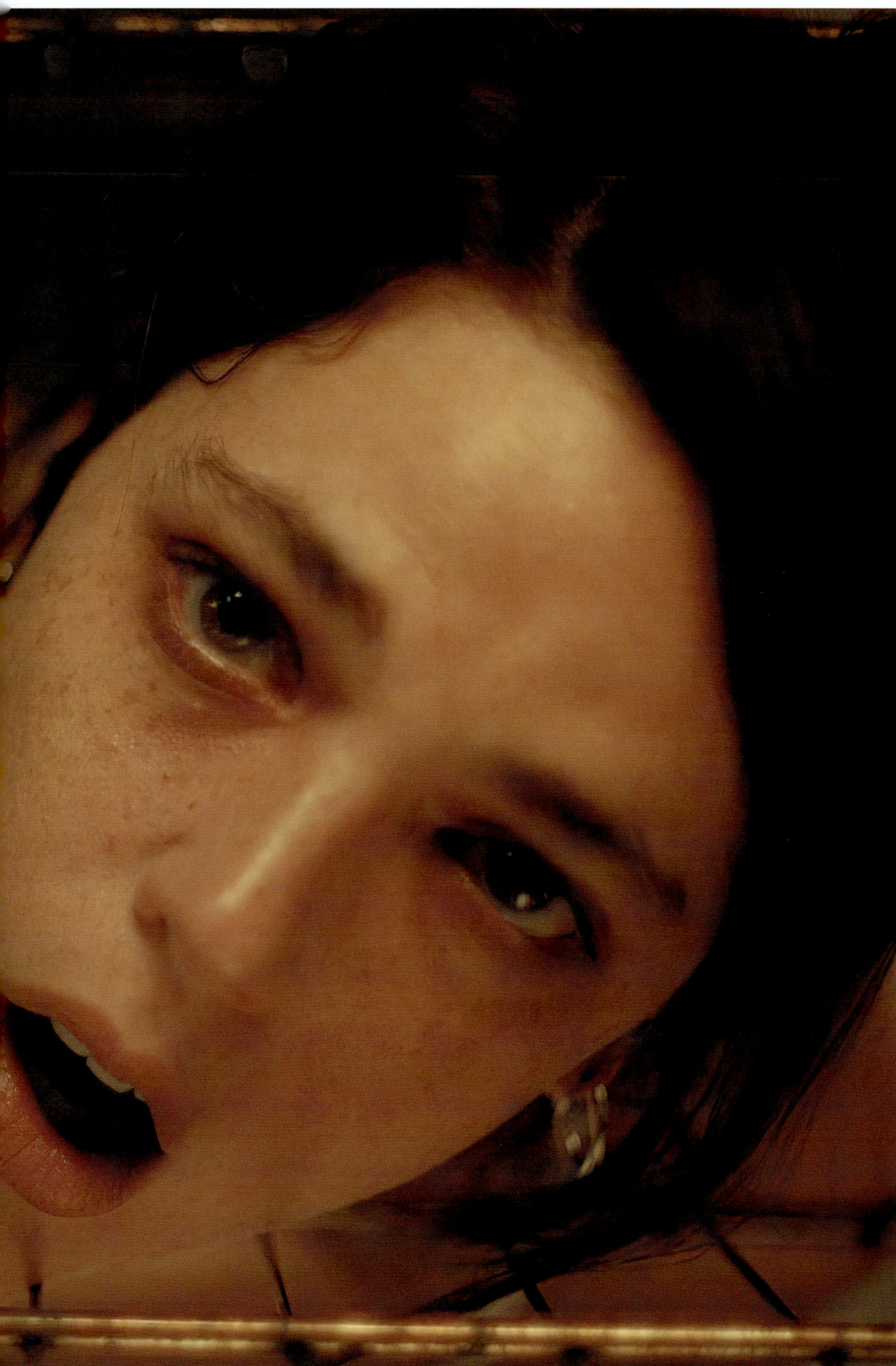

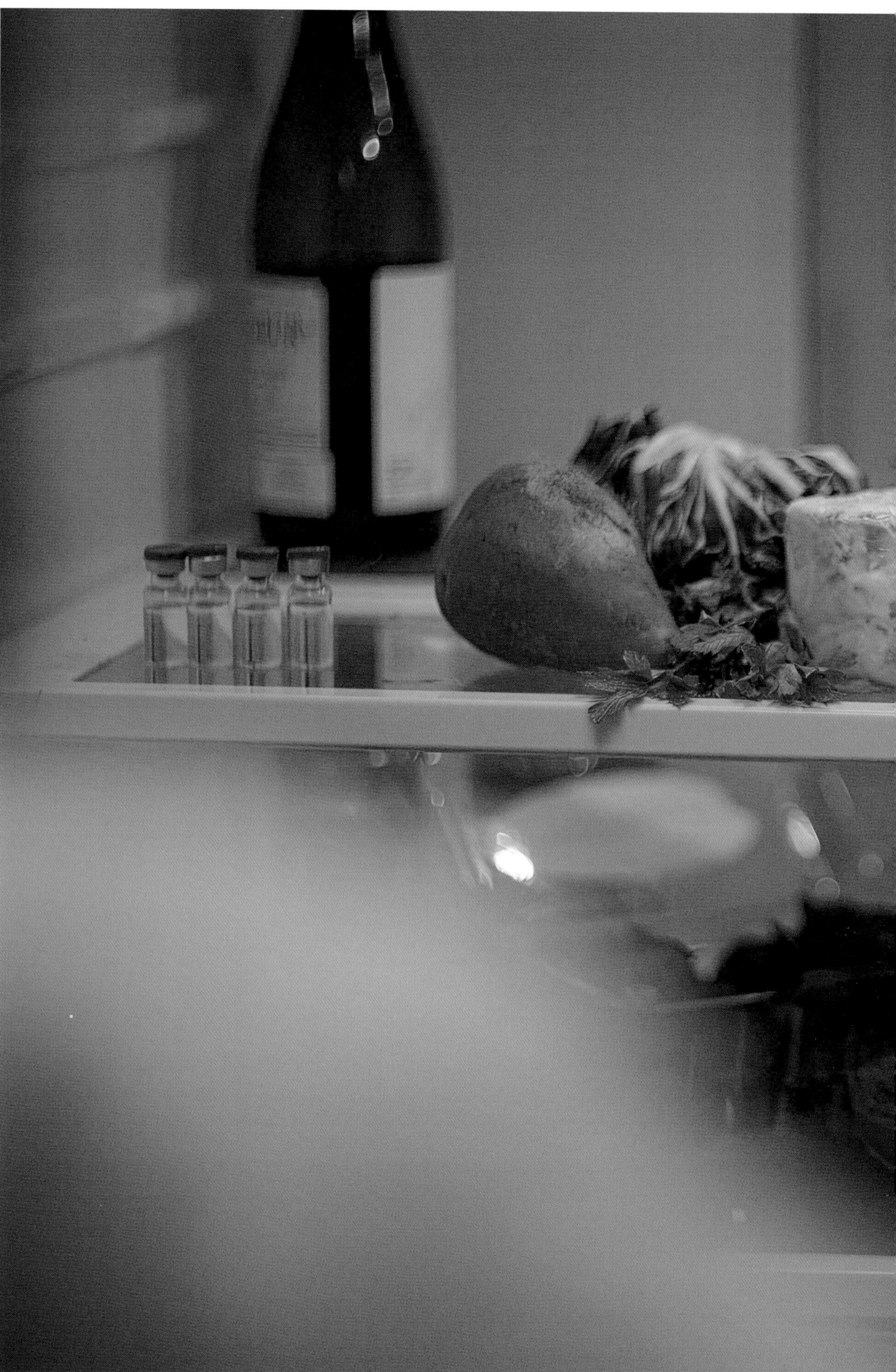

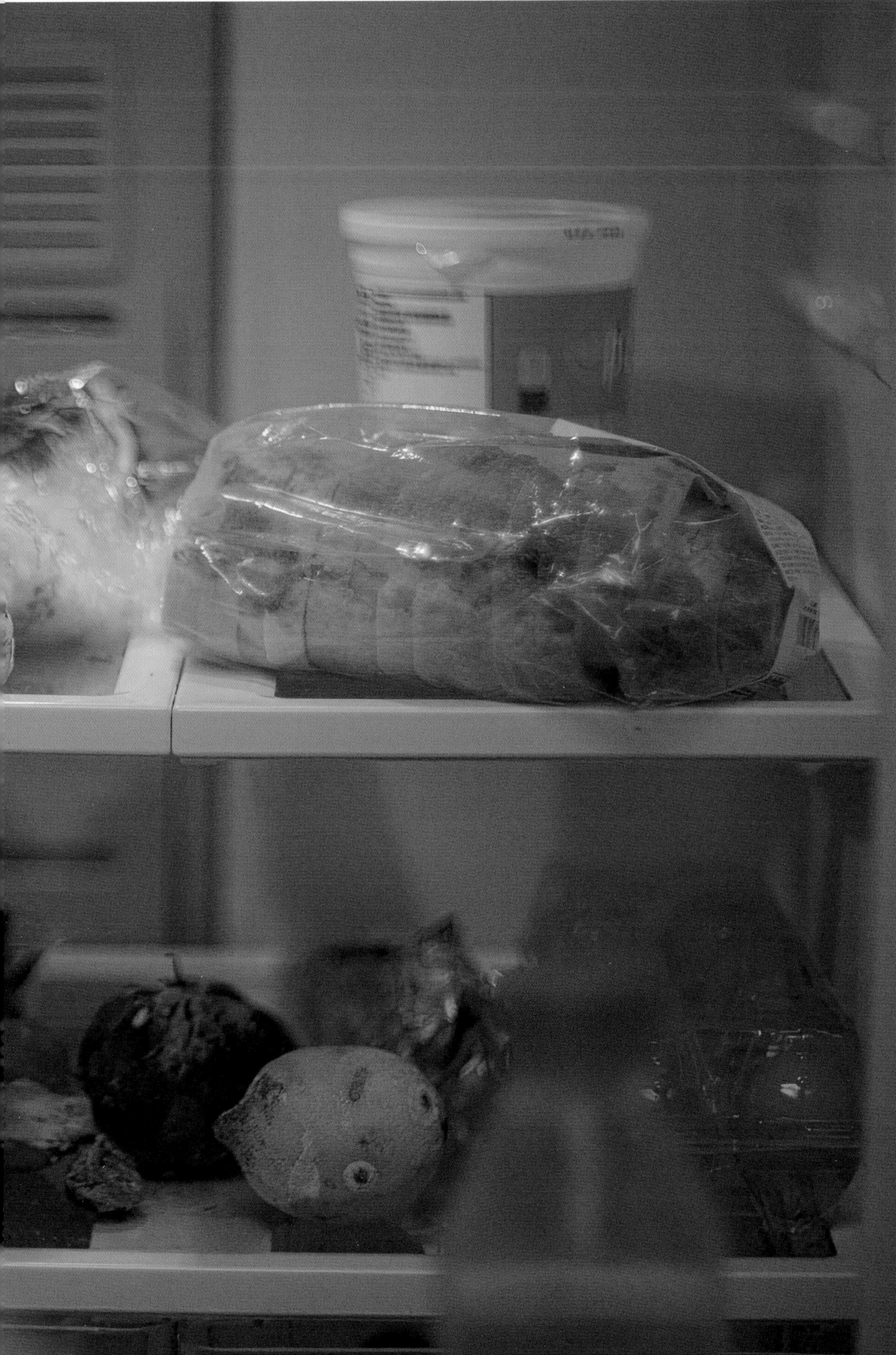

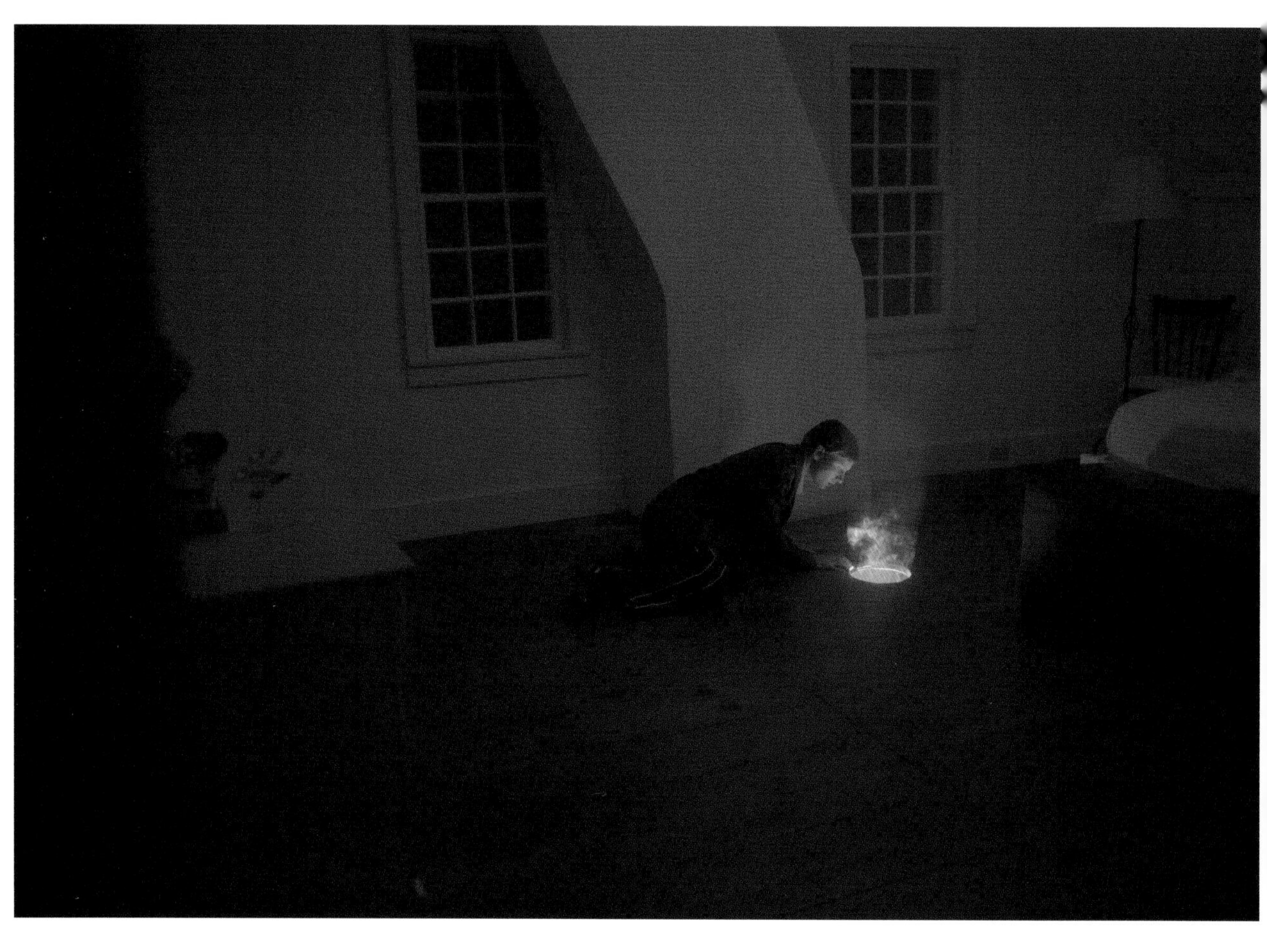

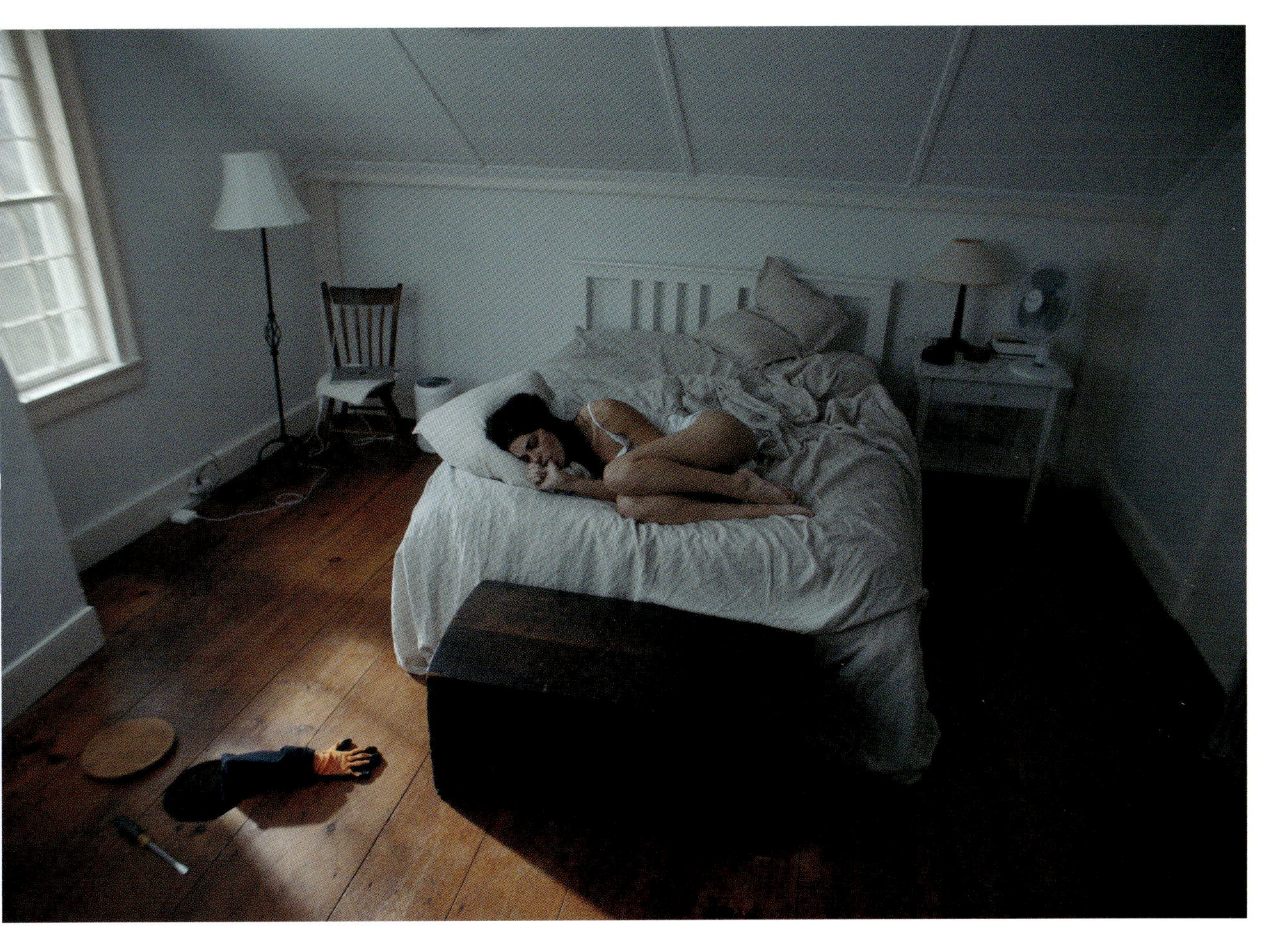

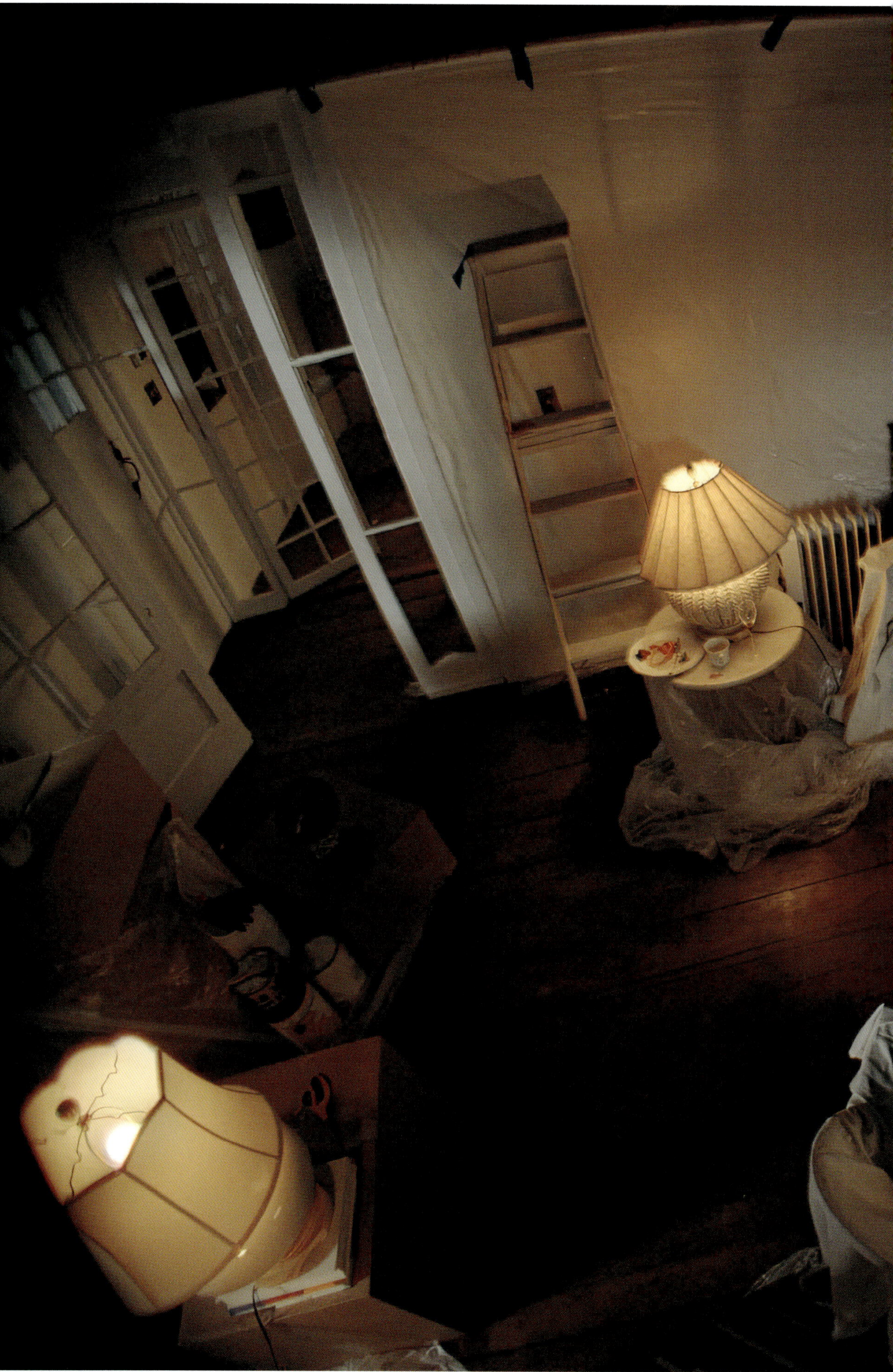

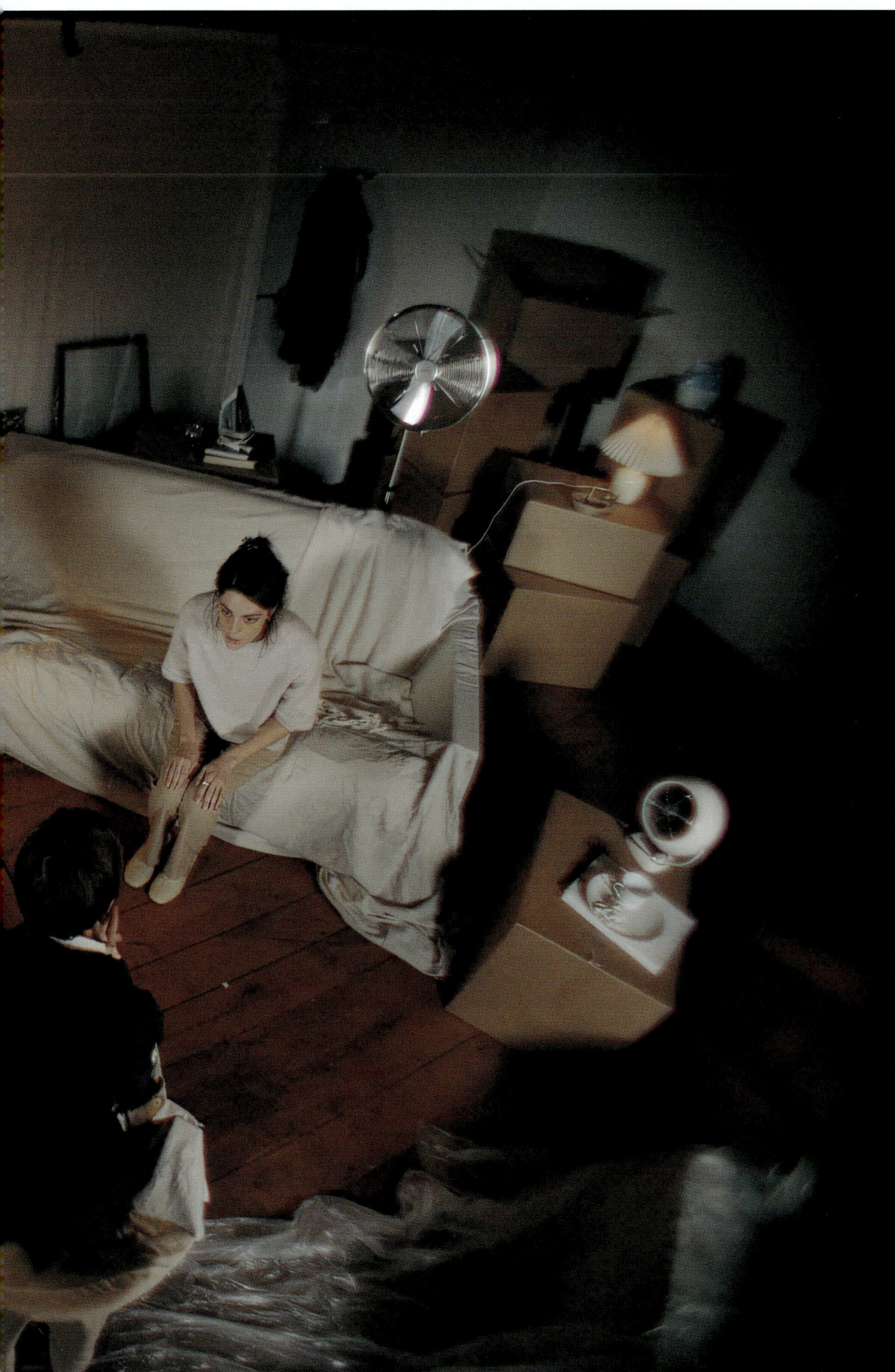

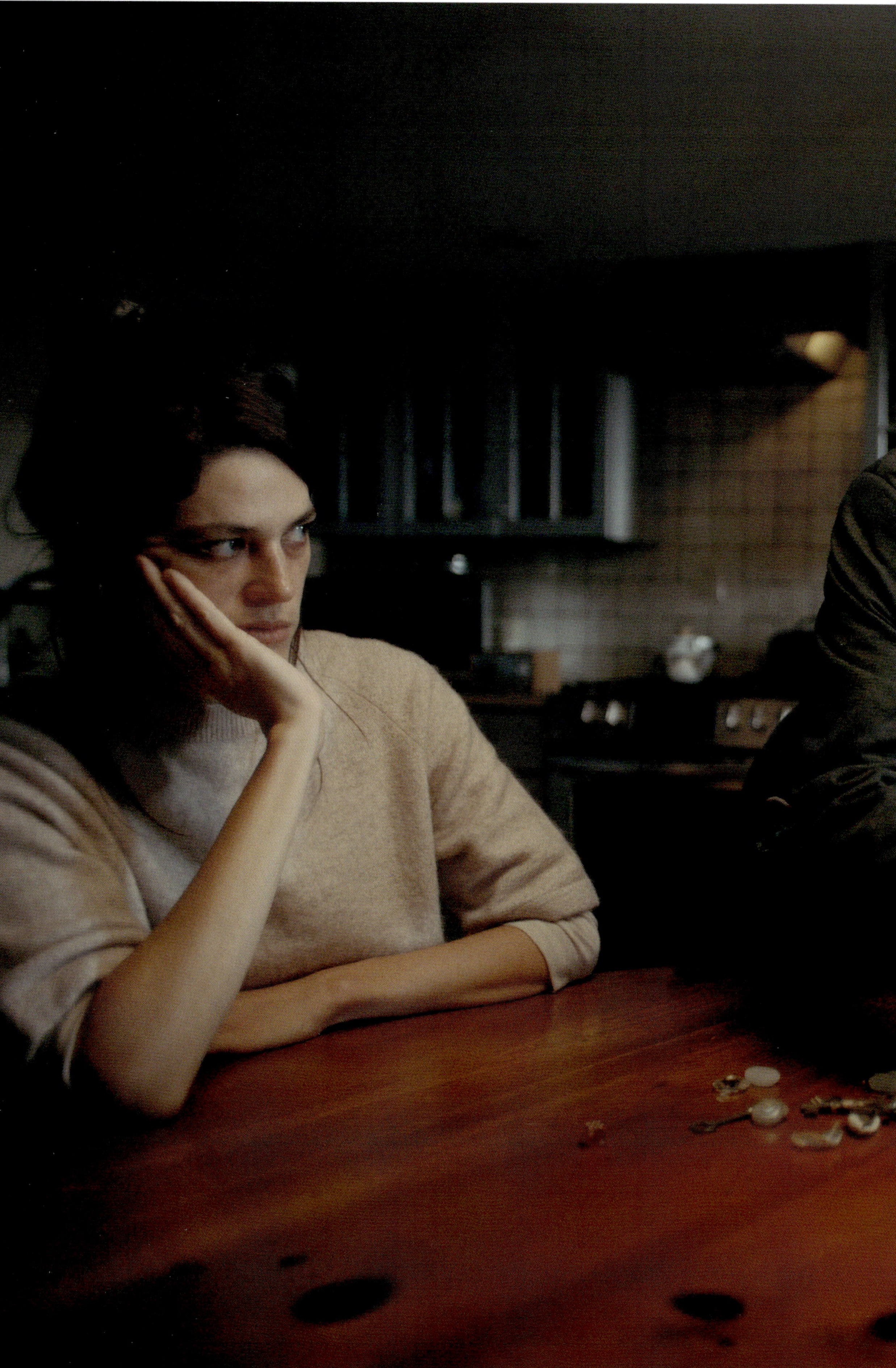

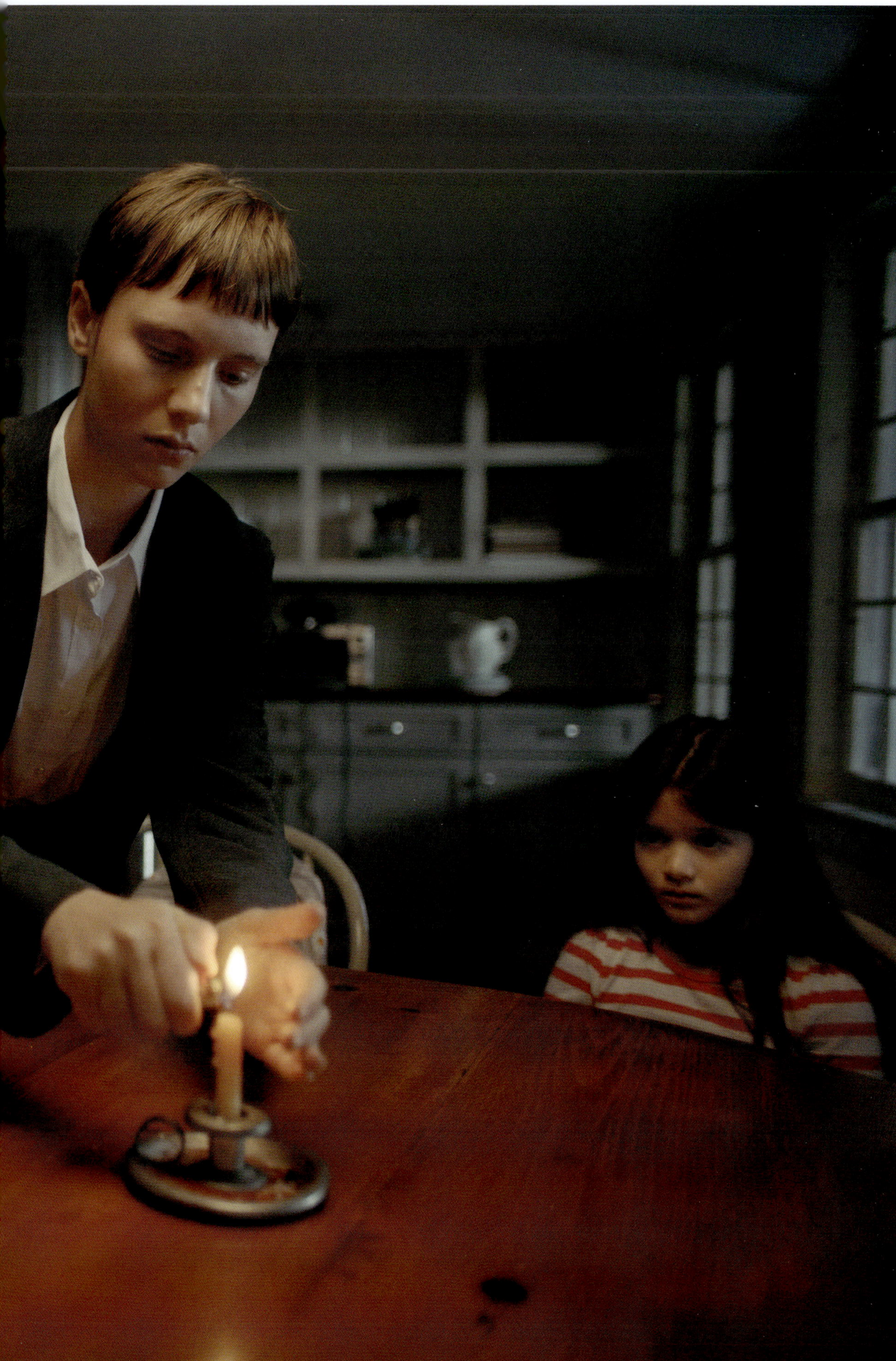

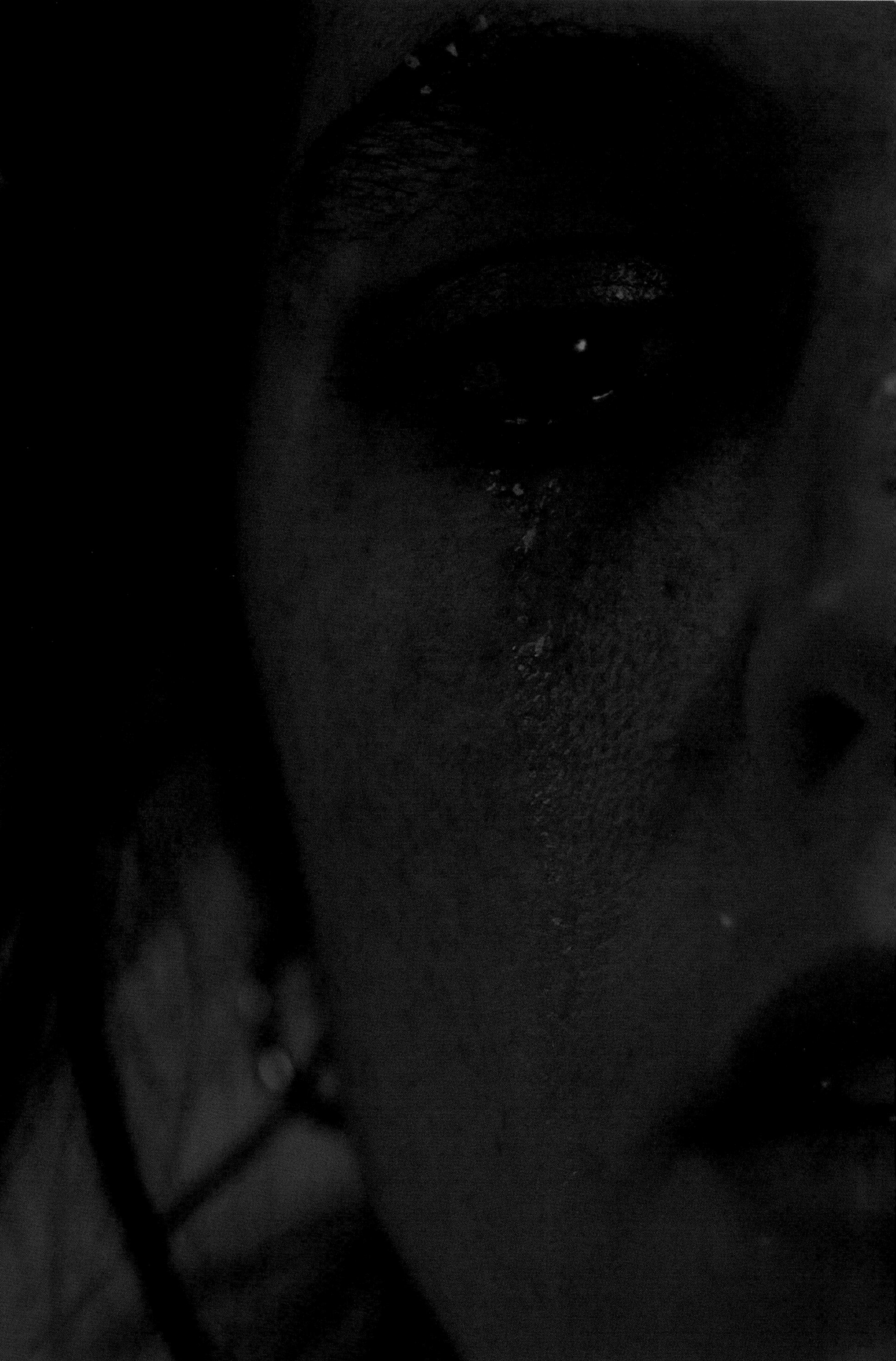

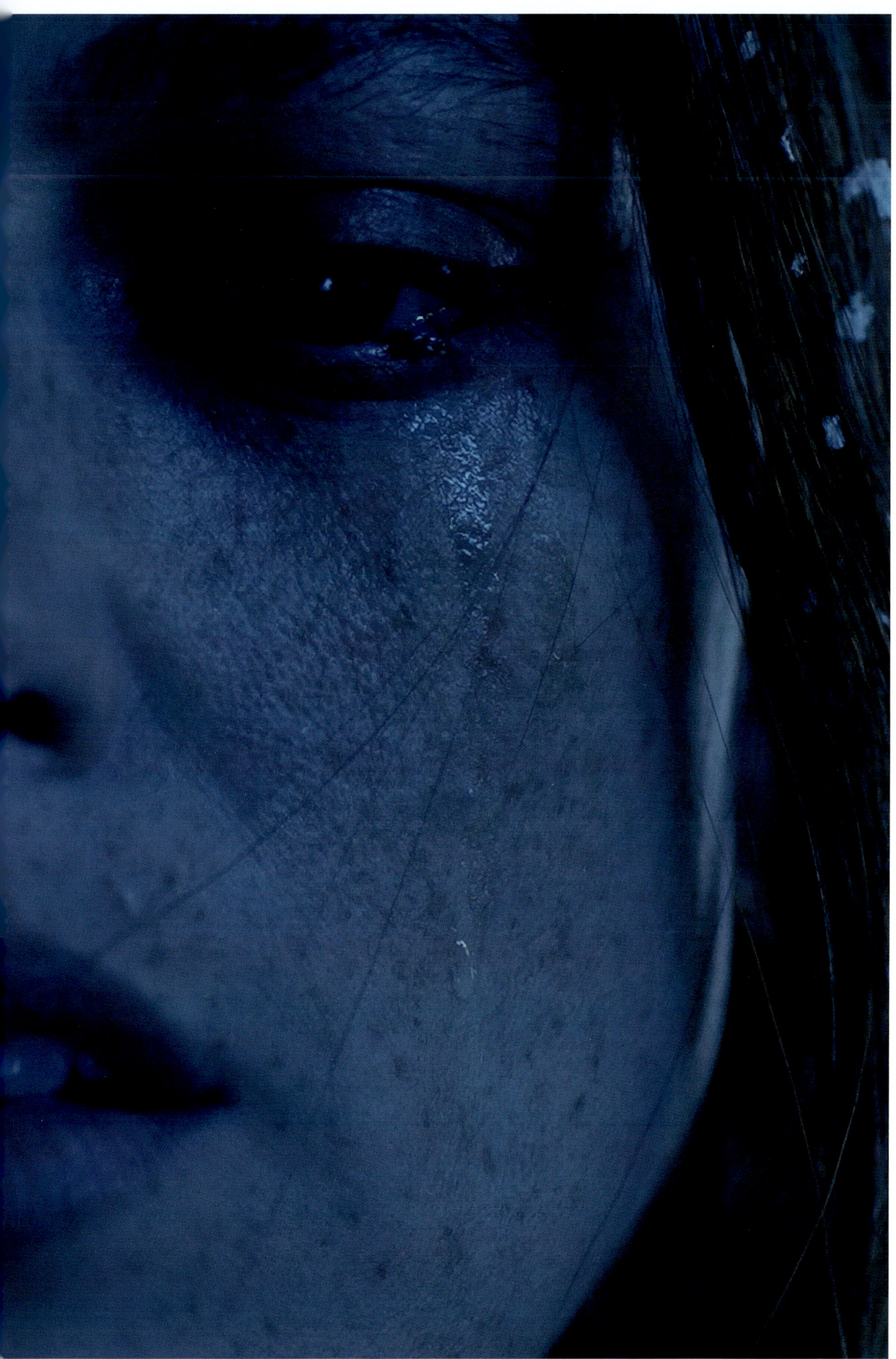

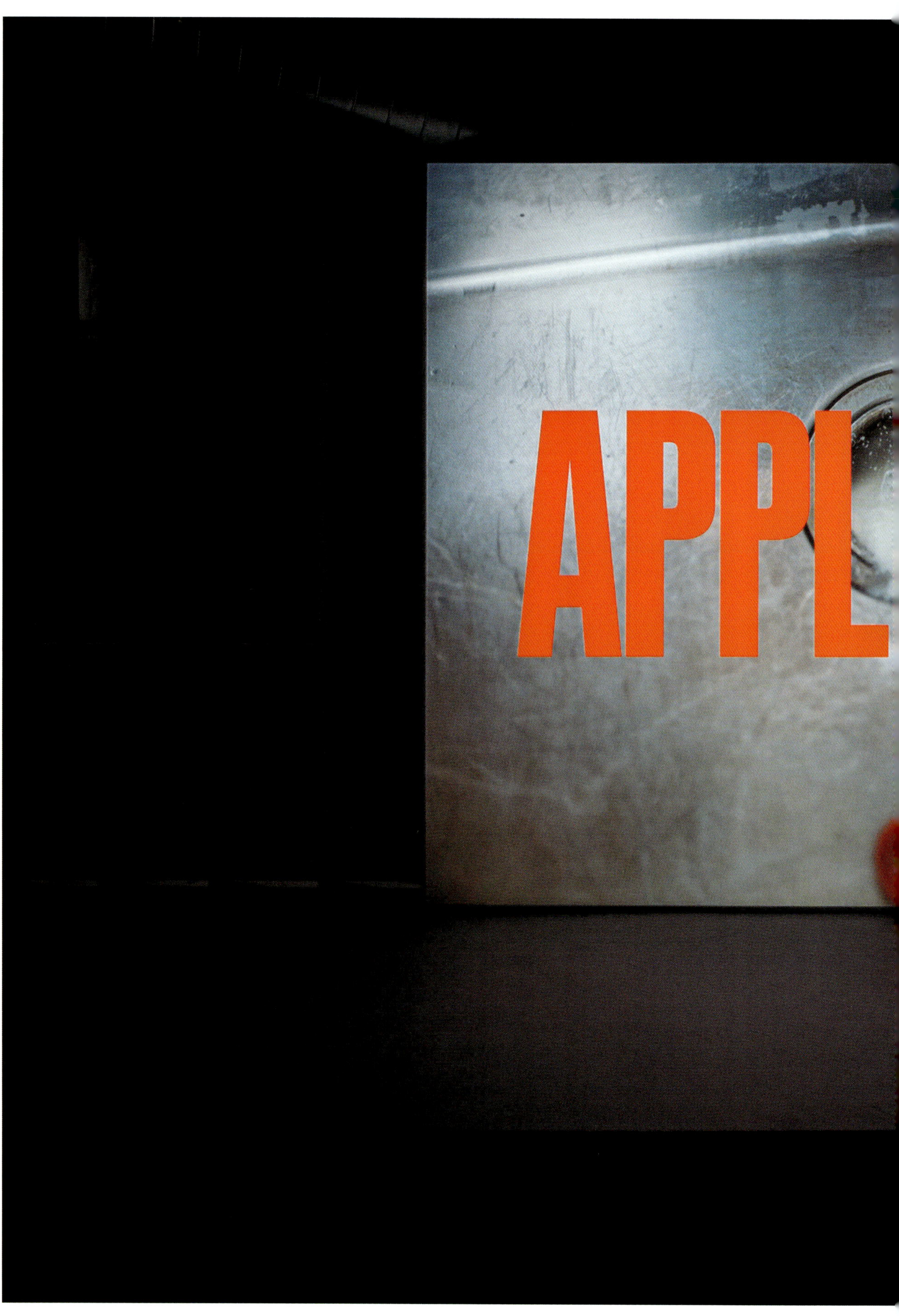
APPL

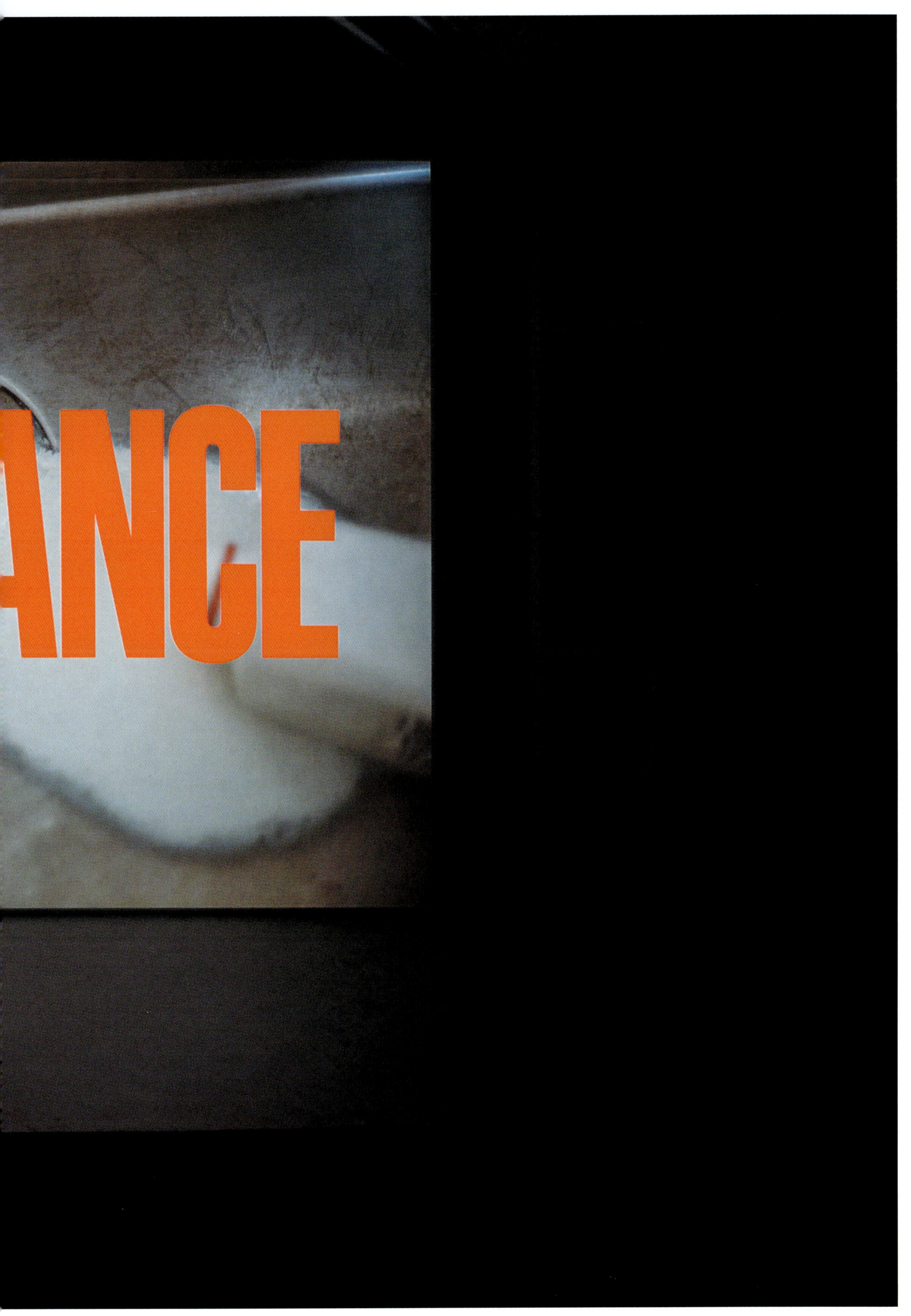

ANCE

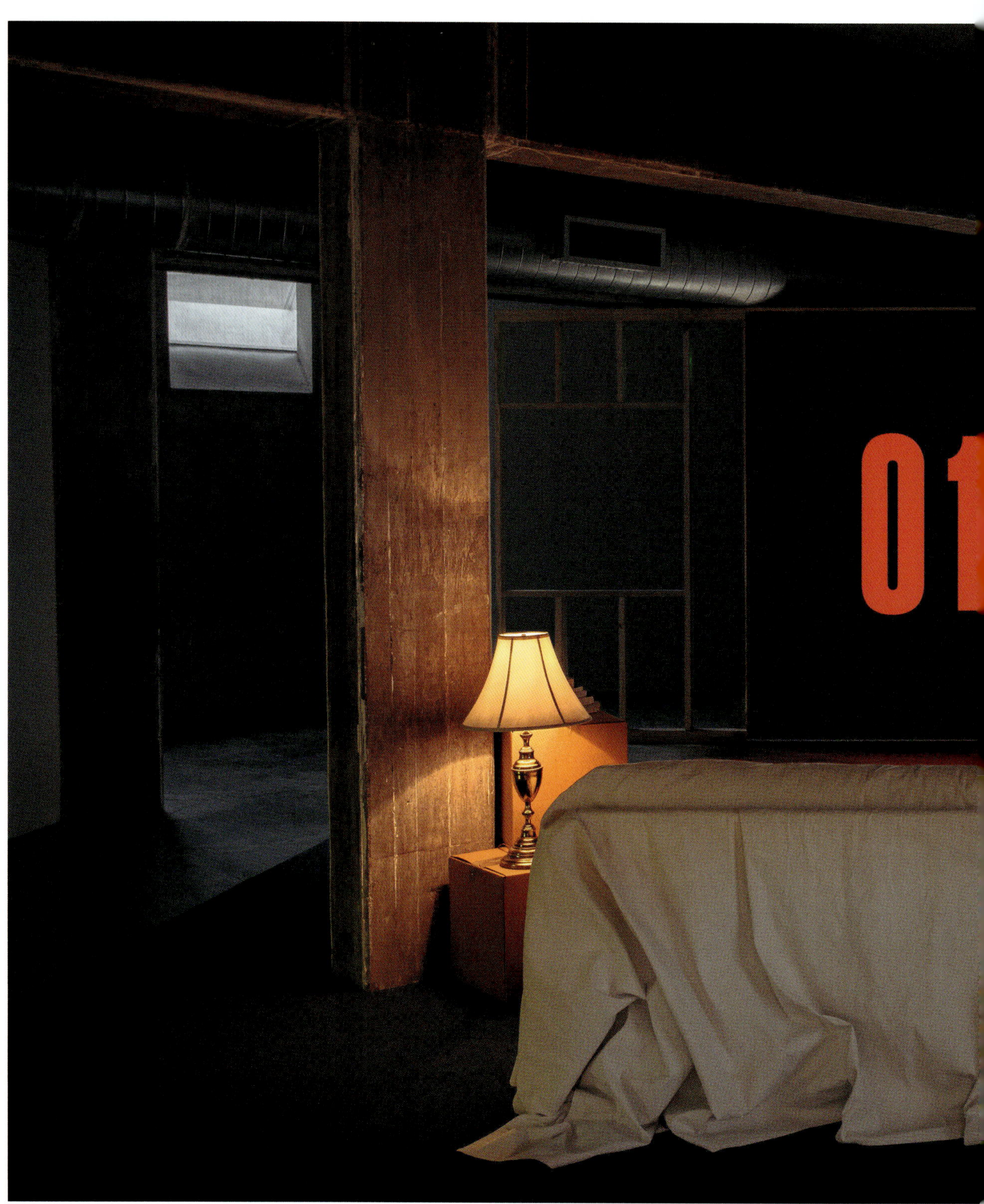
01

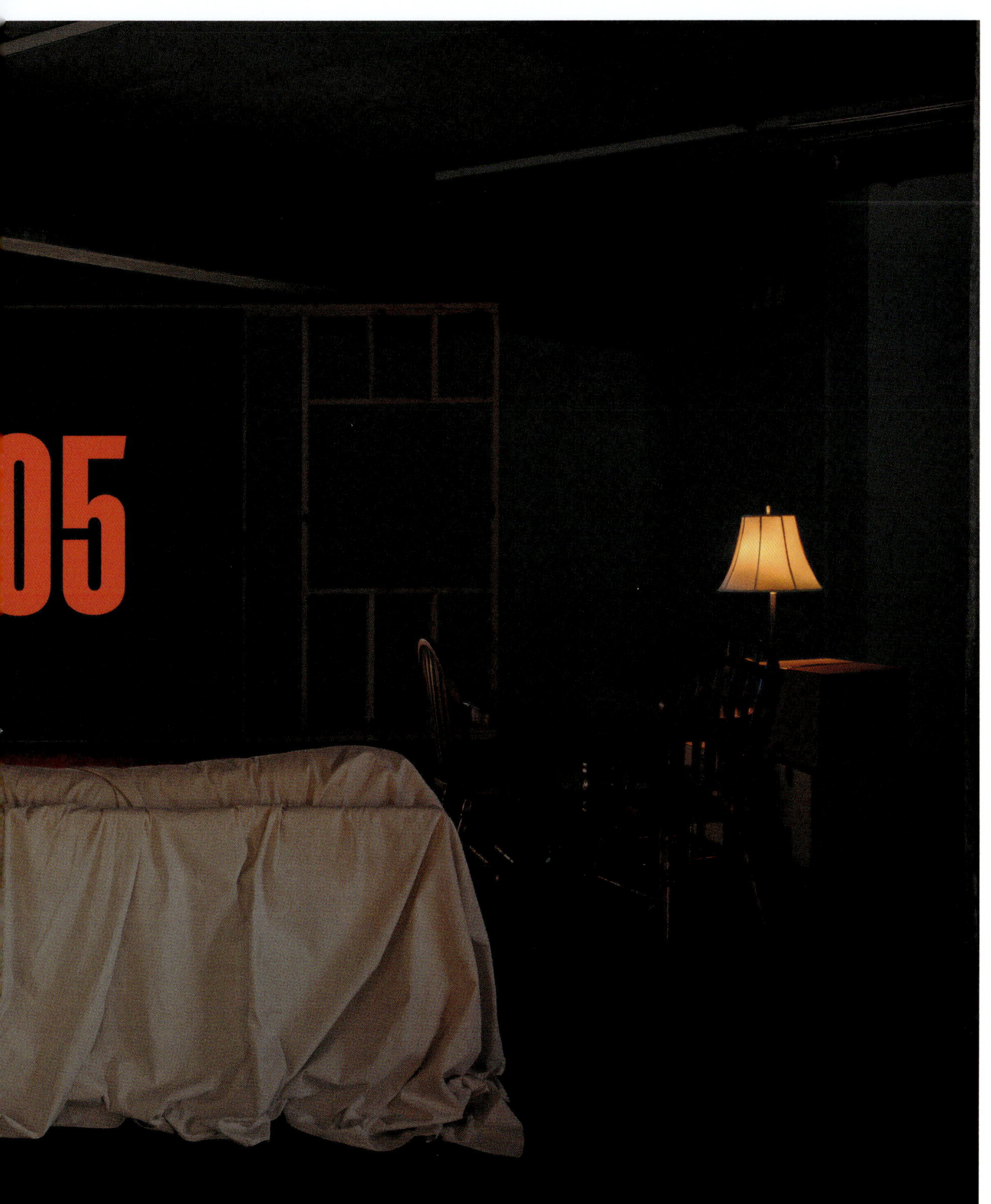

05

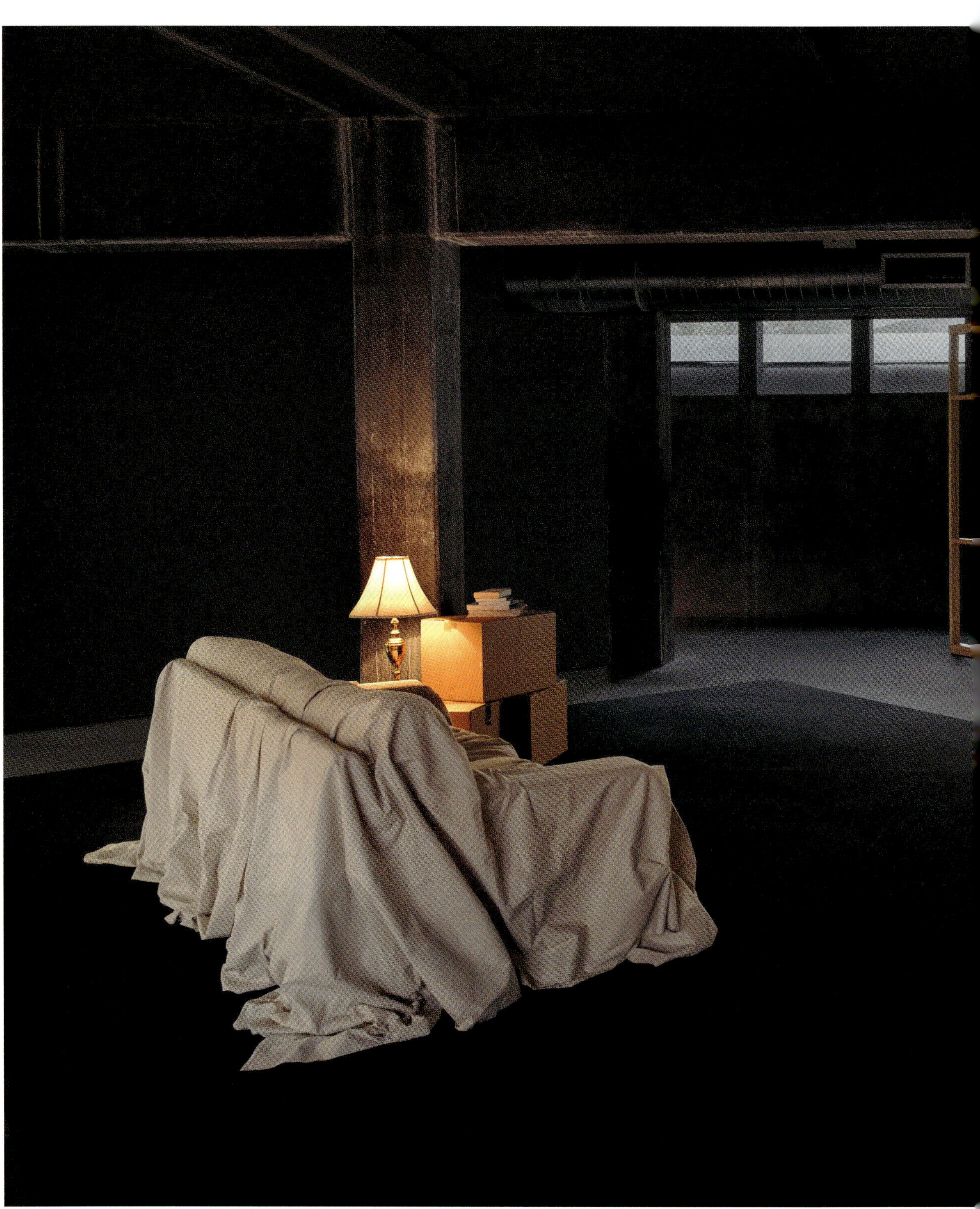

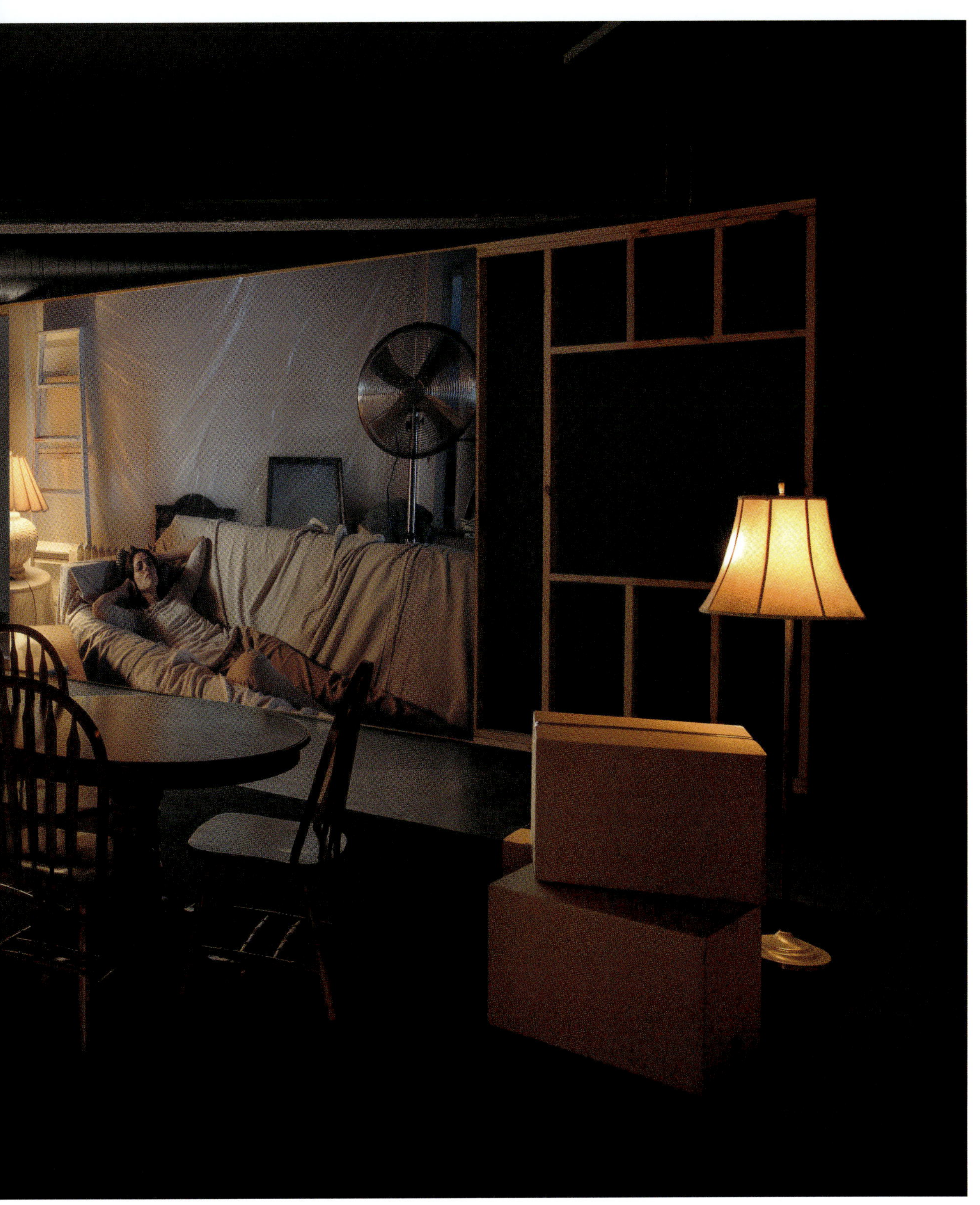

CHRIS KRAUS

If Today Were Tomorrow

For more than a decade, in sculpture, stories, essays, performance, and narrative film, Olivia Erlanger's work has been probing the difficult question of how our most private, internal, and psychological lives are shaped and reshaped by forces completely outside ourselves.

The infinite loop between the self and the world was the central topic of European nineteenth-century novels: the obsession of writers like Charles Dickens, Honoré de Balzac, George Eliot, Gustave Flaubert, and Jane Austen. Two centuries later, the notion of the 'world' has become much more amorphous. The world outside the self has become an ungraspable notion; omnipresent but always elusive; an invisible web. Most contemporary literary fiction prefers to ignore it. Instead, the investigation has been taken up by critical theory, speculative architecture, gaming, sci-fi, visual art, and horror films. Erlanger's work makes excellent use of all of these forms.

"Language and money," the philosopher Franco Berardi wrote in his 2017 book *The Soul at Work*, "are not at all metaphors, and yet they are immaterial. They are nothing, and yet they can do everything: they move, displace, multiply, and destroy. They are the soul of Semiocapital." Growing up in the 1990s and early 2000s, Erlanger was profoundly affected by the global financial crash of 2008. The crash was precipitated by the reckless promotion of subprime mortgages. As details unfolded, it became apparent to all that the single-family suburban split-level homes that fueled the American dream were in fact houses of sand. At a young age, Erlanger began to question the very notion of home ownership, and the unreal reality of global finance.

The chaotic collapse of the housing market during the financial crisis of 2008 is brilliantly visualized in the three snow-globe sculptures that Erlanger made for *Split Level Paradise*, her 2020 Bel Ami Gallery show. In *Soft Kiss* (2020), a generic, suburban split-level house rests on a 'lawn' made of table-top glass, set into the globe. But the glass platform is titled, and covered with weed debris, traces of mold, and artificial white snow. It's a perfect and koan-like metaphor: the dream of private home ownership, upended, and resting on something that's turned slightly fetid. . . .

"Everywhere," Eugene Lim writes in his 2017 novel *Dear Cyborgs*,

> there is no there there. Except for those and that that's fucked. There there's hell. Detroit, Dharavi, Guryong Village, Cova da Muta, Oakland . . . The smoothing of all difference into capitalist civility is remarkably unremarked on. Oh, the omnipotent juices of the market's gut—it eats it all! And maybe the nonremarking is but one other aspect of the digestive process. (How quietly it eats!) . . . Like the city itself the complex is unknowable, one's neighbors are so close yet so far away. . . .

"I had been looking," Erlanger told Rosie Sharp, "around these ideas of systemic crisis, global financial crisis, which is what I came of age in. It's frustrating because we never give these things a language of volume or density."

She was interested, then, in the philosopher Timothy Morton, and in "hyper-objects," a term that he'd coined to describe things like "climate" and "global economy" that are at once very real and completely abstract.

And so, she set out to do this in some of her earliest sculptural works. In earlier exhibitions like *The Oily Actor* (2016) and *Body Electric* (2017), Erlanger found ways to physicalize the sensations caused by these real but elusive abstractions: financial flows. Her sound-piece *I Am No Viper, Yet I Feed* (2016) used data points from Zillow's Detroit real-estate valuations behind a play-list to create a distorted ambient soundscape. And in *Body Electric*, a thick mist of fog and blue light, its rhythm dictated by changes in oil prices, was pumped into the gallery, immersing viewers.

×

In *If Today Were Tomorrow*, Erlanger bisects the museum into four zones: the arrow zone, the planetarium zone, the sitcom zone, and the diorama zone. The sitcom zone is really a theater, where viewers sit and watch *Appliance* (2024), her sixteen-minute horror-genre-inspired film that has been at least several years in the making. Its precursors include her 2022 book of the same name, published in conjunction with her exhibition *Appliance* at Kunst-verein Gartenhaus in Vienna, and the play, "Humour in the Water Coolant," which she wrote and staged for that exhibition. The play's leading characters include the anthropomorphized "Oven," "House," "Lamp," "Shower," and "Fridge," as well as the humans Sophie and Crystal, who have both migrated out of the play and into the film.

Erlanger's psycho-architectural investigation of suburbs began in 2015, when she started work on her book *Garage*, "a secret history of the garage as a space of creativity," cowritten with the Mexican architect Luis Ortega Govela. The original manuscript for the book was called *Hate Suburbia*, and published by Publication Studio. Home, she believes, is a metaphor for the body: the siding its skin, the appliances its vital organs.

During the course of her suburban research, Erlanger studied the his-tories of household appliances: the toilet and shower, the oven, the fridge. The twentieth-century extension of urban space into peripheral zones could not have occurred without the expansion of public utility infrastructure that flushes and fills these machines. Each suburban house is a body, existing alone. And yet, on a poetic but completely material level, it is the appliances that offer a way out of this isolated hell: their pipes and electrical cables con-nect the familiar suburban split-level to the more public spaces of reservoirs, sewers, and grids.

In *Appliance* (2024), Sophie is a young, single woman whose history is unspecified and unknown. She could be an actress. Lanky and white with long glossy-brown hair, she looks like the final girl of every bad horror movie. She's just bought an old house in the country. And, like many before her—the viewer senses—she's fled the city because her chosen career hasn't fully worked out. Her rural escape seems to be in upstate New York, where sadness rises out of the ground.

Sophie's new house—shown to a familiar acquaintance on a FaceTime video tour—could not be more generically, superficially ideal. Whatever history or happiness its old wood plank floors and sloping ceilings might once have contained has been gutted and whitewashed, replaced with the middle-class twenty-first century signifiers of happiness: the gleaming stainless-steel appliances and Kitchen Aid mixer; the white ceramic wood stove; the wrought-iron black faux-colonial latches on the white-painted wood doors.

Like Sophie herself, the house could not be more sterile or sad. Living alone but still craving a child, she's apparently getting IVF treatment, injecting her bruised skin every night with fertility drugs. Sophie sleeps curled at the foot of her bed like a fetus holding on to her phone.

We know right away that things are about to get weird. The house, dreamt as a refuge, assumes a life of its own that maddeningly echoes Sophie's disease and surfacing trauma: the appliances hum, the oven breathes. Mysteriously somehow the fridge has unplugged itself and Sophie's perfect assortment of healthy Whole Foods inside it is covered in mold. As Stephen King observed in his essay "The Modern American Horror Movie: Text and Subtext," horror films frighten us because of the ways they connect the unreal to the real. Horror films depict financial and sociological stress and then move deeper inside, probing out most deep-seated personal fears.

Terrified Sophie consults Crystal, a local exorcist she's found online to cleanse her new home. Despite her nightly and painful efforts to become pregnant, Sophie is taken aback when Crystal arrives at her door after dark with her small daughter . . . the idea of a child being much more appealing than an actual child. True to the genre, Sophie confronts her fears. Wearing a thin, cream sweater, she weeps and then cleans up the mess. But in the last shot she looks up abruptly at something off-screen: is the terror beginning again?

×

Appliance contains so many vital ideas that it's tempting to see the short film as the mother ship or the heart of the exhibition. But *If Today Were Tomorrow* transforms the museum into a single sculptural space, visual themes and ideas are refracted in scale and in shape. Through this refraction, they at once clarify and distort.

Erlanger's two new sculptures *Antimeridian* and *Prime meridian* (2024) consist of two spheres cantilevered out of the wall. Boxy suburban single-family houses erupt from the skins of the planets like boils or cysts, lit from inside with loose electrical cords. Looking closer, the planets are actually three-dimensional aerial maps, depicting abstracted roadways. Space is used up: the planets covered in roads like arterial veins.

The four dioramas in the diorama zone—a city, a mountain, a mesa, and a park—seem to suggest an escape (like Sophie's house) into an idealized world. But looking closer each of these four environments is demarcated, bisected by property lines and surveilled. Mesa obscures the desert landscape with billboards and ads, while Park—inspired by the baroque garden in the movie *Last Year at Marienbad* (1961)—is a 'free' urban space that imparts only a sense of control . . . an order that's been externally, imperially imposed.

In *Eros (When Night Was Last Dark)*, sixteen polished aluminum arrows map a celestial constellation. Each arrow is titled with its own stellar coordinate point: the numeric system that astronomers and sailors once used to position themselves and their crafts. During the last quarter century, light pollution has increased by forty-nine percent rendering celestial navigation all but obsolete. Here, Erlanger recreates the sky over Houston, Texas on the night (January 26, 1880) before Thomas Edison patented the electric lightbulb. It was, she explains, "the last day the sky was dark."

Ecological exhaustion, environmental collapse. All of Erlanger's witty, inventive and beautiful work is built on her deep understanding of structure, from the engineered meshes of highways and grids to the abstracted flows of finance.

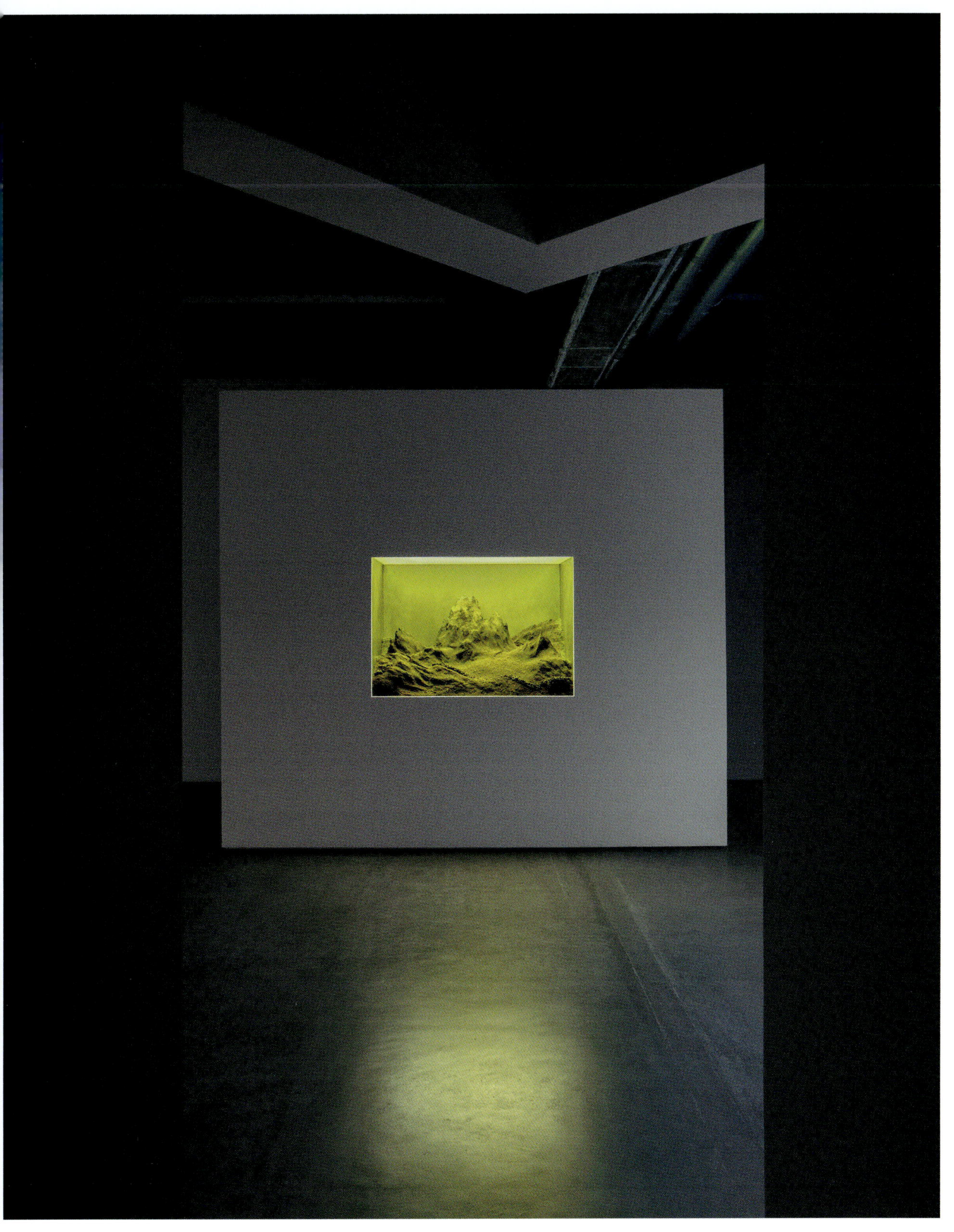

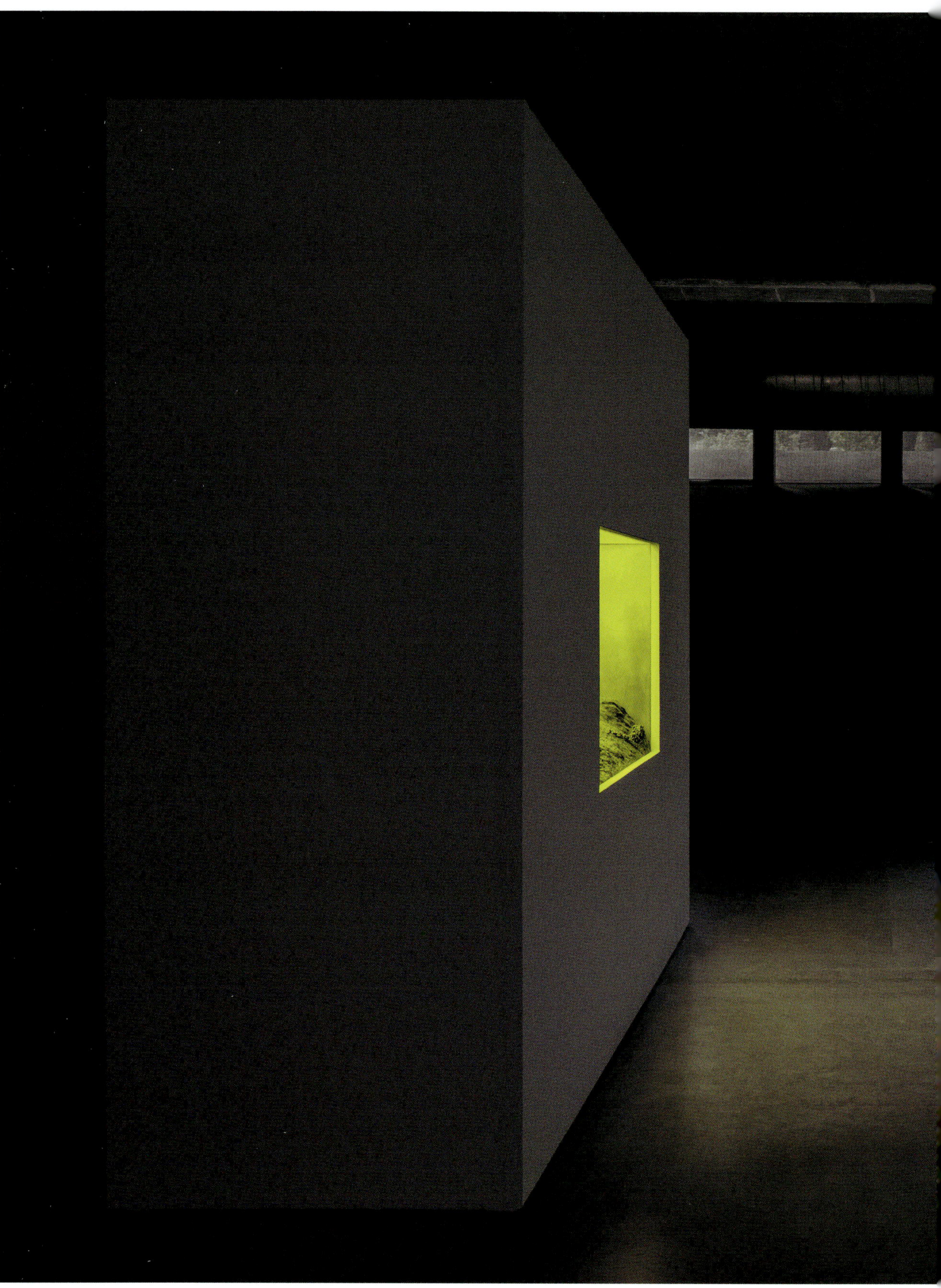

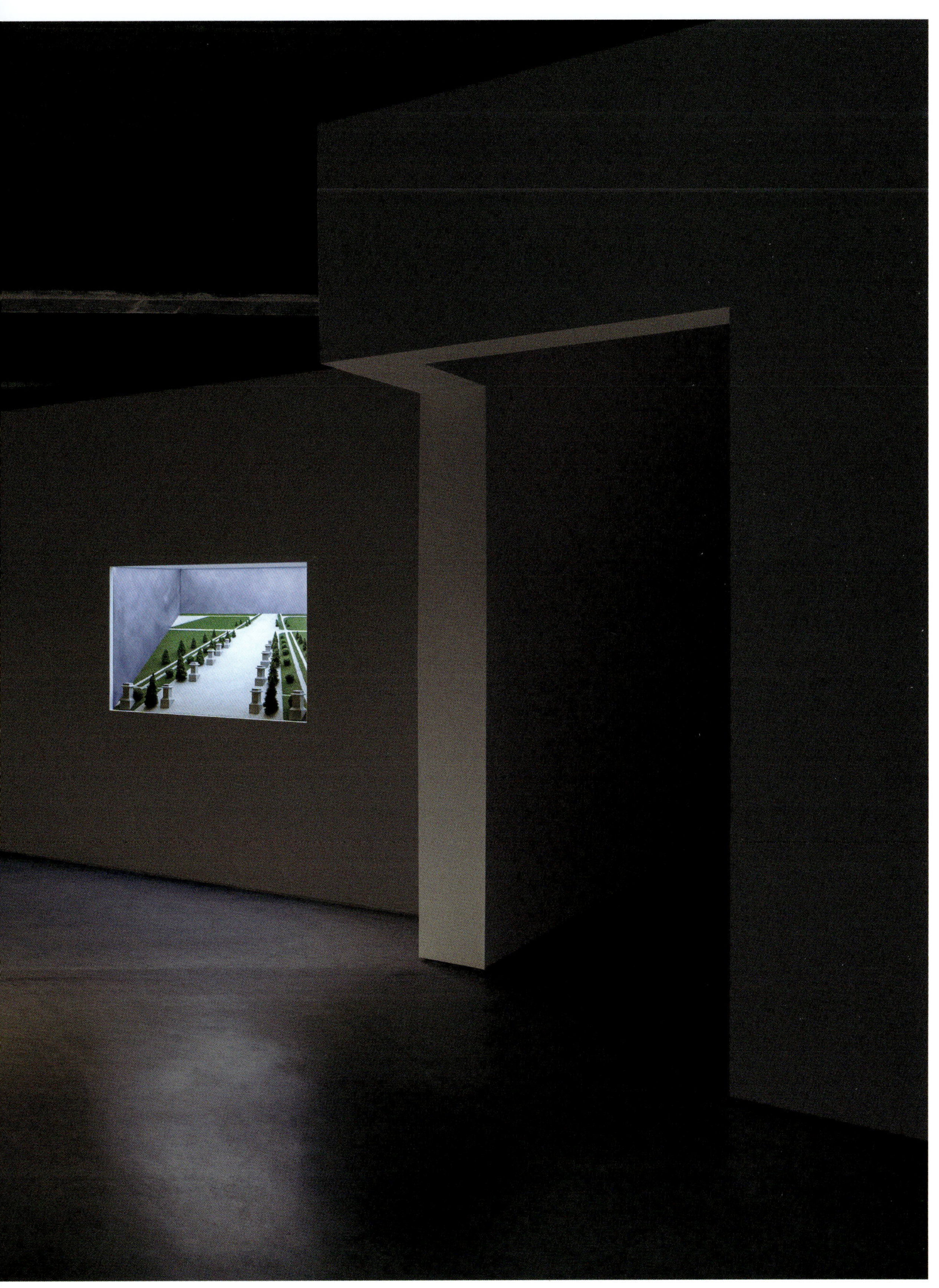

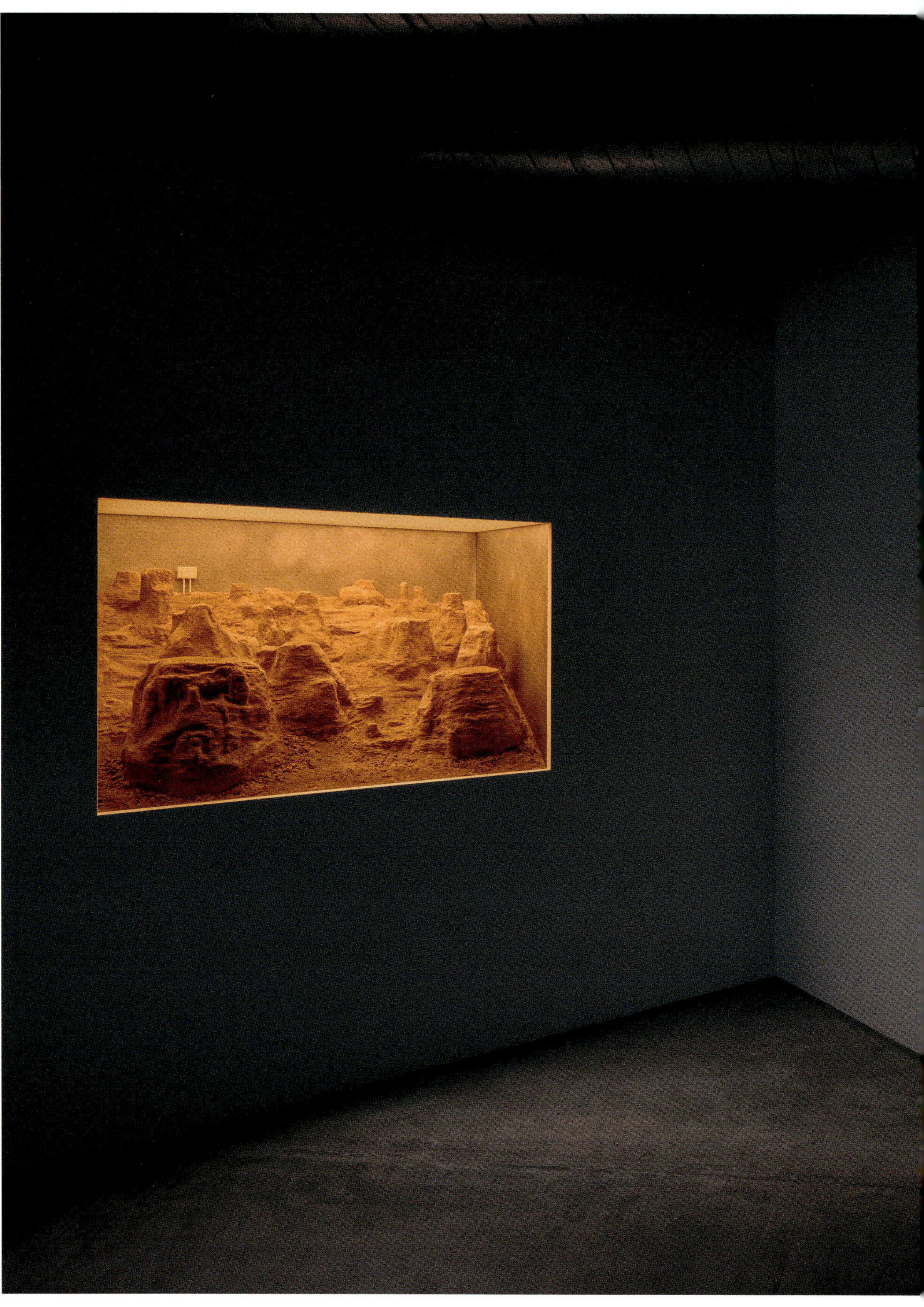

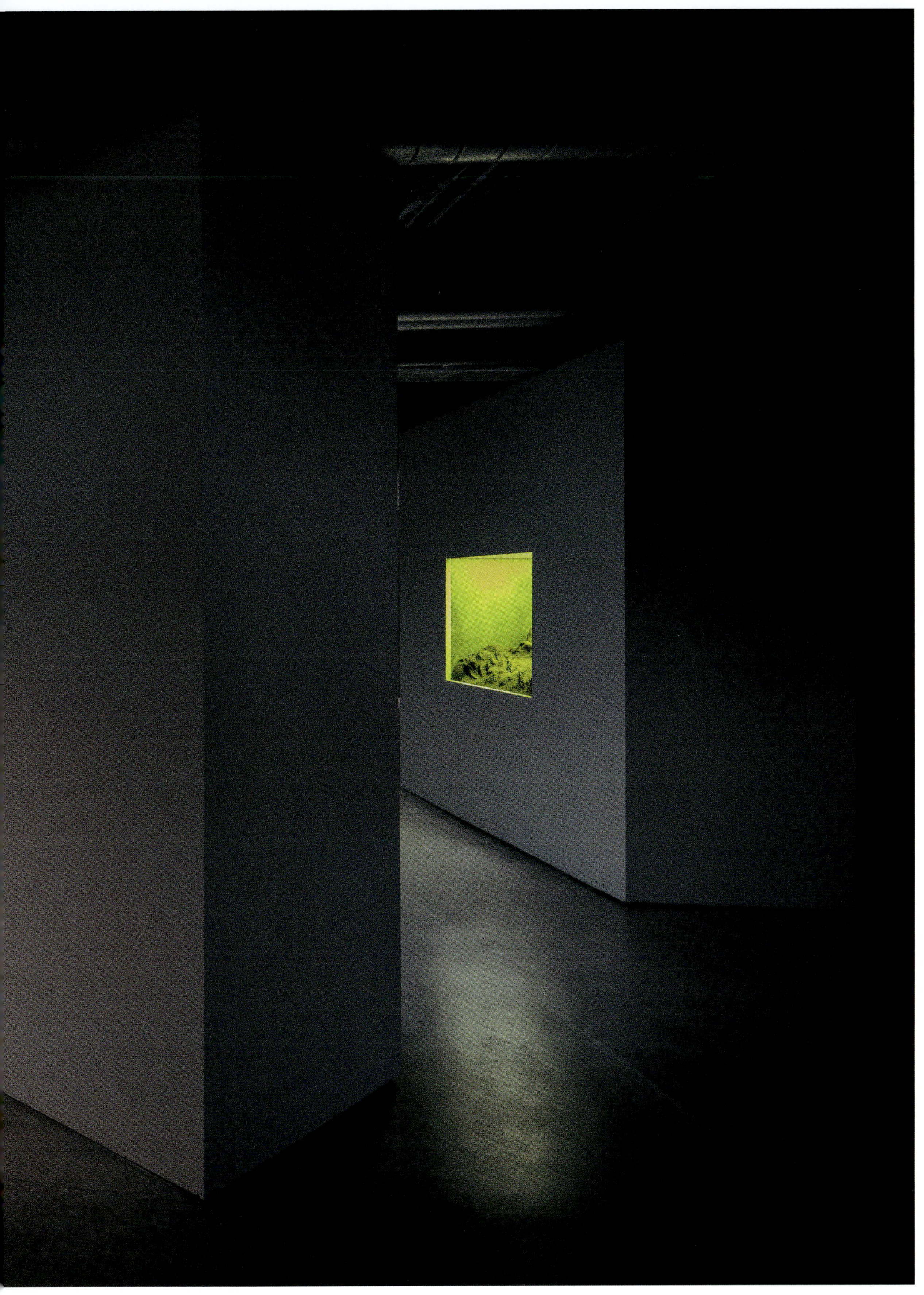

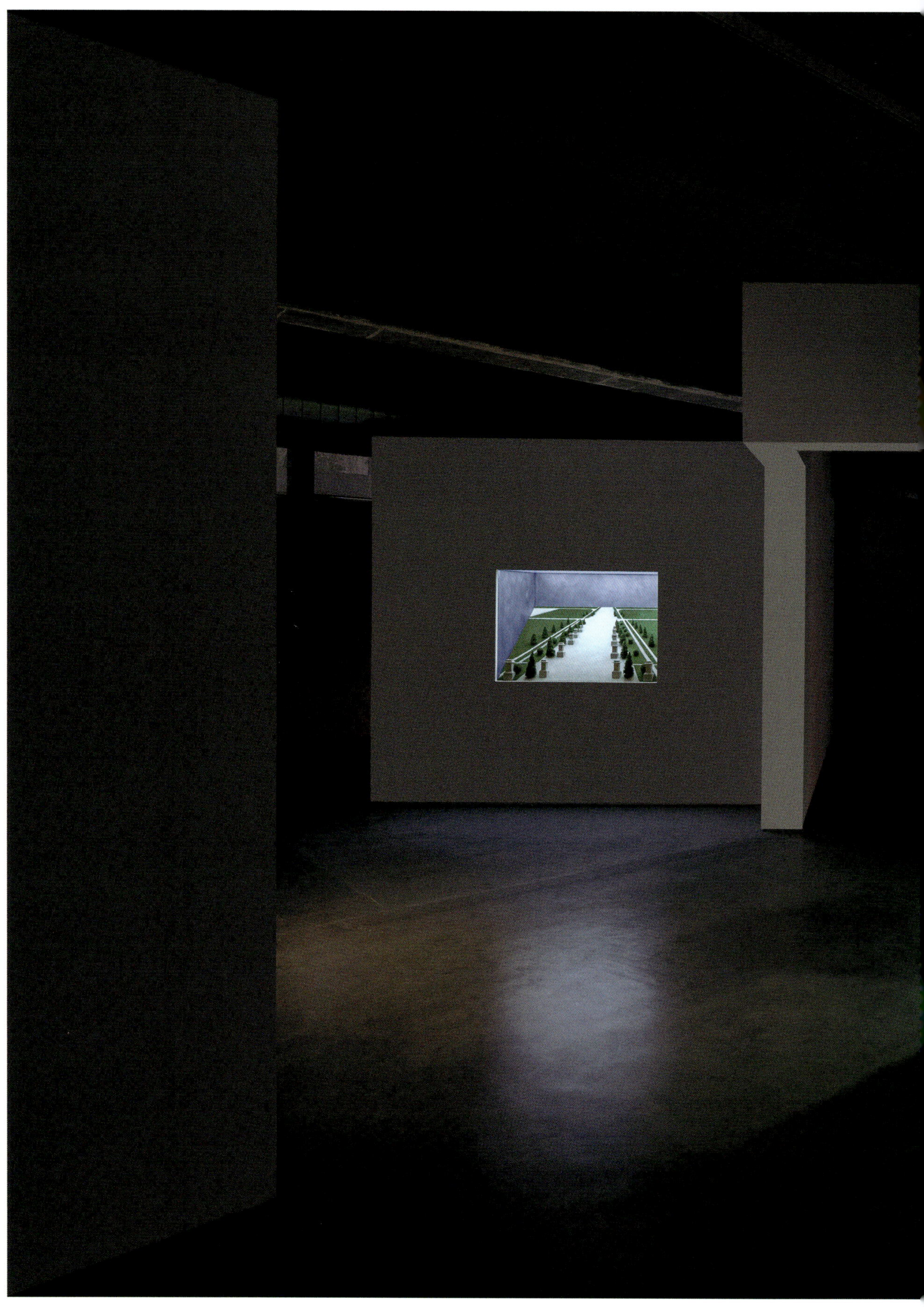

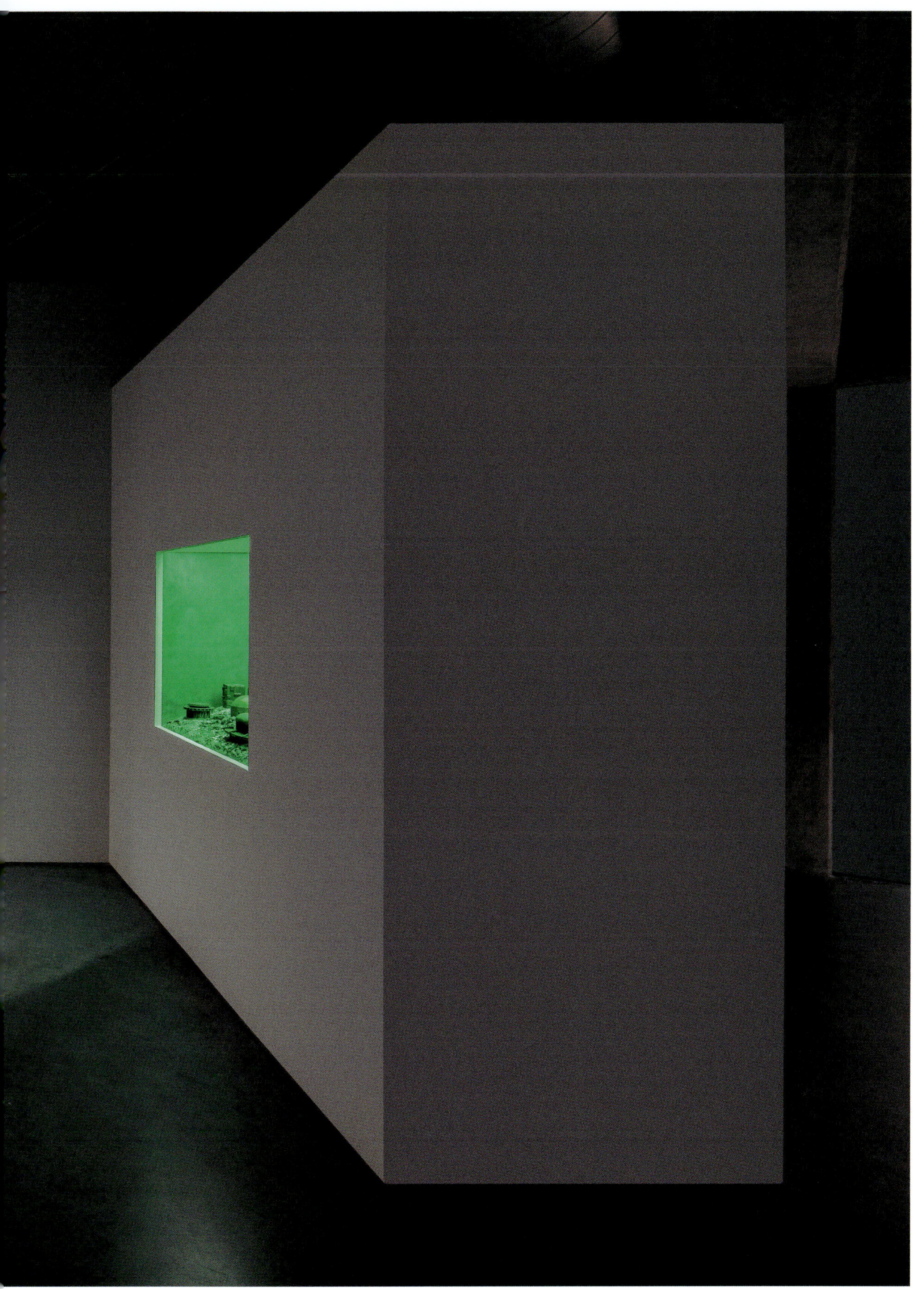

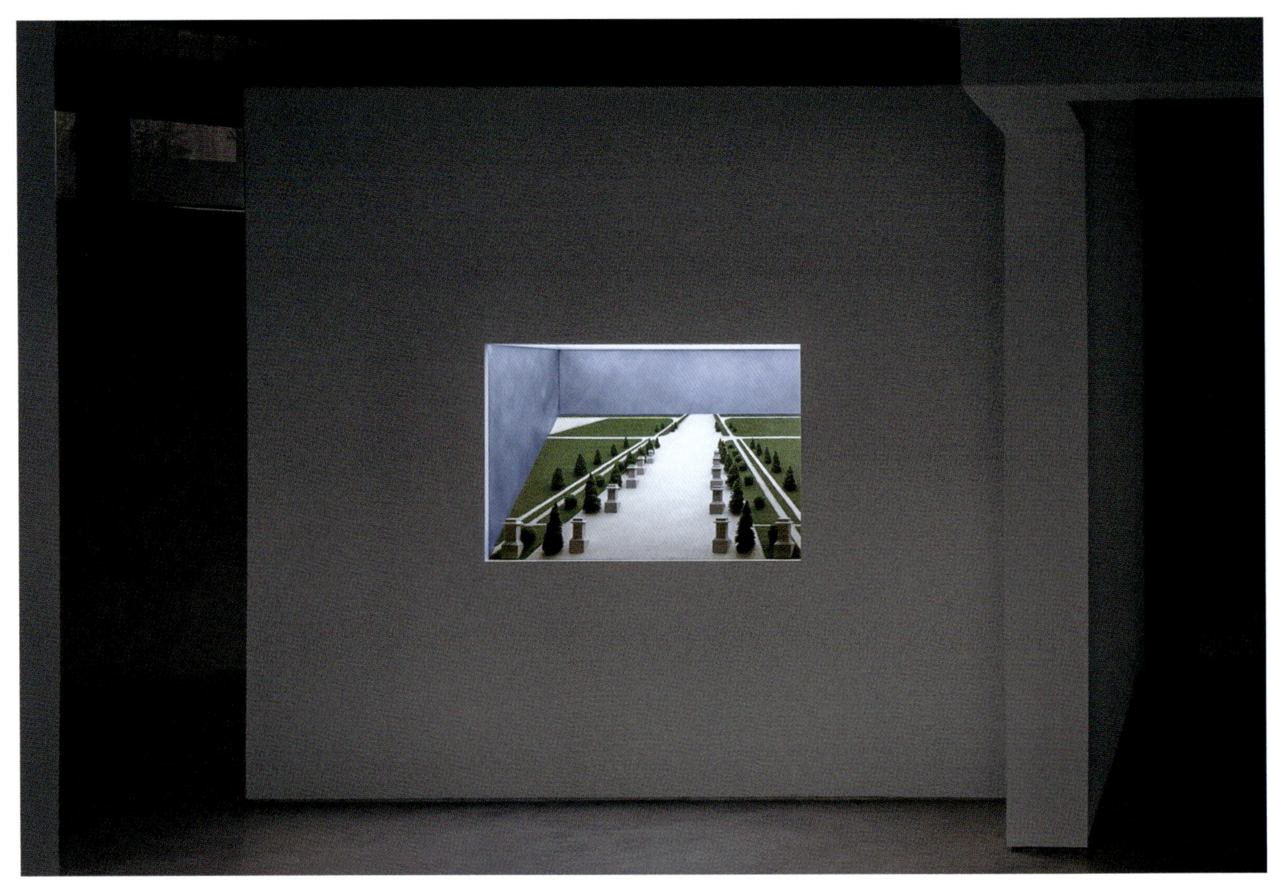

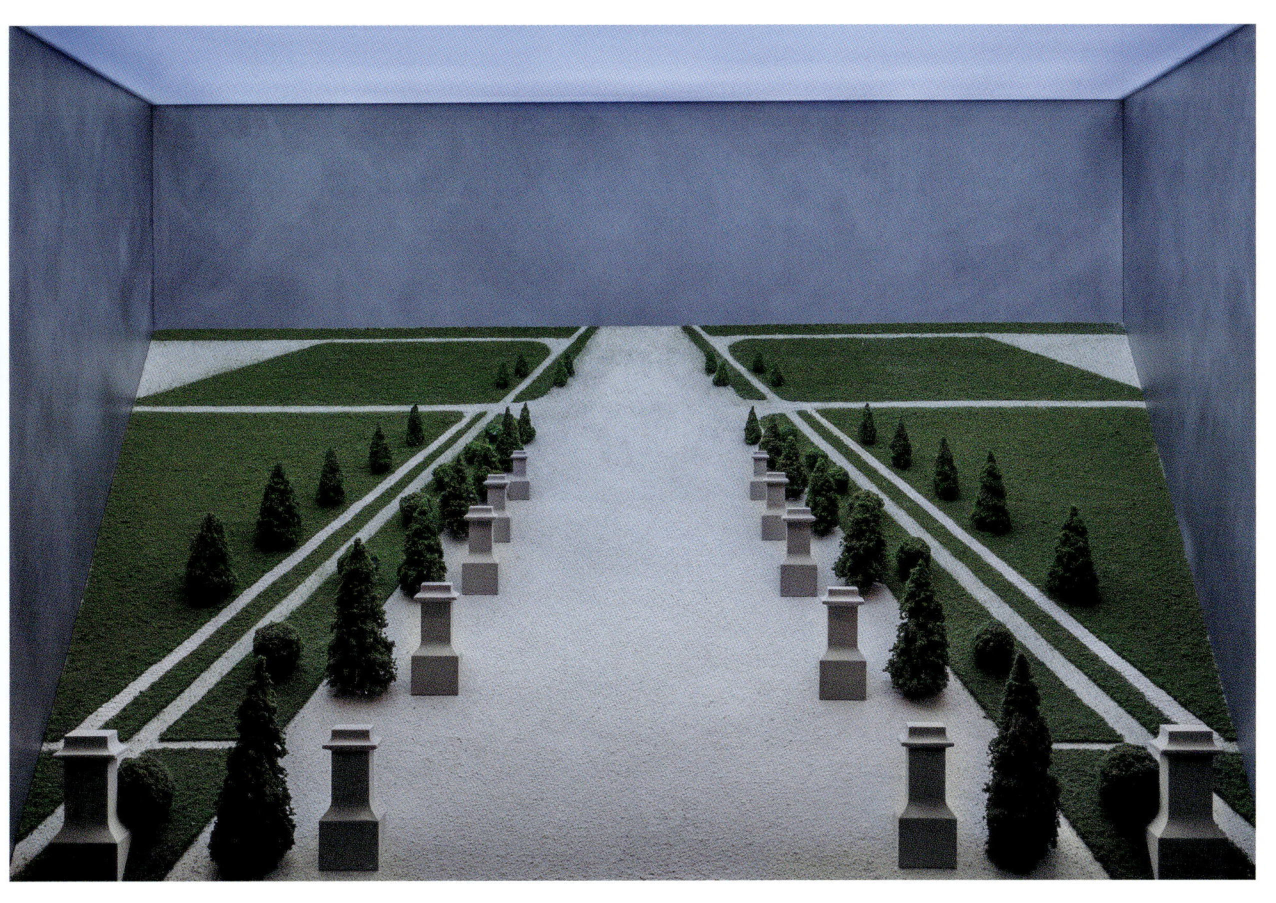

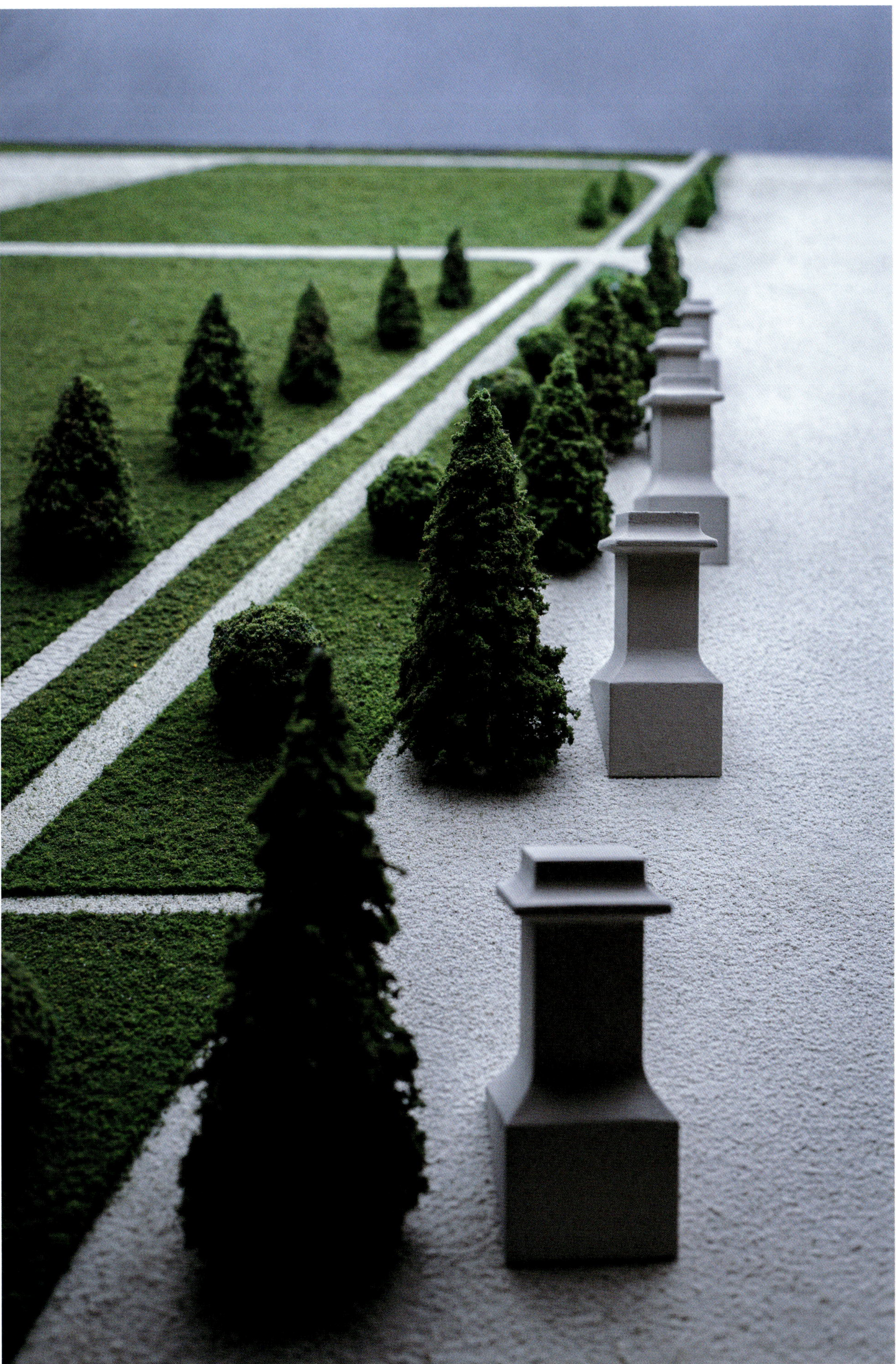

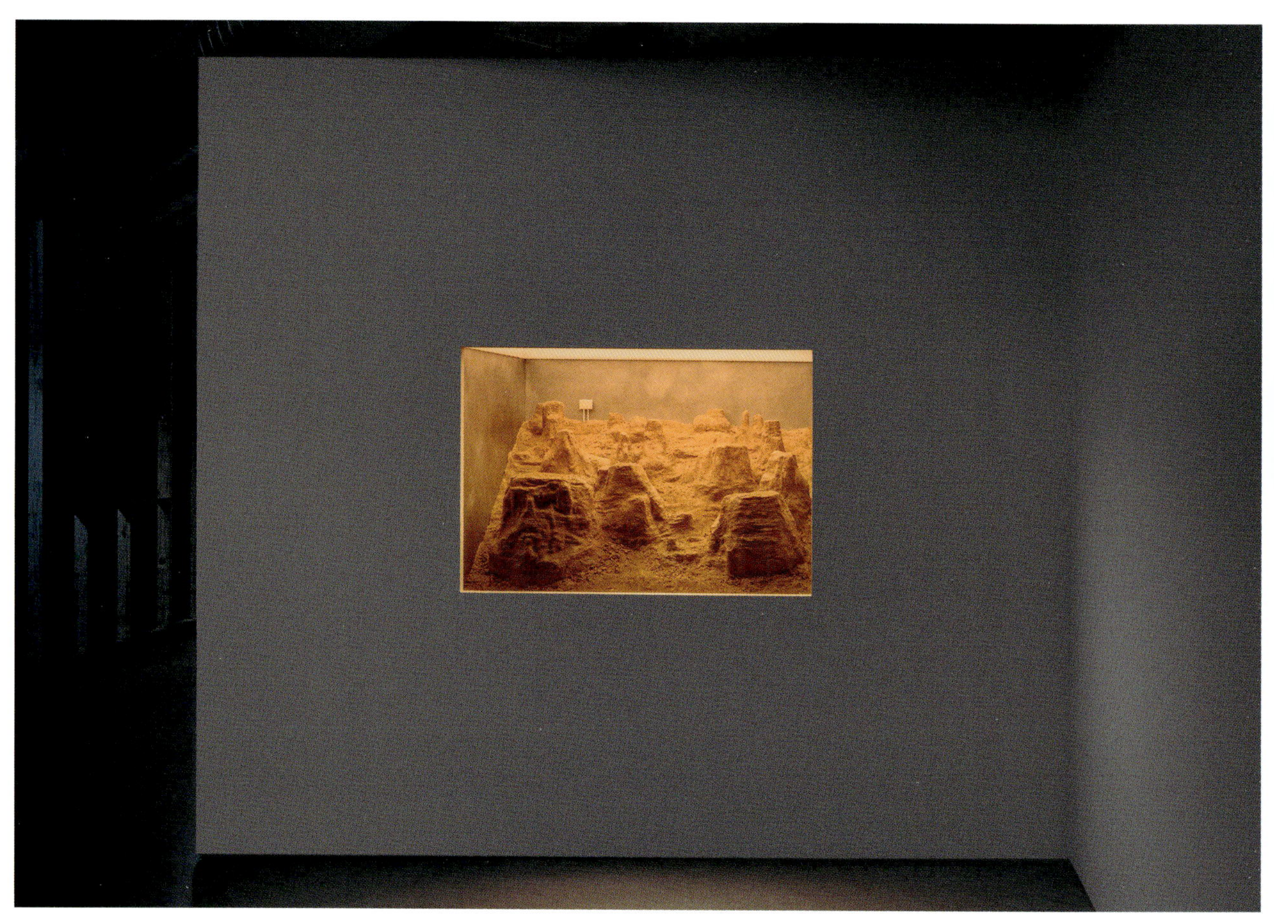

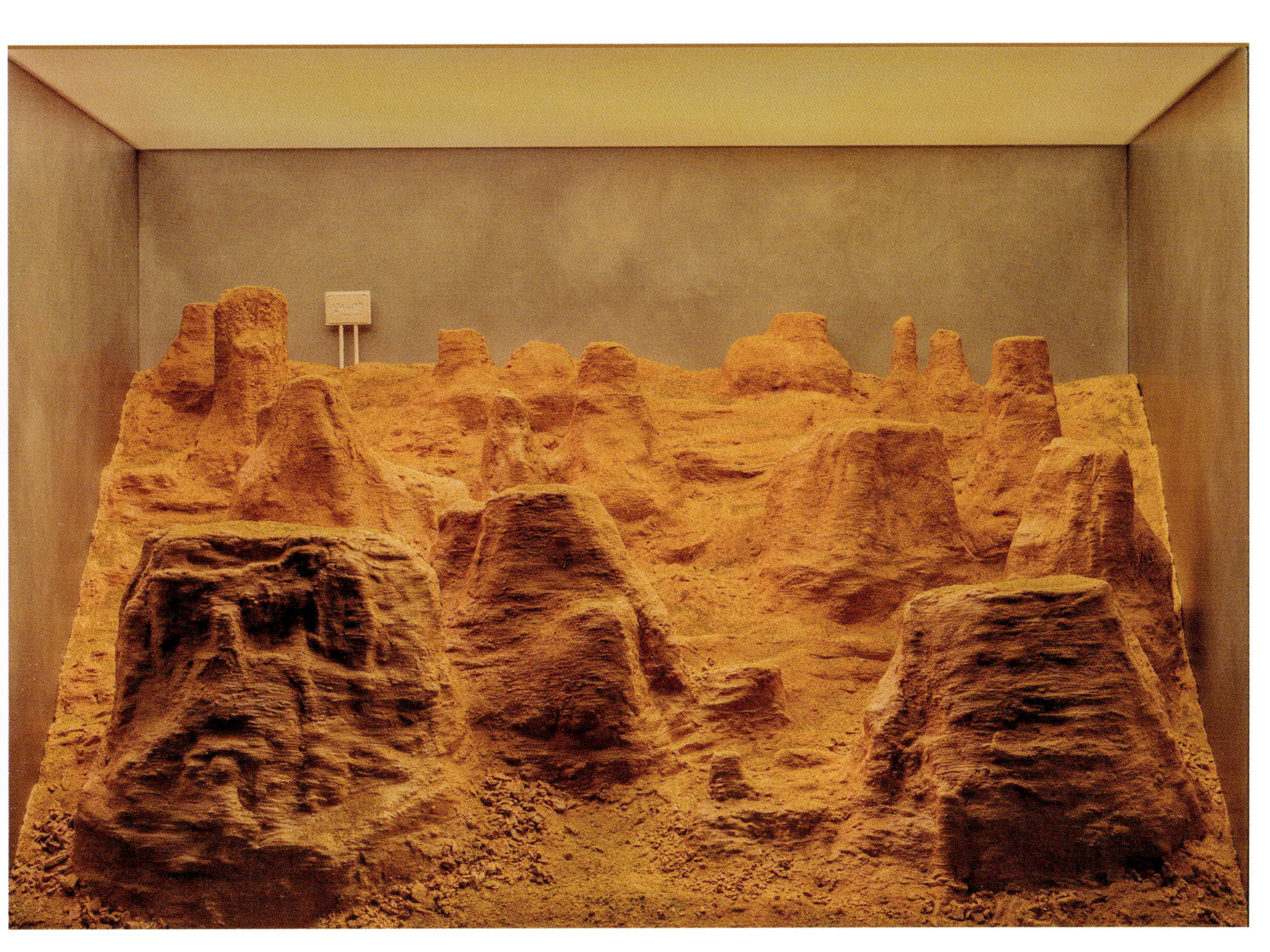

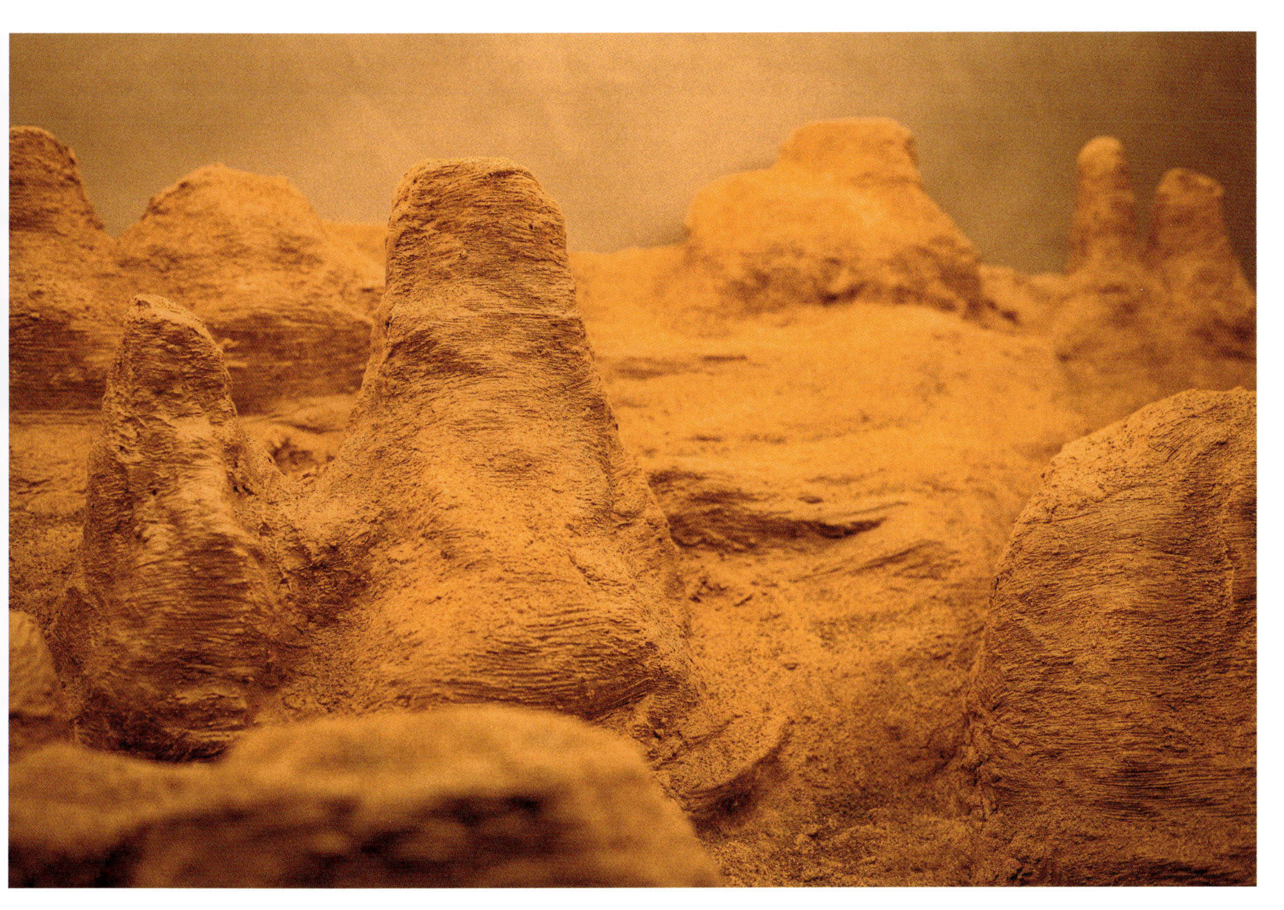

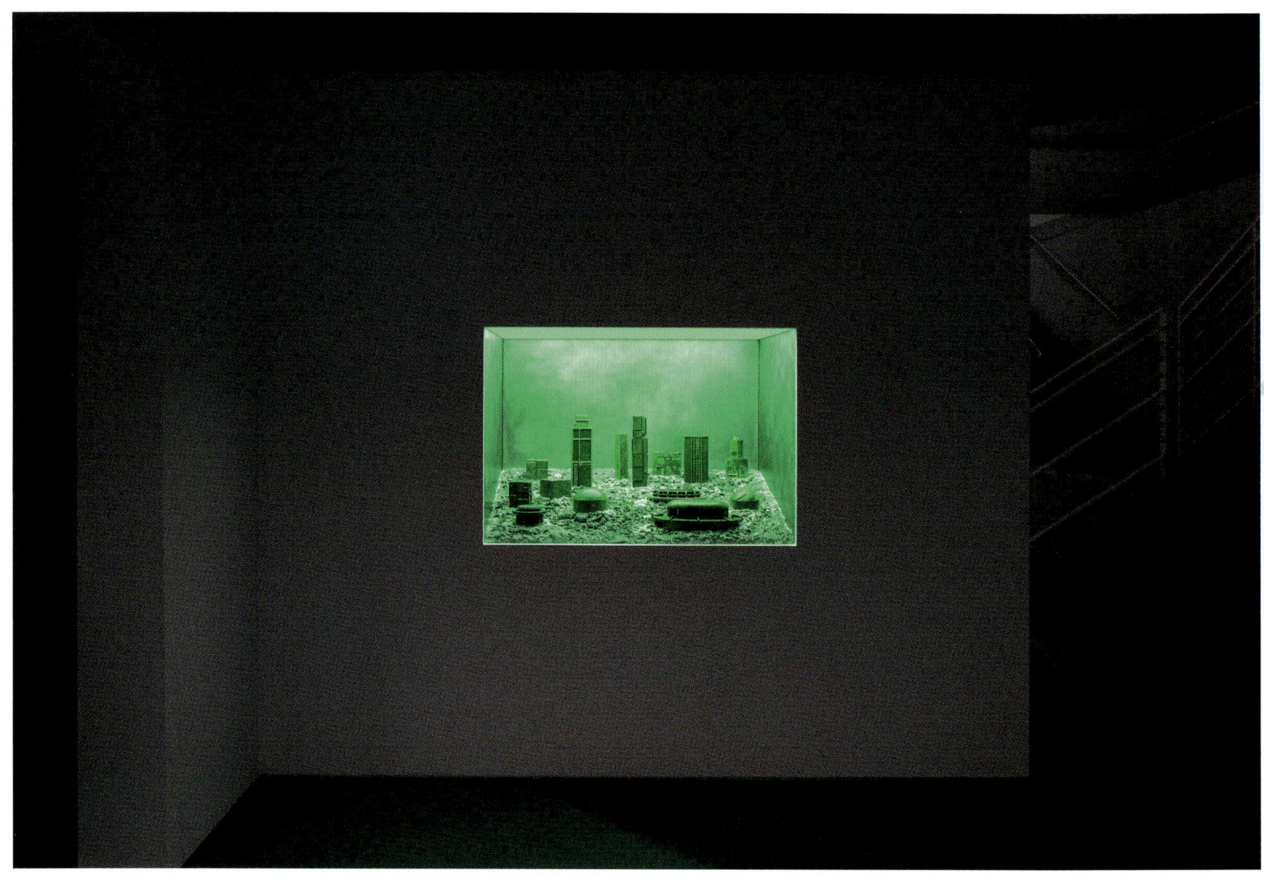

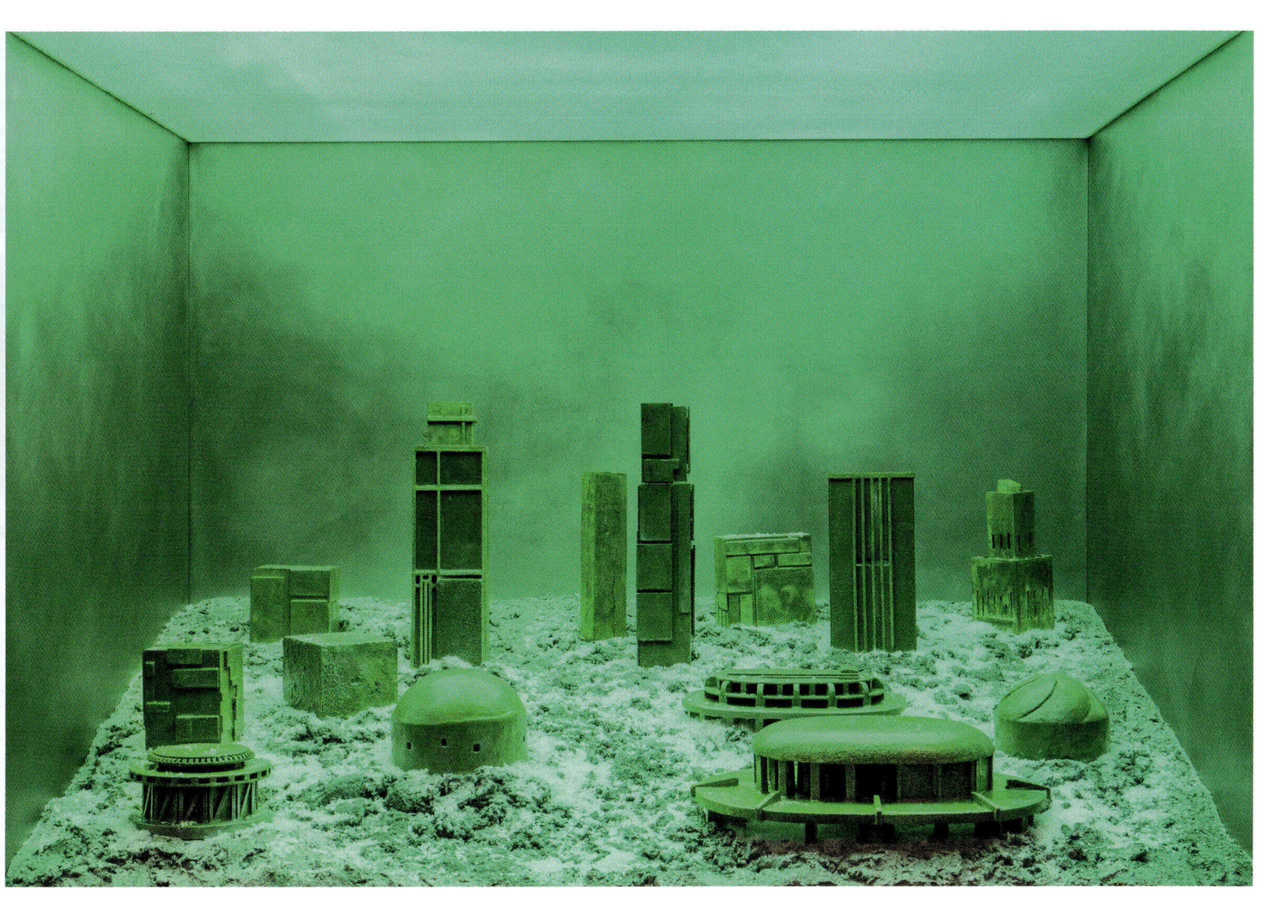

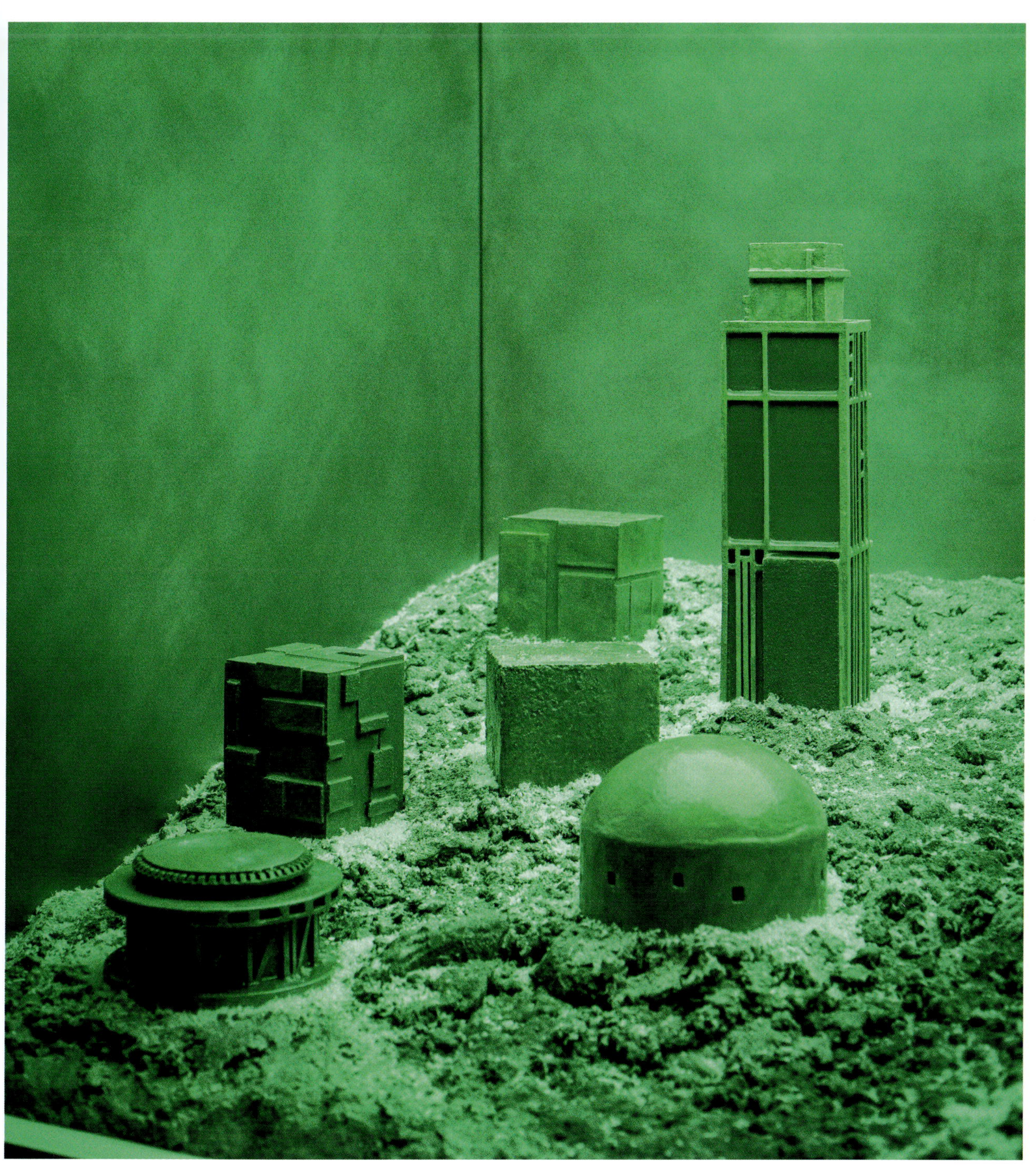

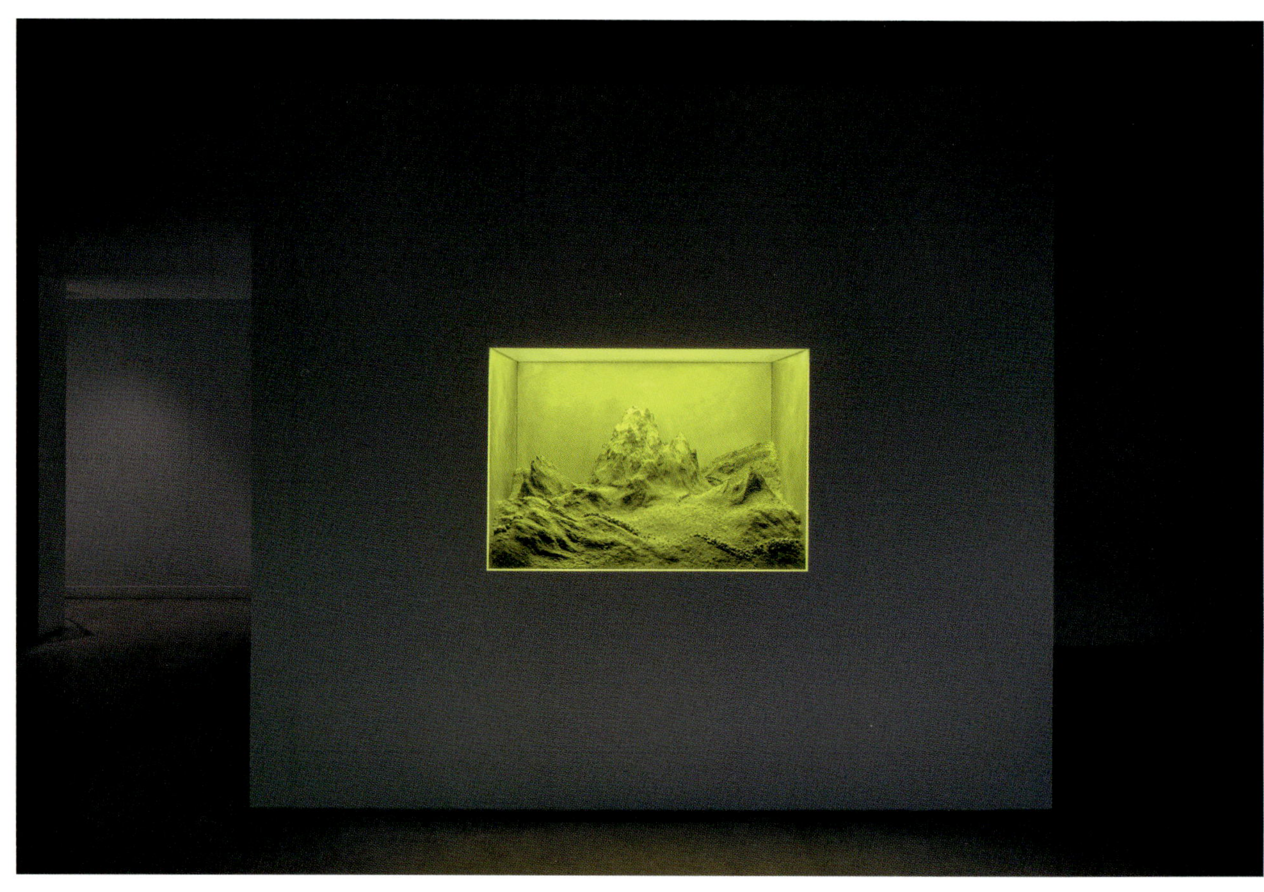

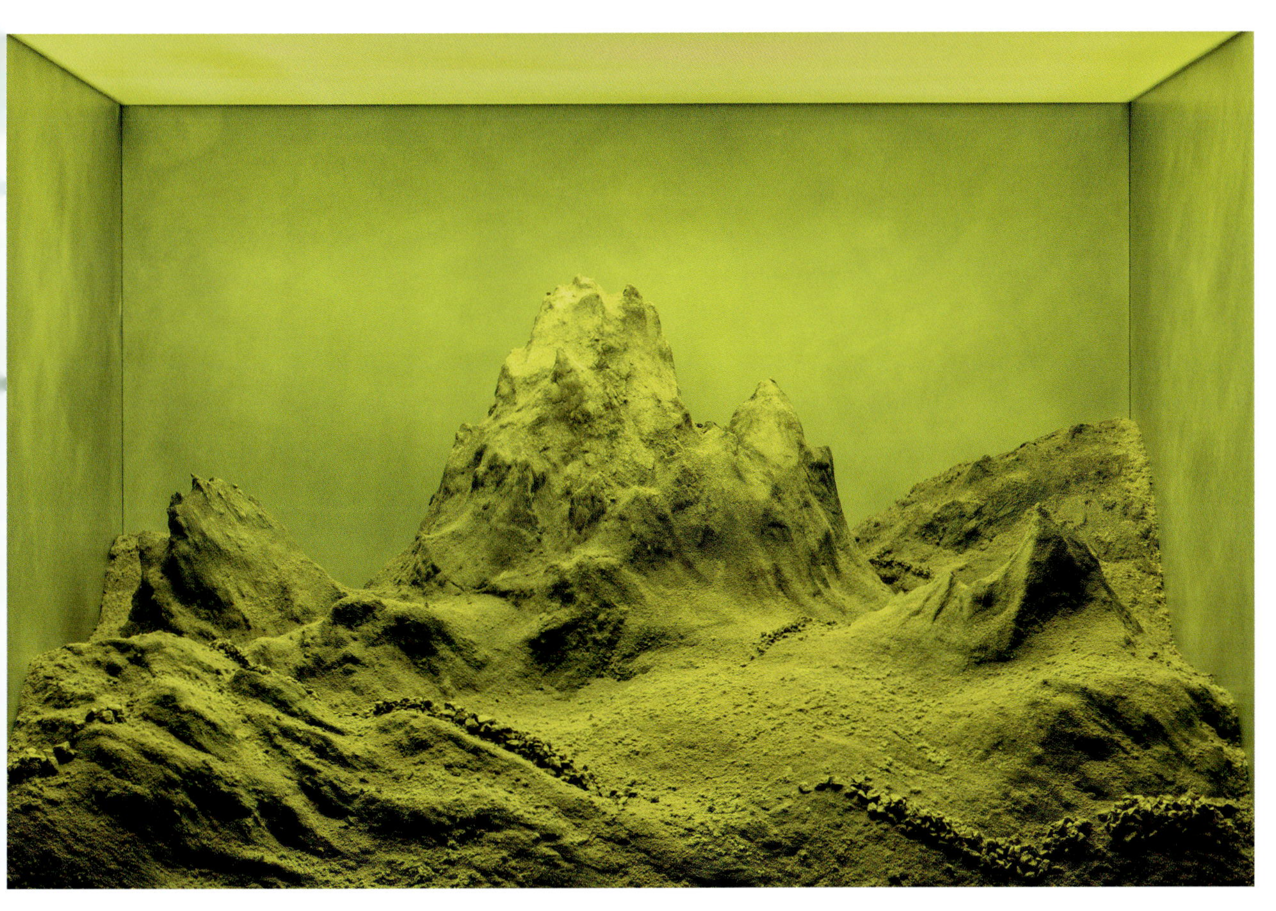

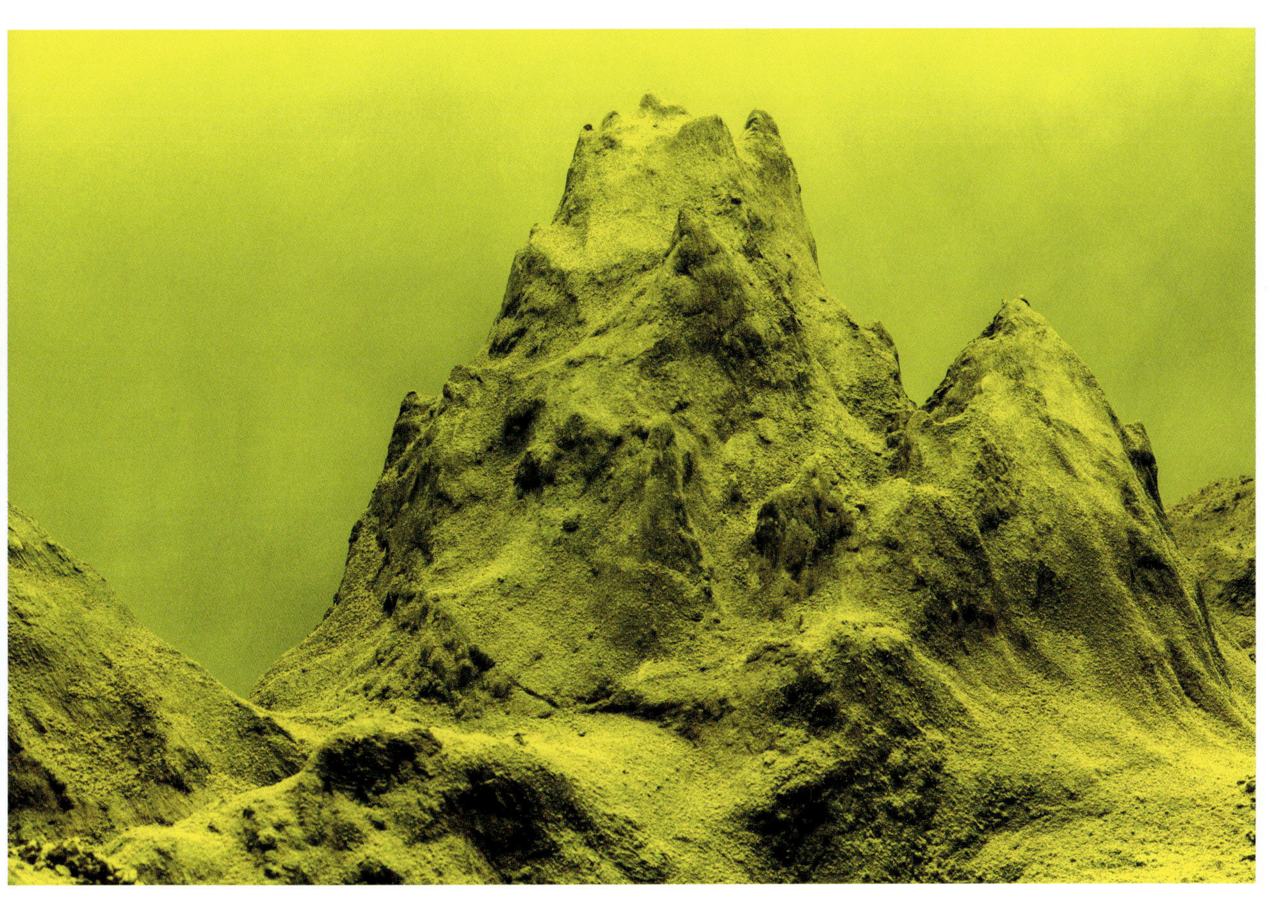

MARK VON SCHLEGELL

OUTSIDE EFFECTS

Where to go? The question, on this stone path along a green-lined arbor, appeared answerable. In the distance ahead there lurked an architecture. A dark-brown door stood closed at the top of a boxed-out wooden stairway.

You were meant to leave the outside outside, like in a dream. To let this new world replace it, you passed through a series of false worlds. Continually entering your mind allowed your body to act, or be acted upon, without your agency. So the corpus could be relied upon to make subtle and perfectly precise actions during your absence, you never lost consciousness. Inside, in a state comparable to lucid dreaming, your constant attention was demanded.

Weren't these sensors all screwy? Pressure at 4.3 psibs. Nitrogen: 1.041 kgf/cm^2? CO^2 4.9 mmHg? CO^2 that high would already risk hypercapnia, at least.

She turned attention inwards. Fast these impressions faded. But the fantasy of being proton-suited against a great vortex or void wouldn't so easily melt away. After such simulations, you never knew when you were not falling. There were those who never returned from such journeys.

As she approached the stair, the arching bower of smart hedge cocooned the walkway of printed stone entirely. Redeeming lunar modernism with archaic revival, this was a creation so full of taste, so readily accessible that, since it came from her own mind, it became for all intents and purposes, natural.

Allowing the world to take life all around sustained the silence of the outside. Wind first, on "skin," and then with the wind came sound—birds, frogs, insects—and aromas of lilac and eucalypti soon covered over the metallic patina of space. Each sensation already struck that peculiar tone between nostalgia and deja-vu with which every immersion experience showed itself artificial. That was OK. Agency, and its realistic point of view remained intact. She would bring the realism. Ambrosia Aberdeen!

The recent past was gone, though. Walled off by necessary ignorance, its silent presence resembled the void that haunted every long-time spacer, always meters or less away in whatever can or cave they sucked their air. The simulation here counted on that first human intuition, to enter the interior, to nestle, stay put.

But her case was special. Ambrosia Aberdeen, on the outside, was a full-on re-gen. This meant she had committed to replacing all memories with fictions, and building her new POV from a self-created, artificial identity. This actually made it more difficult to immerse into further autofictions. Maybe it explained why she was already doubting everything here.

Yet she herself most-likely designed at least the approaching wooden structure, keeping this particular stage set for inner Kyōgen perfectly screened away from whatever she needed not to know she needed to do. Did she need not know? That was all also obscure. But it seemed for such a realistic environment to exist it would have to project in full concert with her own will.

She stepped casually, but with a flicker of superstition, and used the banister to climb the stairs. She knocked at the door.

"So you're finally here."

Aberdeen looked around. "Who is it? Where are you?"

"We're here." The voice was now embodied, female, from behind the door. "Talk to us this way."

"Mainframe? Is that you?"

"Mainframe? No, um . . . better call us Monika." But the use of the plural pronoun signified an artificial intelligence, who were required to reject singularity.

The brown door—lab-wooden apparently—stuck for a moment, and then popped open. A personage Aberdeen preferred not to look directly at stood back, and ushered her into nothing that she expected.

She entered a smart modular habitat, not at all the wooden sort of interior the entry had announced. The floor was stone, and cool under the bare feet. This was a planetside ad-apt, with oxygenating plants placed about to soften the brutalist aesthetic. The far wall was all window—perfectly transparent. Surprisingly the broad view showed Mars, apparently, red-rocked and be-shadowed by flattering magic-glass. One might have been standing outside, under an overhang or slab.

Against this uncanny planetscape, a sarcophagus was visible, a bookshelf, a gnomecooker, a kitchen counter, a harness, shelving, and an omni-noder.

Except the sun was the size of a fingernail, outside it might have been earth. The Sahara, or Arizona.

"Shall we get on with it?" Monika spoke from behind.

"Yes. Get on with it."

A wave rippled through what had been solid. Monika disappeared. Aberdeen had emerged into a smartfloored, otherwise natural cavern in the pale beige stone. A pair of handy slippers waited there where the perfect printed stone ended at a pool. Wispy mists inveigled distant corners, as great brooding ferns rose in the distance to obscure any view beyond.

She recognized the look: an augmented interior carved into a water-rich Saturnite, or moonlet. A pool filled half the cave and disappeared under the inside wall; the glow promised further fictions beyond. She stopped at the slippers.

"How's my nitrogen?"

Monika answered, from behind. "Stable. Why? Any warning signs you'd like to report?" A note of impatience in her tone. But she seemed not to have detected any change.

"Just the usual discomfort with invasive presences like yourselves, it seems. What is this software exactly?"

Without thinking, Aberdeen stepped into the perfect slippers. They wrapped her toes warmly, like she seemed to remember from her imaginary childhood.

"We're scripting interface on the fly, actually. But anything you see there has been created by your own mind. Our script essentially prompts you to build, as you please, an architecture that complies with our algorithms."

Architecture always complies, she thought. And an immersive environment is determined by the current state of surveillance. "Is my sense of time at all in sync with time outside?"

"Negative. Here time is passing far slower than on the outside. Large scale sudden changes can be put down to outside effects."

"I see."

"Why are you still not looking at us?" Monika pressed.

Aberdeen thought for a moment. "As a voice it's easier to accept an outsider here," she said. "Whatever body you're wearing, well, even that will be the creation of my mind. That's worrying me somehow. It's me, not you."

"Yes. Well, shall we get on with it?"

"Yes, of course."

The sky was pink. She stood now out from under the slab, outside and exposed on the Martian surface. A well-worn path or track stretched out before her, leading down into a canyon pockmarked with smaller craters. Wispy clouds drifted past rugged, distant mountains.

Far in the distance, a habitation flashed out—steel or glass catching sun apparently.

There were even plants in the distance. A large dome? Perhaps this was supposed to be Earthside. Cacti poked out from craters and dark fractyl crags, and here and there on the broader plain she spied wispy, leafless trees.

"Ambrosia? Are you leaving us?"

The voice that came from behind her was no longer Monika's. It sent shivers down her invisible spine to hear it.

"Ambrosia?"

Now what the actual—a quick turn around and Aberdeen caught the image of the interlocutor—a personage she had never somehow seen so clearly. In fact, this kind of other was not supposed to be present. Artifacts of deep memory? This is exactly why Aberdeen had gone to the Orangerie for re-gen to begin with. So certain persons, and she felt this person in particular, had been such a one, could no longer live here. This was unfair.

"Wait," Kathy said.

Kathy.

"Oh no," Aberdeen objected. The rectangles contributing to her vision came apart before her. Paradoxically, the glimpse of the dreamlike, parareality which came to her now, did so with the shock of the real. Colors combined, blended, and then faded, shifting from vibrant hues to deep, abyssal shadows. The threads pinning together the fabric of reality were loosening wherever she looked, shadows imprinting the curious tiny etchings of rolled, and folded dimensions hidden to conscious comprehension. Strange whispers echoed through the thickening ether. Murmurs of voices came from everywhere and nowhere at once. It thrilled her to hear the sound of a multitude. They spoke in languages she only just began to recognize, each word like the fragment of another forgotten dream. Aberdeen tried to speak them, but found she had no mouth. Like everything else here 'she' was a cobbled-together idea. A head without features tumbling along a maelstrom of gravity; her own floppy left rabbit hand appeared beside her, flipped shockingly backward.

As she fell away, turning helplessly into winding nausea, something black and moth-like flickered into focus, falling between her feet far below, above, trailing yellow lines on both sides all the way to her flying arm.

"Wait."

Kathy shook herself back to the moment. She looked again at the mirror, at her left eye. There was some sort of yellow ring around the socket, but otherwise it looked OK.

"Wait." This couldn't be her. She was repelled by this persona. Without thinking, she stepped forward, into the mirror altogether.

Did causing one's own sudden change have outside effects?

But she had come nowhere new. As she walked through the yellow gardens, among the gray stone monuments, she understood their time had passed. This world held no future, only a wide expanse of aging artifacts bearing undecipherable hieroglyphics. She had never seen an earthside cemetery, but imagined this is what this was like, and where she had had to leave Kathy, whoever she was, behind.

But the scene was not quite lifeless. An improbable banana tree waited ahead, and as Aberdeen approached, a bird landed, an incongruous piebald parrot. Its gaudy coat seemed intelligently designed to provoke wonder. In her, it provoked annoyance, a sense of interruption.

"Please don't talk to me," Aberdeen said. "There's no point. Parrots make clever noises. But they don't know what they're saying."

The parrot jerked its beak.

"See? You don't really need to talk," Aberdeen said. "You just needed to move your head. You're just routine. You know less about language than a real parrot, to be honest."

The Parrot jerked its beak.

And just like that, she could see through the slope behind, the other claw of the crab-like architecture bleeding through the hill. She was back inside the original ad-apt, looking out that same broad window. But now she could see that wing as well visible outside mirroring this one. They had been inside all the time. The so-called abrupt changes were shifts in augmentation of the same architecture.

Tiles on the floor now lit up to lead the way to the gnomecooker (that's what her generation called the multipurpose microwave oven/grills that made uncountable hovels dug into hostile worlds something like hospitable). On the counter in the kitchenette, there was a folded note. She read.

Darling, we'll be home tomorrow. In the meantime, have a popcrake!

Popcrake! It was impossible to express the longing that came over her. Not only the tone. But also the shape of the letters, the flow of the ink. But it also sickened her that someone would use these emotions to essentially enslave her mind this way.

She had always wondered what happened to the past. Where it went. She herself apparently ate it up like popcrakes.

"For X sake," the Parrot said, from behind. Its cage cast bars of darkness across the scene. "You really are a difficult collaborator."

The churning emotions immediately directed her challenge to this unjust accusation. But there right up close to her on the counter, the egg-shaped gnomecooker made its characteristic *ding*. She held back.

"Let me out of my head," she said.

"A moment ago you were accusing us of being 'a dead thing.' Now you think we're reading your mind," the Parrot said.

Aberdeen turned—spun around, more like it—to catch the augmentation off guard. But it was she who was pancaked. The real past hit her full front and flat on—in the shape of an ice-crusted, asteroid-sized sphere driving her backward into the void.

> I don't know where I'm going
>
> I don't want to see
>
> I feel the world below me
>
> Looking up (Looking up, looking up)
>
> Looking up at me . . .[2]

A colossal popcrake? She tried not to know. To bring darkness and silence to extremes in the visible and aural fields. And as she turned herself over, spacetime engulfed her like a womb. She could not remember any such state, having almost certainly been lab-bred in a Saturnite zygote farm. But she recognized the primeval silence or space into which the hard velocity of the planetesimal on which she now perched directly curved. The frozen marks of a billion-long dead worlds scattered old yellows like Father Time's teeth across the sky. Even as the shared velocity careened, you could touch the stillness as it met the shockwave of the present's scream.

But a yellow line was visible curling up against the high void from where her arm had once been. And where it led to, a perverse hand had traced a cauliflower of darkness deeper than the void into the void. And against this shadow of a hypercube, on its emergent edge, a silver sliver warmly gleamed gold. A habitat.

Here she was magnetically fixed, gently, but firmly, to an orb somehow orbiting that entity. She could even stand, and like the little prince, look out into space. She could see a habitat. And then she saw her own white detached arm floating between.

She was fully proton-suited, immune to radiation, unless losing that appendage had changed things. For some reason it was impossible to call up mindscreen for the suit's readings.

As her orb rounded the black-sailed ship, Saturn's big beige suddenly intruded, weird rings askew from this angle. Memories began to trickle back to Aberdeen, including flashes a music career that had nothing to do with this place. She wondered if she still believed in them.

"We made it," a voice said, telepathically.

"I lost an arm."

"That was an extra welder's glove attached to the suit."

"You knew I would react exactly as I did in there," Aberdeen said.

"While cruising at hundreds of kilometers per second through the Saturn System, we have successfully space-walked, launched and fallen through seven-thousand plus meters of open space to land successfully on our target: a small, fast moving, hostile Morgov Sphere. We can no longer cut directly through the skin of the sphere, it's true. But we're ready now for the next far more dangerous segment of the mission, nonetheless."

"Actually, you're wrong," Aberdeen said. "We're still inside. We're staying right here until tomorrow. And there's nothing you can do about it." Her heart pounded excitedly.

The kitchenette gridded out easily into the snug ad-apt. Aberdeen popped open the gnomecooker, and removed a steaming, fluffy perfection—what can be described as the popcrake of dreams.

From a cage hanging before the view of Saturn, the Parrot fixed her in its dead black disk of an eye.

1   Ray Davies, *This Time Tomorrow* (London: BMI, 1970).
2   Ibid.

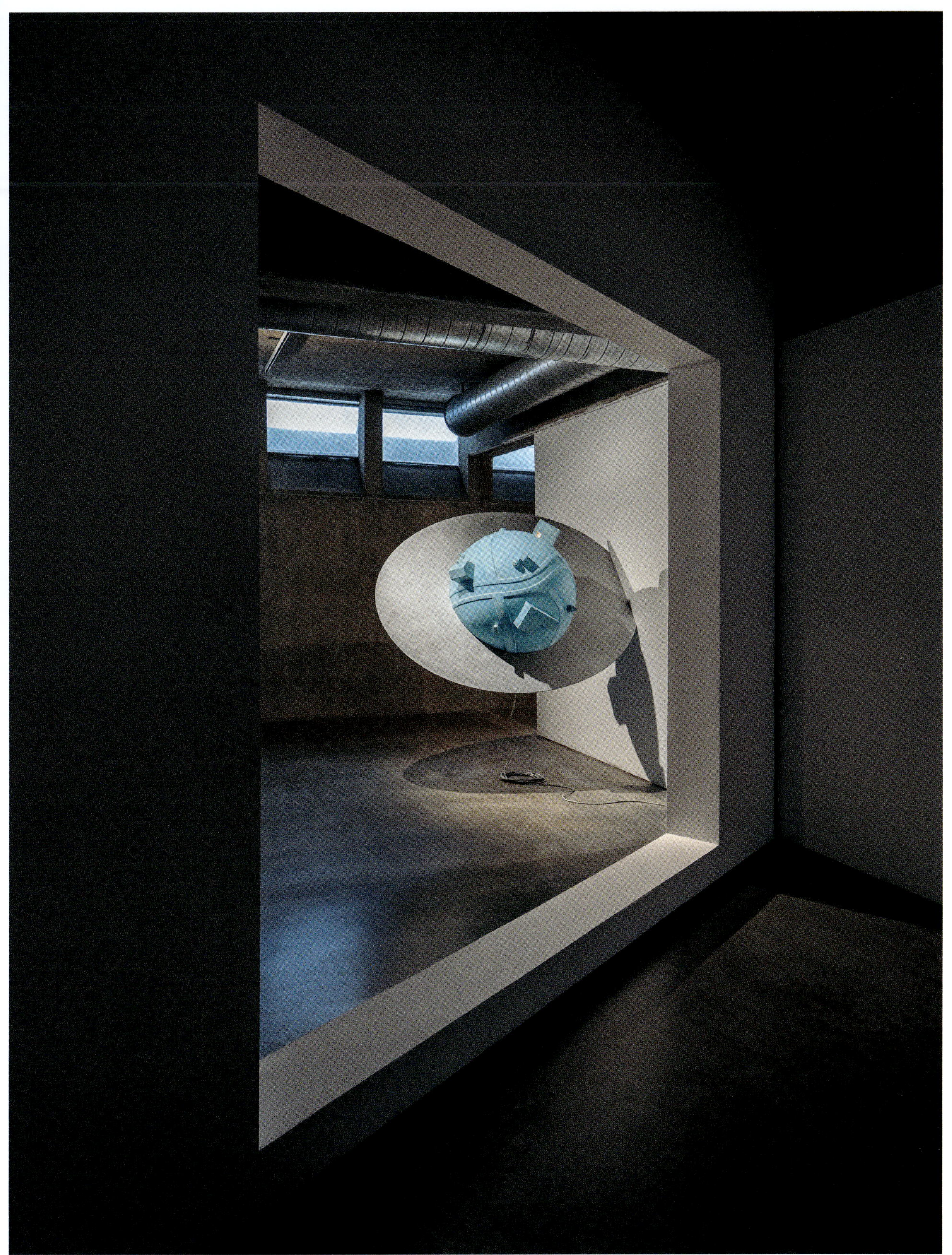

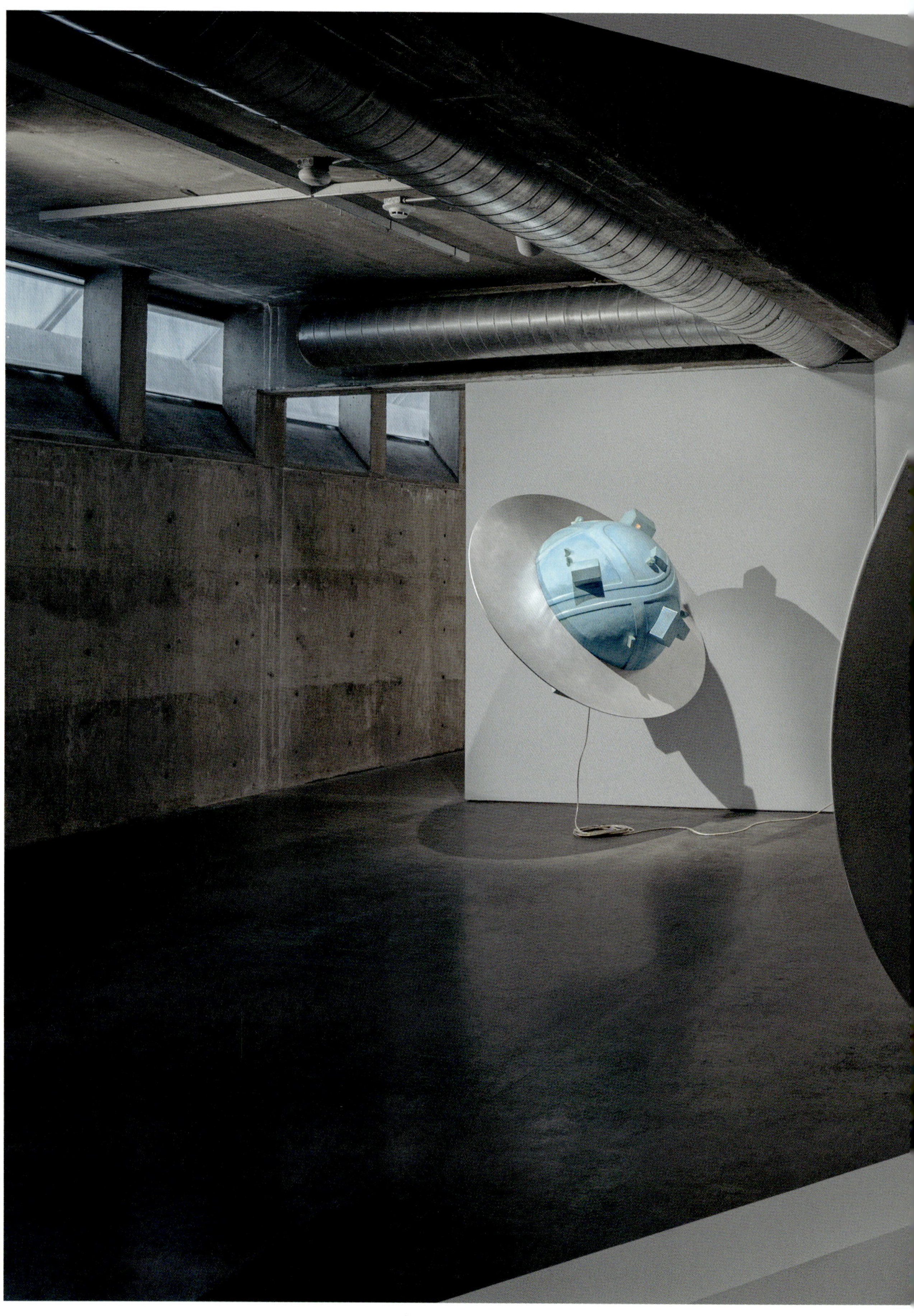

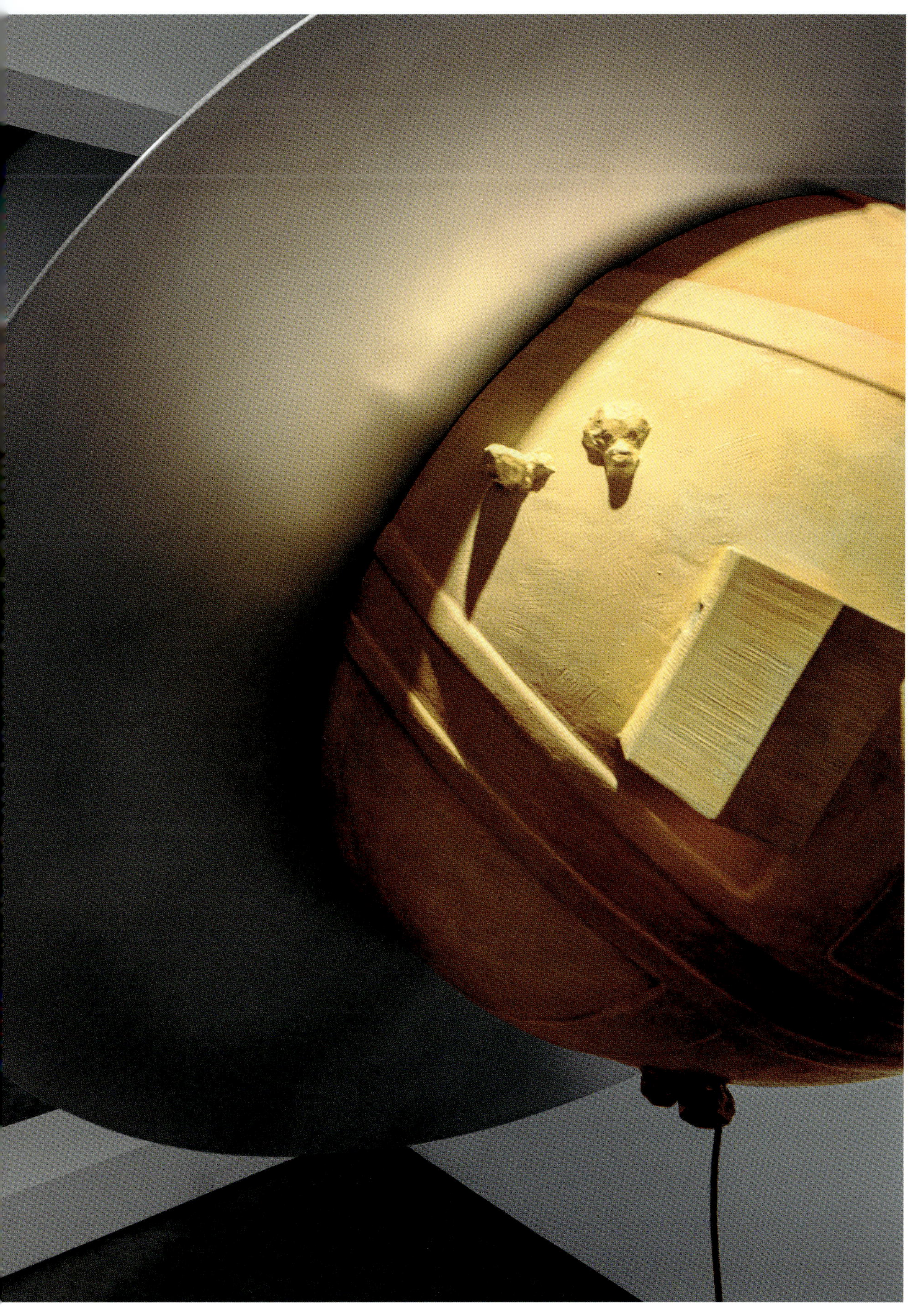

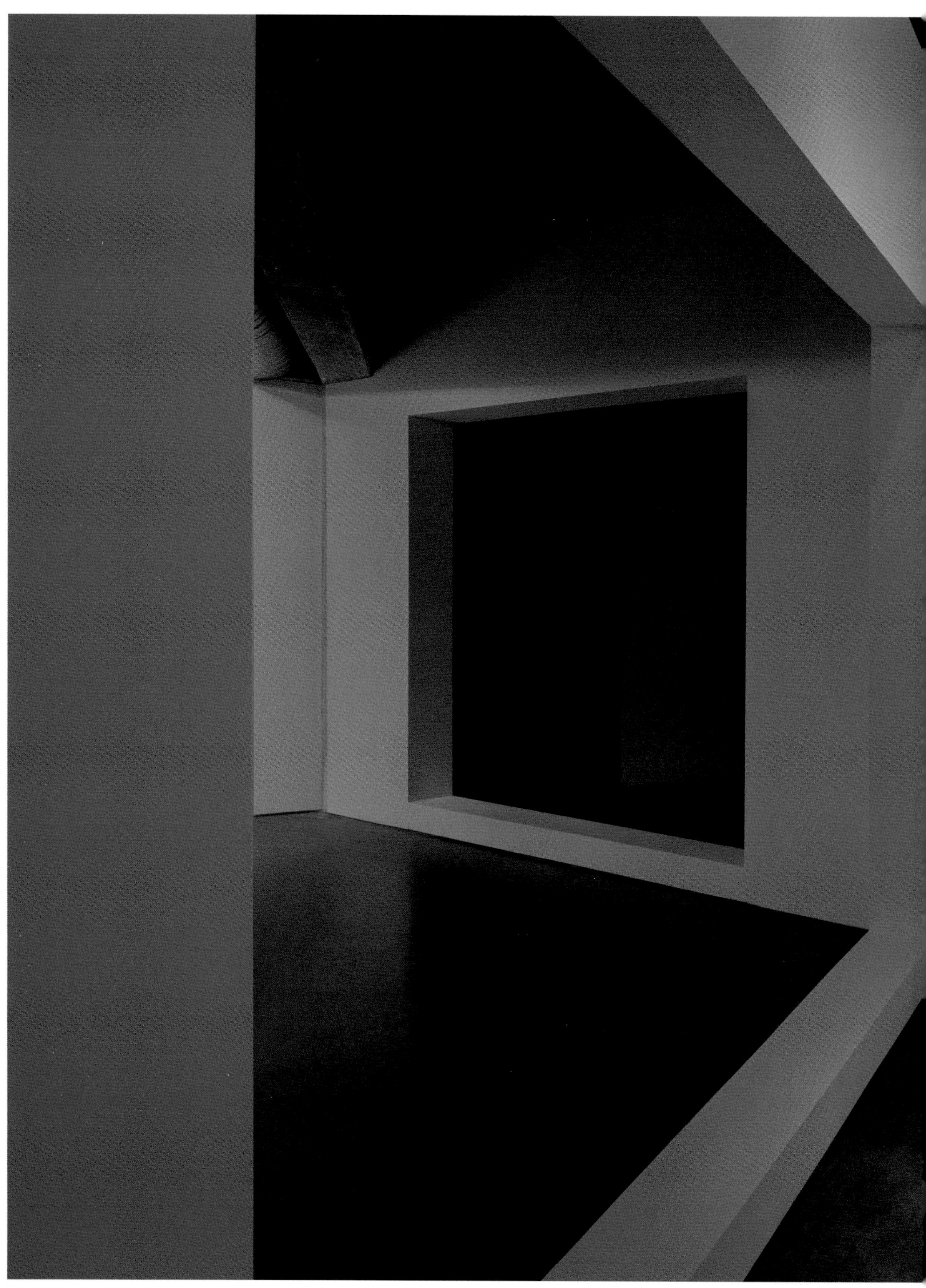

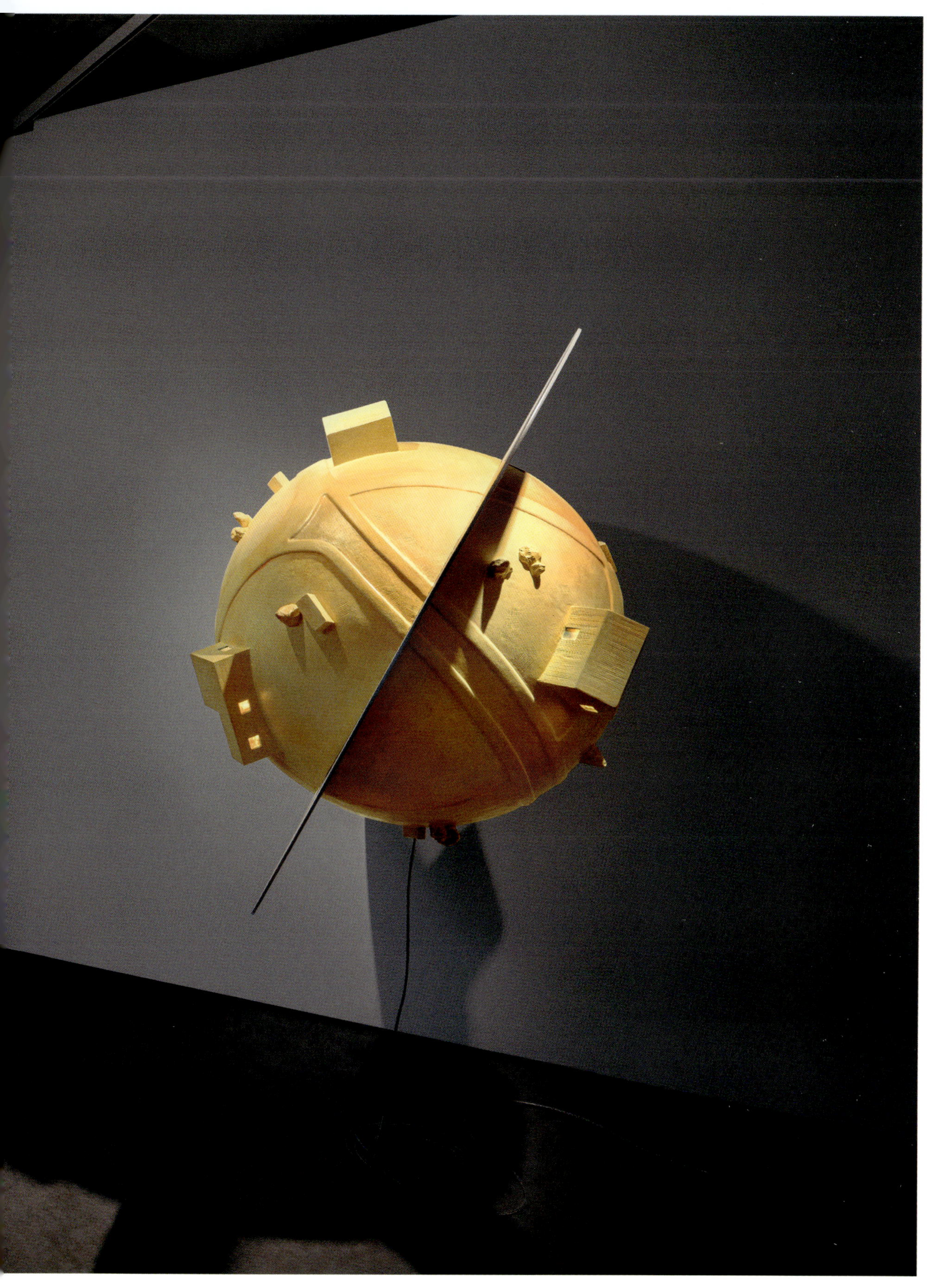

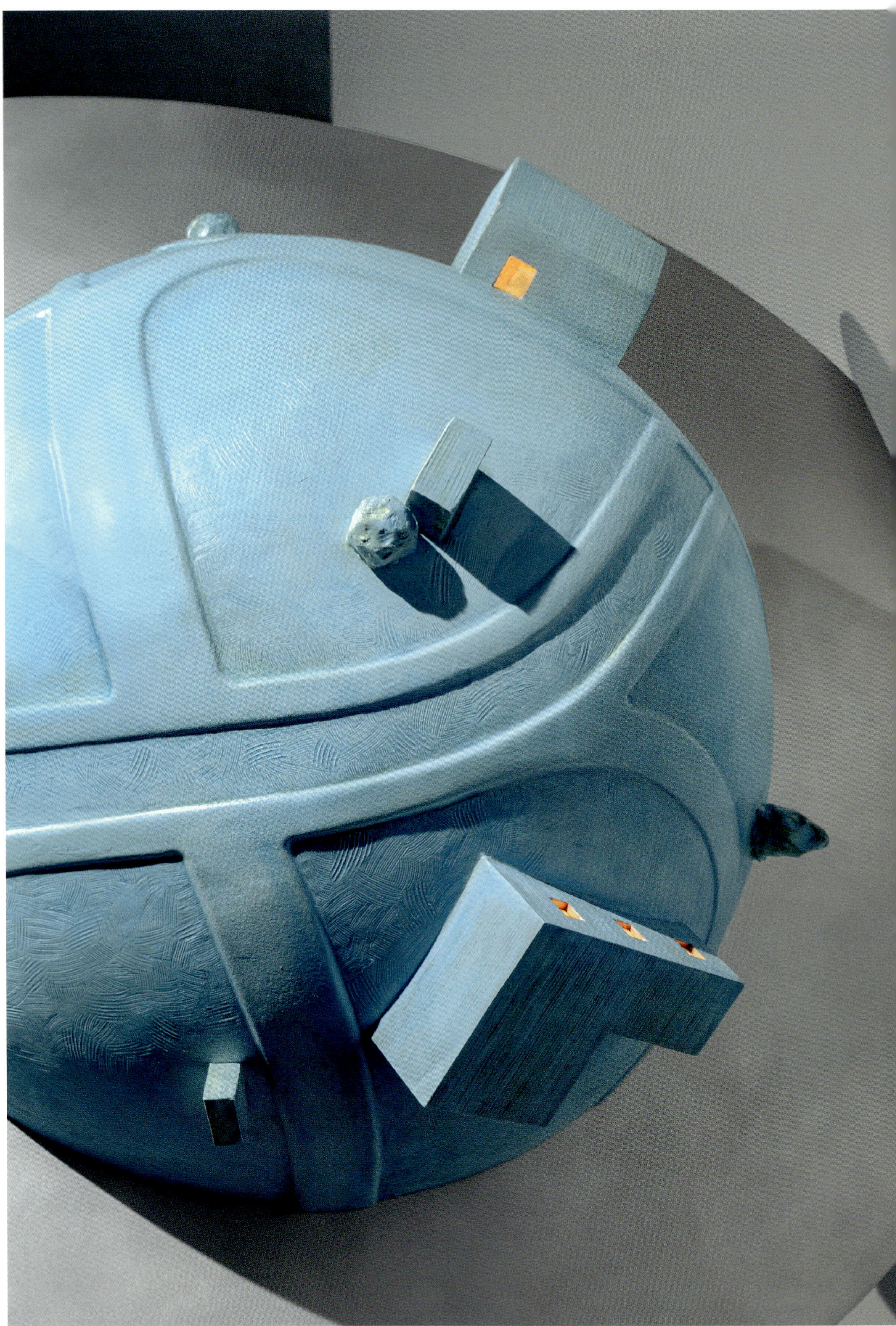

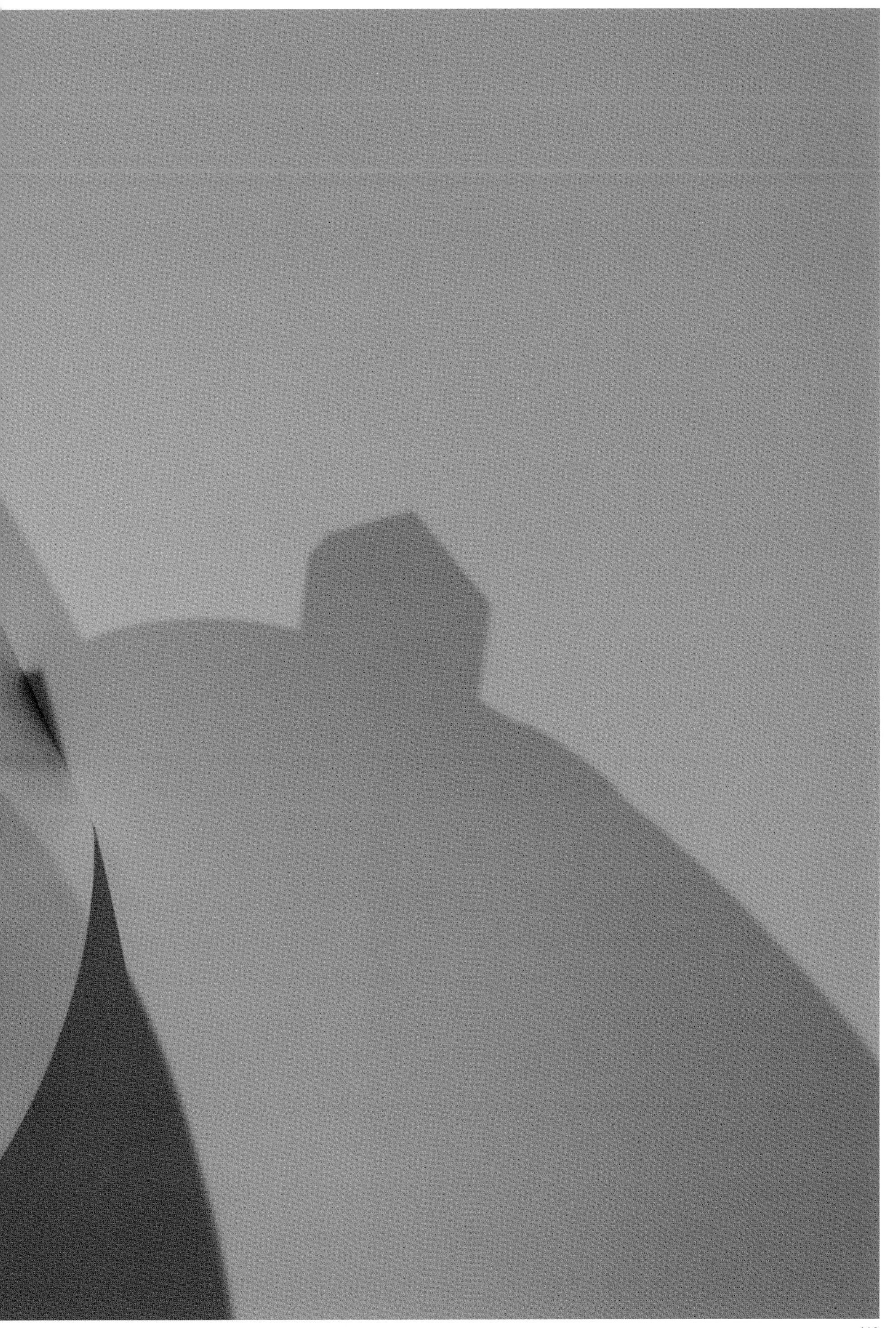

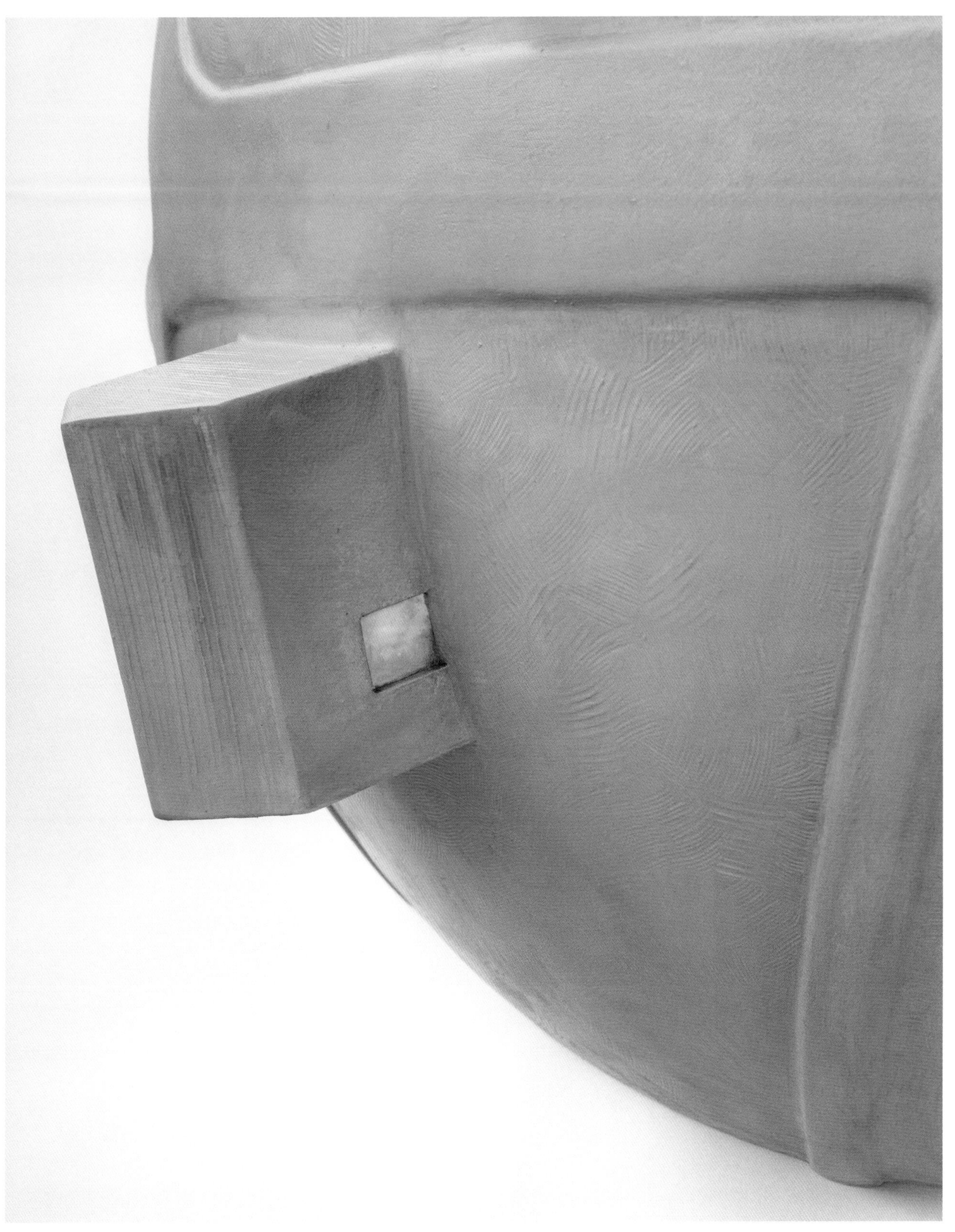

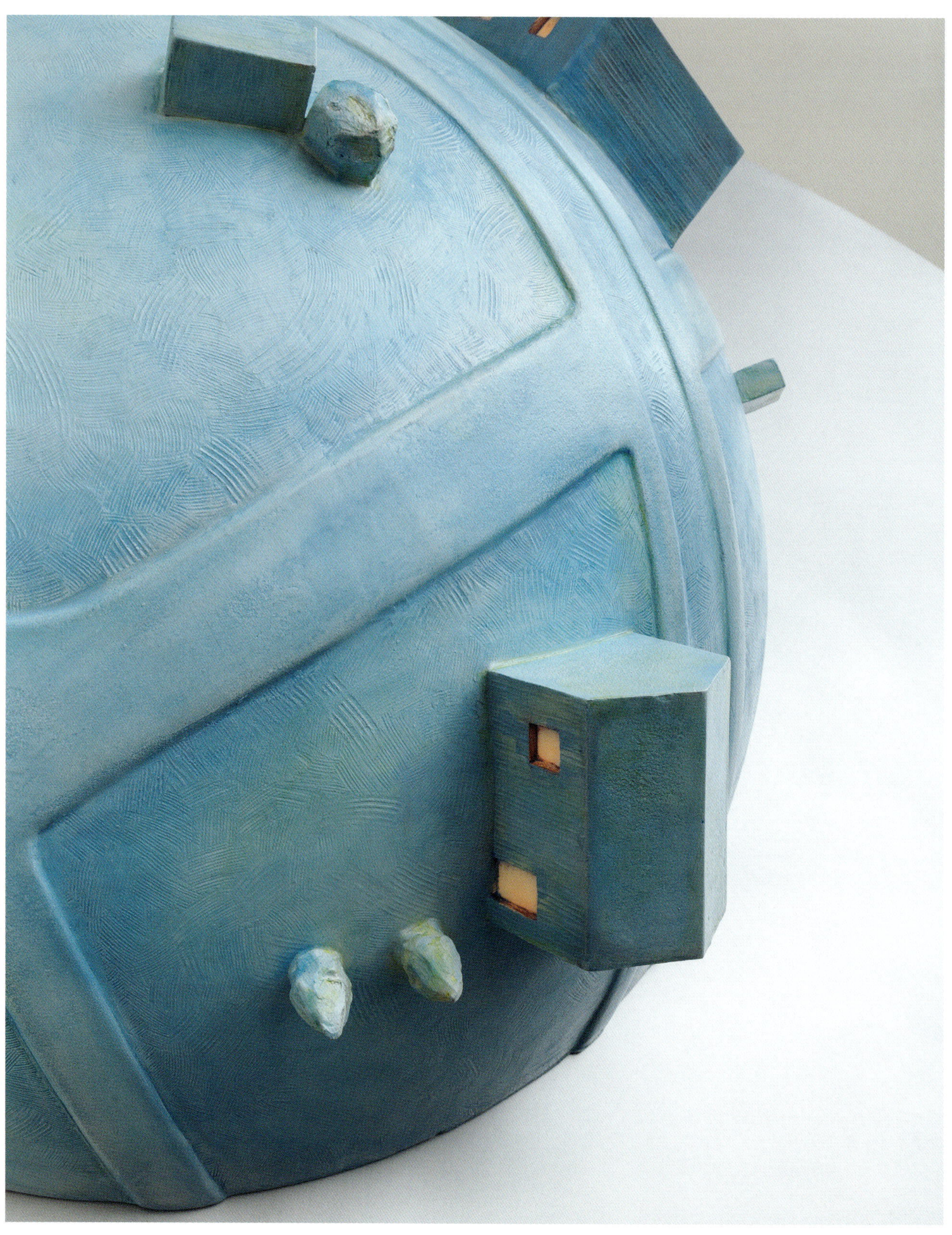

LYDIA KALLIPOLITI

Olivia's Disobedient Homes

By far, one of the most carefully constructed institutions of the postwar period is the institution of the American home. Equipped with air conditioners that recreate the summer breeze indoors, Tupperware that miraculously preserve food, TV screens that bring the outside world to your dining table, kitchens with technical brains rendering manual labor unnecessary, and garages that host mysterious machines and tranquilizers stowed in plastic cabinets, the home is not just a physical space that assembles the constellation of all these artifacts. The home is a planet; one that is designed anew as a synecdoche of a "better" earth, or at least a version of the earth that is compliant and manageable in terms of its housekeeping.

Indeed, the home and commercial structures are the only self-standing structures in Olivia's planets and their orbits, as if everything else has been erased from the surface of the earth. [Figure 1] What is emphasized is the home and the power grid: a nervous system that illuminates the microcosm of each home from the inside. Like the pandemic has taught us, the world has turned inside. This erasure of context, of the tissue of society and the displacement of the urban fabric that bonds communities, is no accident. In fact, it is telling of the myth of American individualism, the supremacy of human ego and the crafting of an ideology that the home is the institution that shelters the world, as imagined by the self, and by extension, the nuclear family.

American Home magazine promoted in 1966 this voluntary self-containment as a position of privilege enabled by technology:

> In your living room, all is serene and comfortable. With space-age insulation and sound-conditioning, you might as well be on a remote Caribbean Island. Your form-fitting chair—the design of which evolved from the seats made for astronauts relaxes you. The best is yet to come.[1]

Such ideas did not only project the body anchored inside a self-contained domestic enclosure, but at the same time, promoted this enclosure, the detachment from context, as beneficial for environmental purposes. One could argue that the longstanding American need for sequestered individualization found home in the astronaut's capsule: an "intra-uterine" bubble absolved from the city and its discontents. Life could now be reinvented with long leisure time at home.

The striking fantasy of *American Home* was nowhere more evident than in the televised moon landing three years later. Apollo 11's landing on the moon in 1969 was one of the biggest television events in history that transported another planet inside each home [Figure 2]; in turn, this live broadcast rebuilt the bubble of the home into a planet itself. The climatically calibrated interiorization of the living room was analogous to the space capsule. The staging of this transposition—zooming from the planet to the home and vice versa, from the home to the planet—was arguably more important than the moon

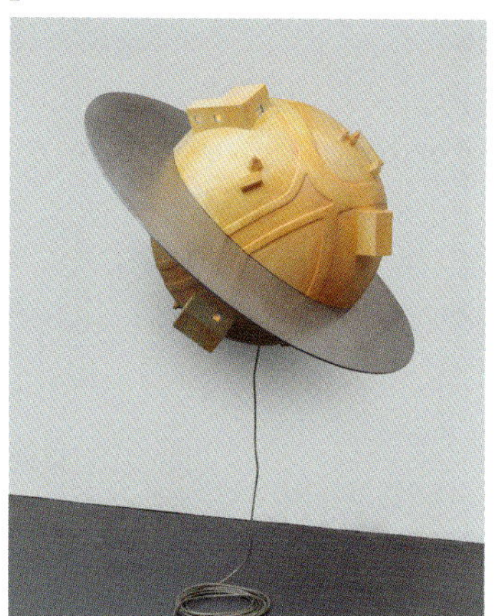

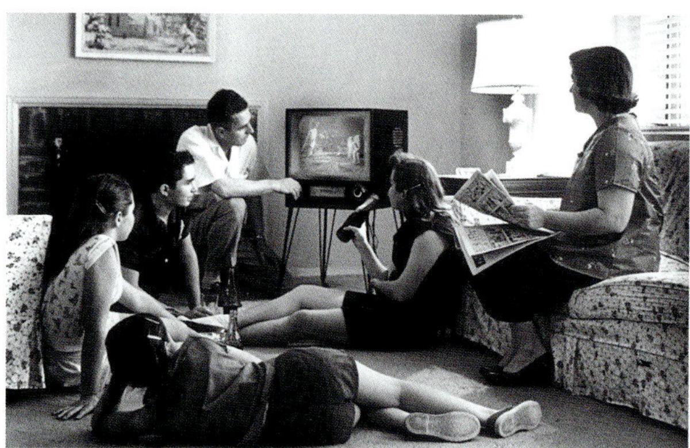

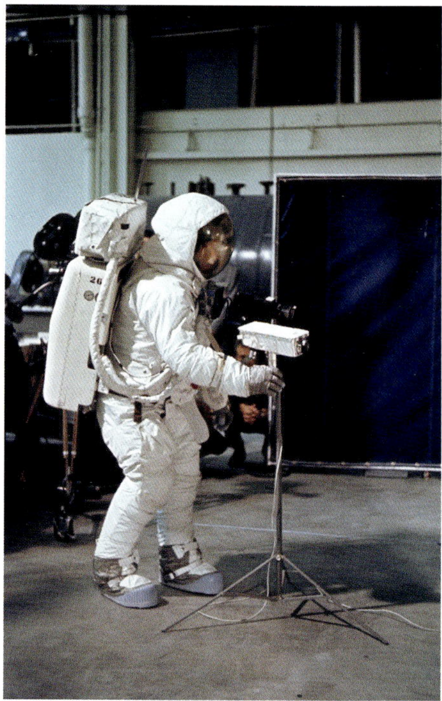

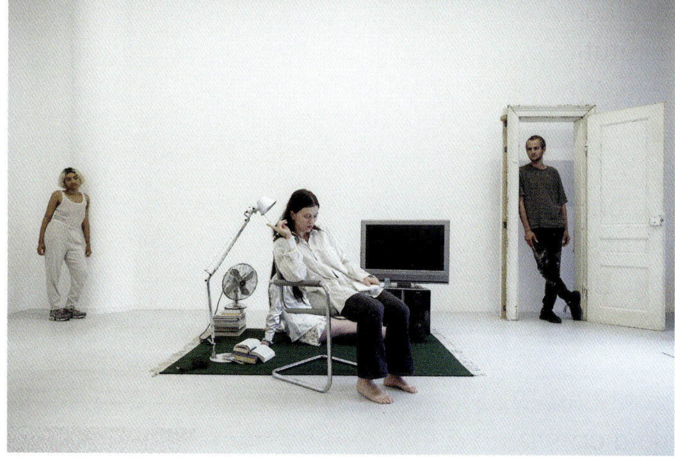

1 Olivia Erlanger, *Prime meridian*, 2024. Forton, fiberglass, aluminum, metal mesh cord, LED, and LED driver. Image courtesy the artist.
2 Family watching television in their home, ca. 1958. Image courtesy Evert F. Baumgardner.
3 Neil Armstrong positions the TV camera during Apollo 11 crew. April 22, 1969. Image courtesy NASA.
4 Olivia Erlanger, *Humour in the Watercoolant*, 2023. Performance, Kunstverein Gartenhaus. Image courtesy the artist.

landing itself. In fact, the deployment of a TV camera to transmit signals to earth was a critical flight objective of the Apollo 11 mission. Neil Armstrong and Buzz Aldrin trained tirelessly to use Hasselblad 500EL Data Cameras for their moonwalk while sweating in their spacesuits. [Figure 3]

Olivia is no stranger to staging events that engineer historical narratives. Like the moon landing, her installation and performance *Appliance* (2024) reveals how domestic appliances shape cultural imagination, with objects forming very specific interrelationships—bonds that cannot be broken—and subjects immersed into specific roles of labor, gender, and posture that signal the hysteria of prefabricated domestic bliss. [Figure 4] But aside from the meticulous orchestration of scenes, the crossing of scales from the home to the planet and back to the home deserves further inquiry.

Like the moon landing, as well as Charles and Ray Eames's *Powers of Ten* in 1968, Olivia's work, is tied with an umbilical cord to the journey of crossing scales and the performance of zooming in and zooming out. Planets floating into intergalactic space, appear as prime real-estate views of domestic interiors, and inversely, houses are the only built artifacts that occupy planets in the scale of continents. From the kitchen oven to arrows pointing to the celestial sphere, zooming becomes the right of passage between different times, territories, and protagonists in a cosmic cloud. Yet, the moon landing, the *Powers of Ten* and the celebrated Earth view, which had only just become visible to the public eye, sponsor a systemic analysis of the universe; one where all imaginable physical artifacts, energies, and human resources are linked in a complex global scheme of unity.[2] Olivia's homes are disobedient to the institutionalization of this unity.

Just like the home and the shaping of its identity within the context of Cold War politics, the earth was more than a celestial body sustaining life. It was in fact an ideational scheme for interconnectivity, with the idea of unity projected onto the cosmos, and moreover, attaining divine stature. Pieces on different scales would discover their position in the complex web of cosmic order. But in Olivia's work, there is noise, cracks, things that escape from the ghost of holism. This is a kind of disobedience. If the term is vague, it is because I can find no better word to describe the cracks in the apparatus of power, the holes and crevices, where things creep and fit into niches. A mermaid comes out of the laundry machine; a hand creeps from a hole in the floor while the inhabitant is silently sucking her thumb in the bed [Figure 5]; the "enslaved oven," as Olivia puts it,[3] calls in her pray; indeterminate creatures live halfway between the floor and ceiling; cabinets, are eaten by mysterious animals and stuffed with unwanted clay and porcelain newspaper that don't fit it. These things that creep in and erode unity, as a regime of power, counter the artifacts of the perfect home and the whole planet: the efficient kitchens that nurture happy housewives, the technological miracle of the TV that anchors the body and subjugates it to atrophy; the compliant body that serves the organization. As Olivia writes, the oven "acts as an apron to directly address domestic servitude and the oppression of the female body. Subservient and pliant, the body quickly becomes a metaphor of an appliance, the womb embodied by an oven."[4]

Somewhere in the crevices, Olivia's disobedient homes are assembled out of systemic malfunctions. They constitute a type of indigestion of how the house processes its inhabitants. These objects that cannot be digested, displaced from context, become tools of resistance to the institution of the American house as a planet, and as a constructed interiority detached from context. They resist the illusion of identity engraved within the nuclear home.

The disruption of unity is as much about space as it is about time. Planets, arrows, dioramas, and houses exist in a stretched version of time that defies the arrow of linearity. We cannot be absolutely sure whether these objects, spaces, and stills speak of the past or the future. In this cycling process, ideas, objects, and phenomena circulate and travel in distinct orbits, with definite points of semantic gravity.

The *cycling* of ideas also offers a means of resistance to a project's linearity or causality to respond as a solution to named problems; *cycling* becomes a disruption to an idealized continuum, or a productive distraction to the arrow of time. As Heinz von Foerster, the father of general systems theory, argued, "It is favorable to have some noise in a system. If a system is going to freeze into a particular state, if inadaptable, it may be altogether wrong—incapable of adjusting itself to a more appropriate state."[5] For it is not only information that matters, but also noise. What may appear as noise at one level of reference—one scale—may be useful input in another. Such is the case in this book. The surplus of means and mediums that are byproducts of other mediums leads to an intentional view that is "out of focus." It reflects the conditions of the world as a heap of waste: a coagulation of ideas, bodies, platforms, objects displaced from their context, and history—in short, our world of climate emergency, health crisis, and social inequity.[6]

1   "Will you live in a Space Capsule House?," *American Home* (September 1966), pp. 82–83.

2   For a full account of the image of the earth and its impact on visual culture, see Volker M. Welker, "From Disc to Sphere," *Cabinet* 40 (Winter 2010/11), pp. 19–25; and Simon Sadler, "An Architecture of the Whole," *Journal of Architectural Education* 61, no. 4 (2008), pp. 108–29. For the history of the first earth image, see Denis Cosgrove, "Contested Global Visions: One World, Whole Earth, and the Apollo Space Photographs," *Annals of the Association of American Geographers* 84, no. 2 (June 1994), pp. 270–94; and Robert Poole, *Earthrise: How Man First Saw the Earth* (New Haven, CT: Yale University Press), 2008.

3   Olivia Erlanger and Luis Ortega Govela, *Garage* (Cambridge, MA: MIT Press, 2019), p. 3.

4   Olivia Erlanger, *Appliance* (Vienna: Wild Seeds, 2022), p. 48.

5   Heinz von Foerster, "On Self-Organizing Systems and Their Environments," address given at the Interdisciplinary Symposium on Self-Organizing Systems in Chicago on May 5, 1959. Originally published in M. C. Yovits and S. Cameron (eds.), *Self-Organizing Systems* (London: Pergamon Press, 1960), pp. 31–50. See http://e1020.pbworks.com/f/fulltext.pdf (accessed December 6, 2012).

6   Michael Marder, "Being Dumped," *Environmental Humanities* 11, no. 1 (May 2019), p. 184.

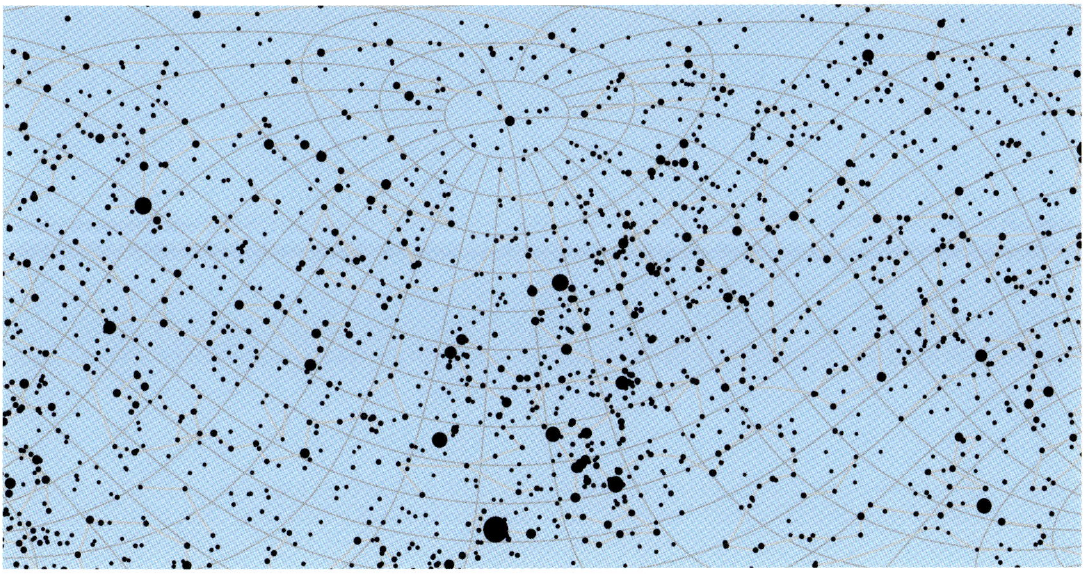

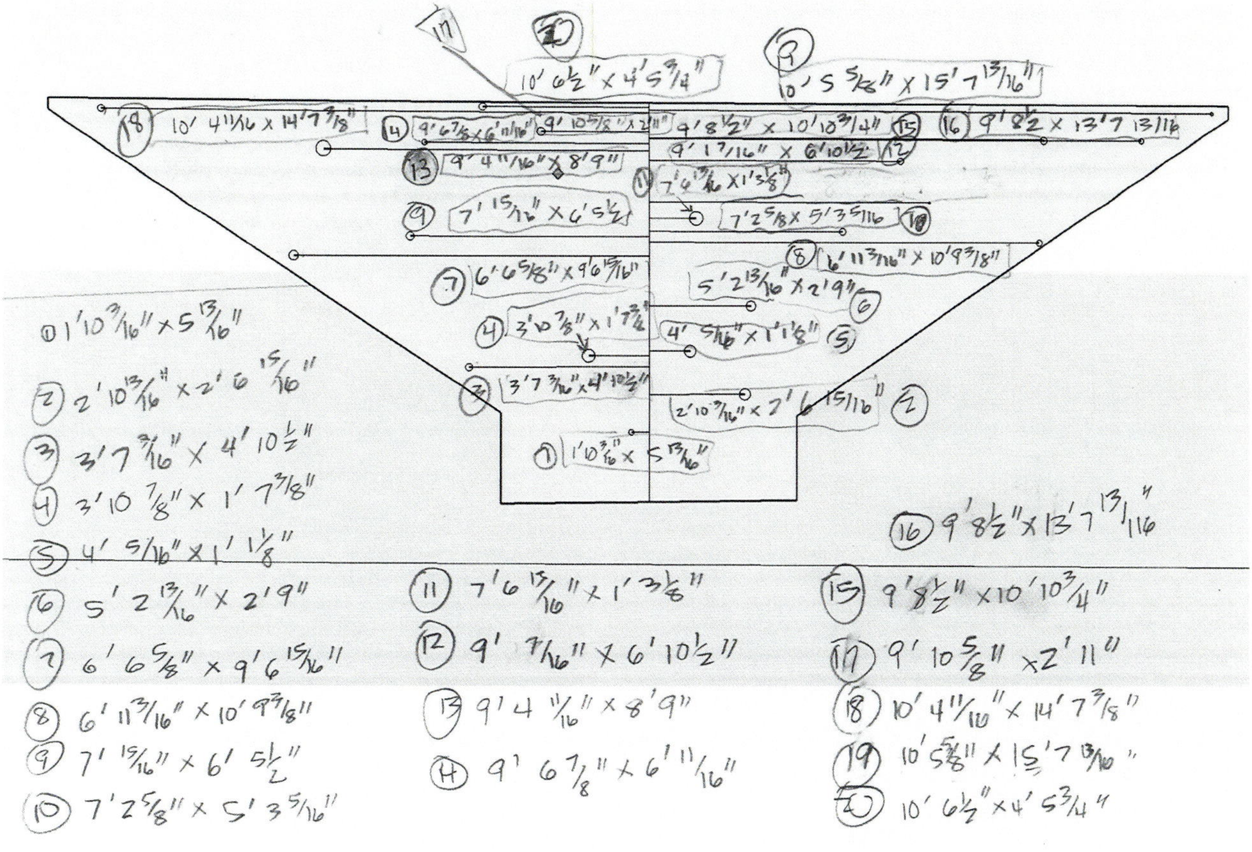

1 1'10 3/16" x 5 13/16"
2 2'10 13/16" x 2'6 15/16"
3 3'7 3/16" x 4'10 1/2"
4 3'10 7/8" x 1'7 3/8"
5 4' 5/16" x 1' 1/8"
6 5'2 13/16" x 2'9"
7 6'6 5/8" x 9'6 15/16"
8 6'11 3/16" x 10'9 3/8"
9 7' 15/16" x 6' 5 1/2"
10 7'2 5/8" x 5'3 5/16"
11 7'6 15/16" x 1'3 1/8"
12 9' 7/16" x 6'10 1/2"
13 9'4 11/16" x 8'9"
14 9'6 7/8" x 6' 11/16"
15 9'8 1/2" x 10'10 3/4"
16 9'8 1/2" x 13'7 13/16"
17 9'10 5/8" x 2'11"
18 10'4 11/16" x 14'7 3/8"
19 10'5 5/8" x 15'7 13/16"
20 10'6 1/2" x 4'5 3/4"

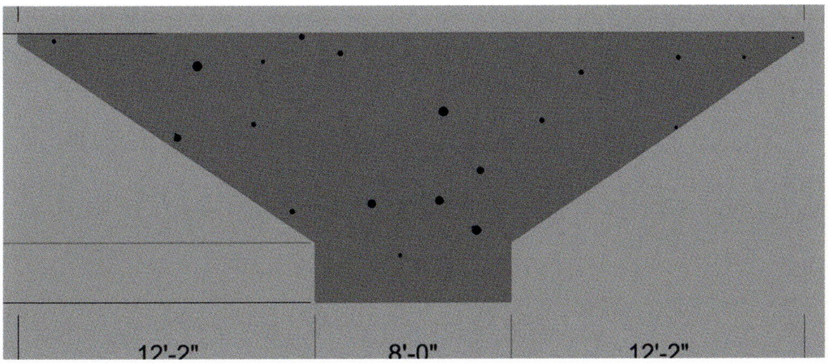

12'-2"
8'-0"
12'-2"

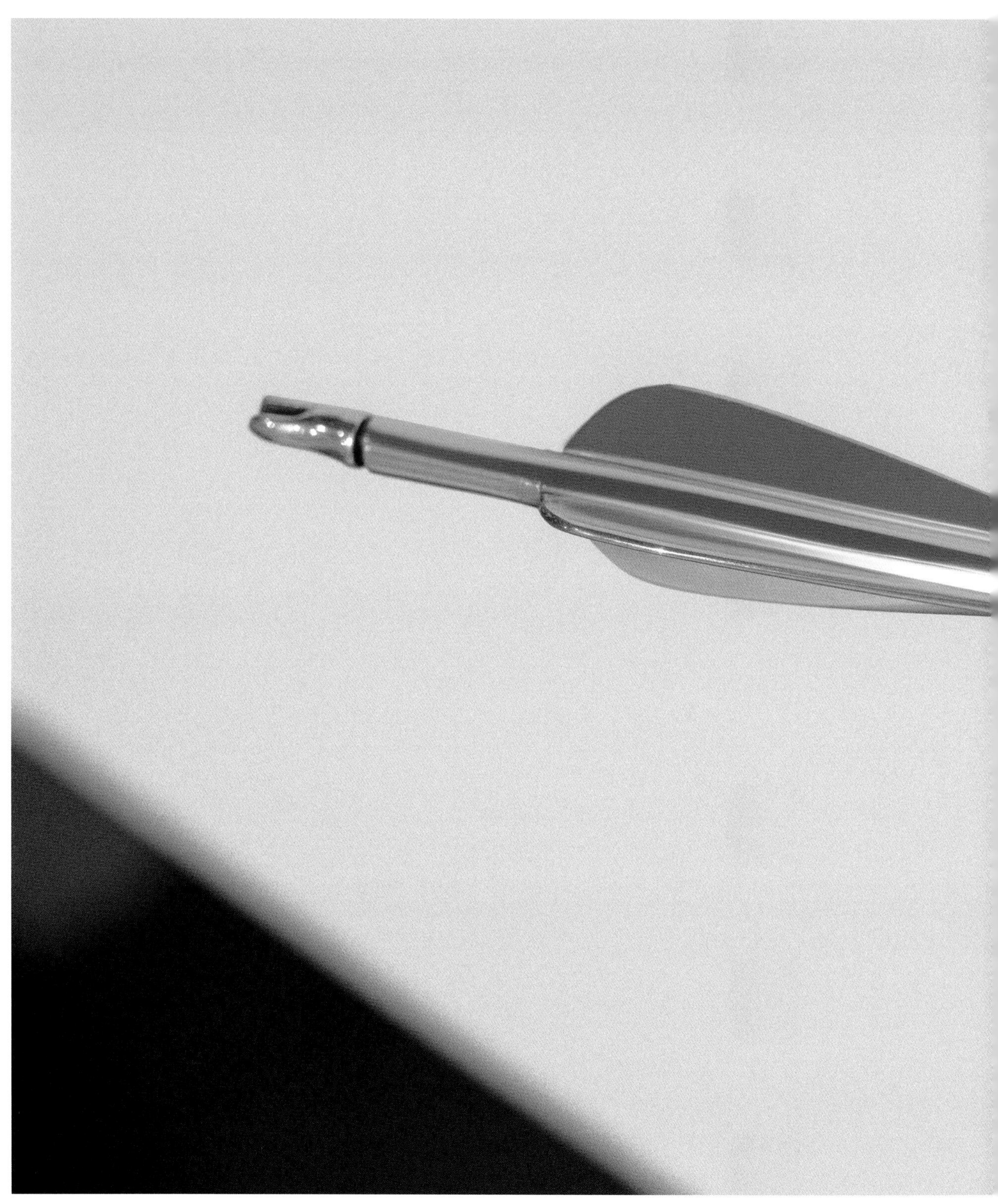

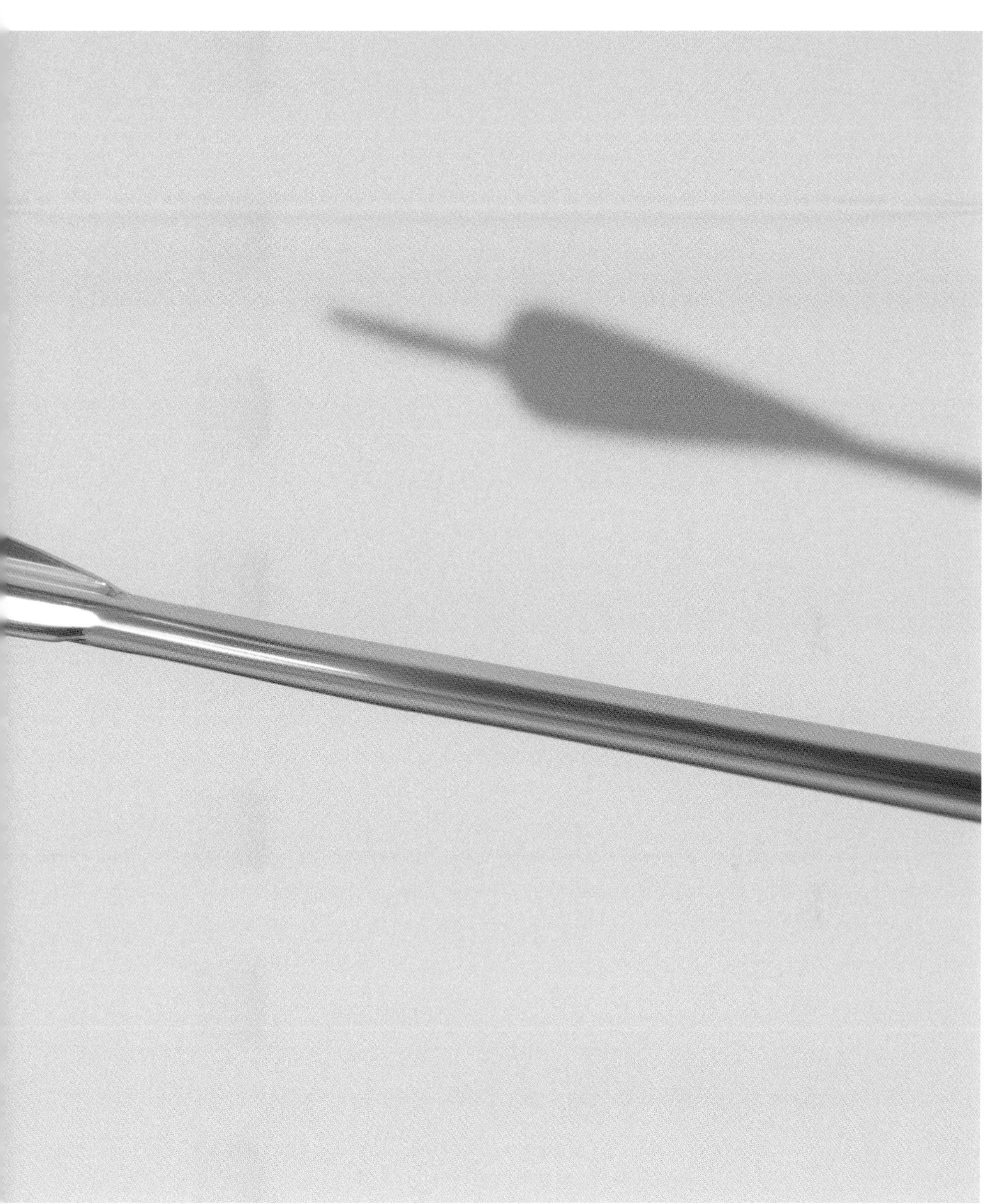

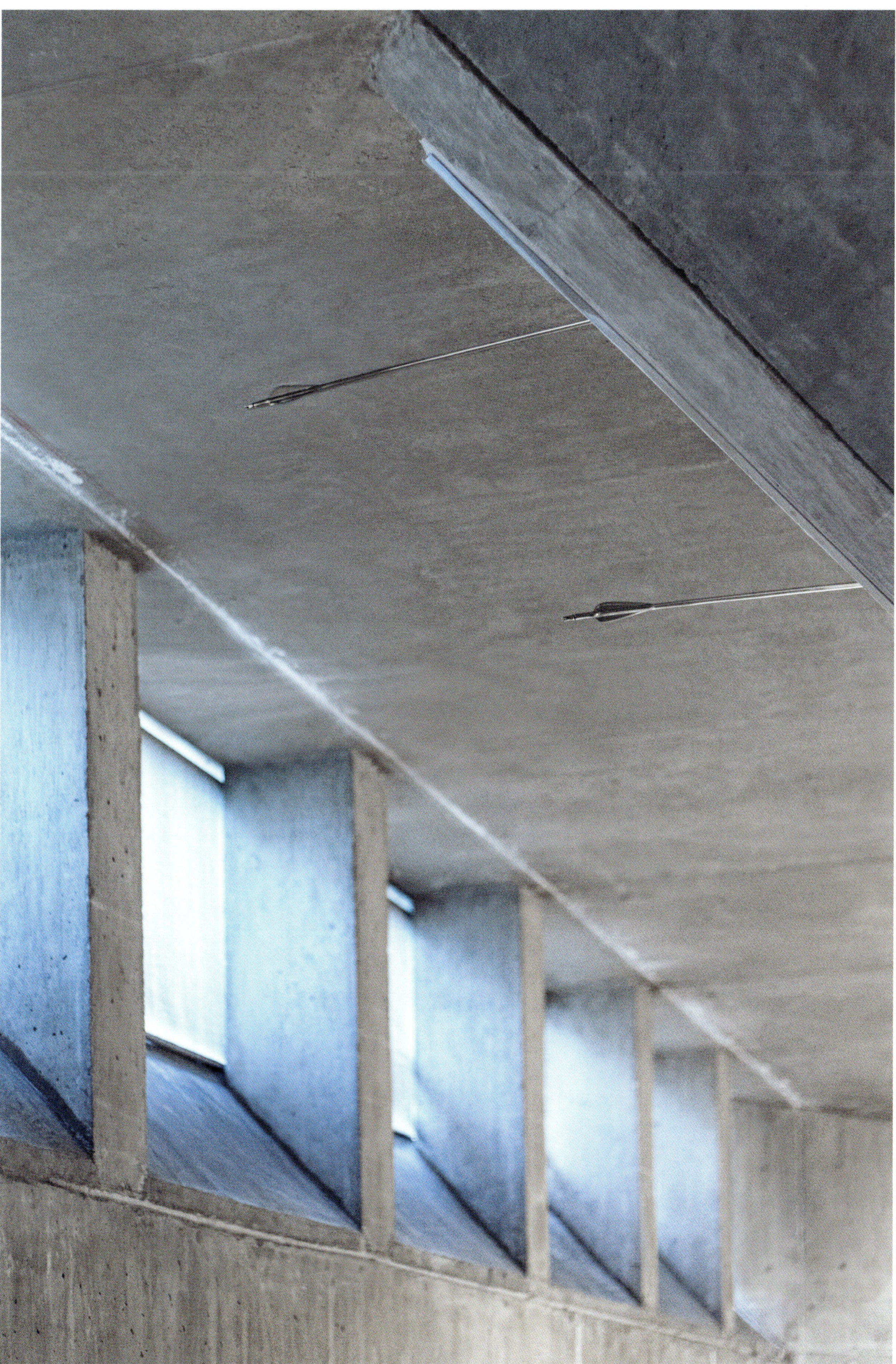

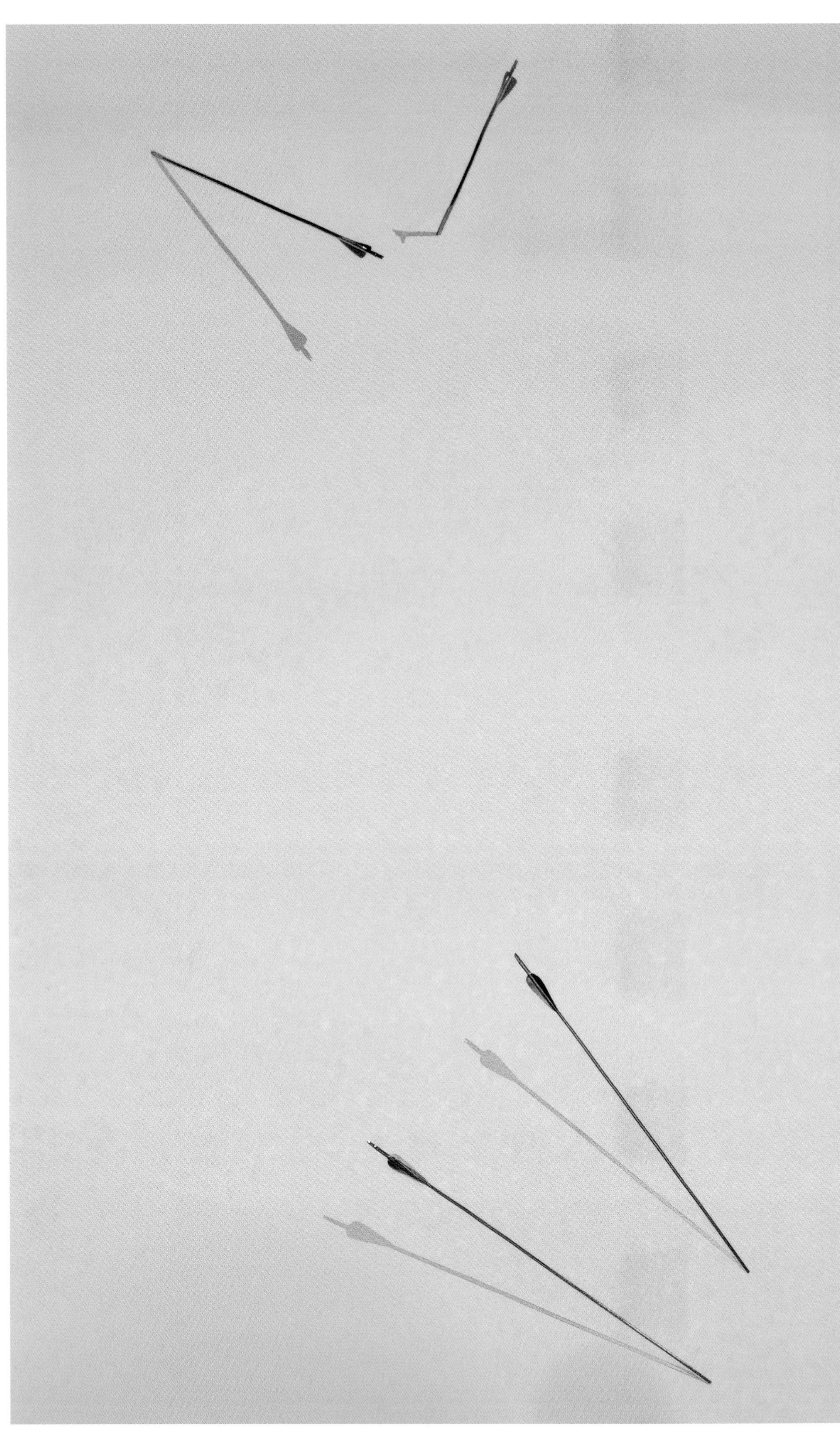

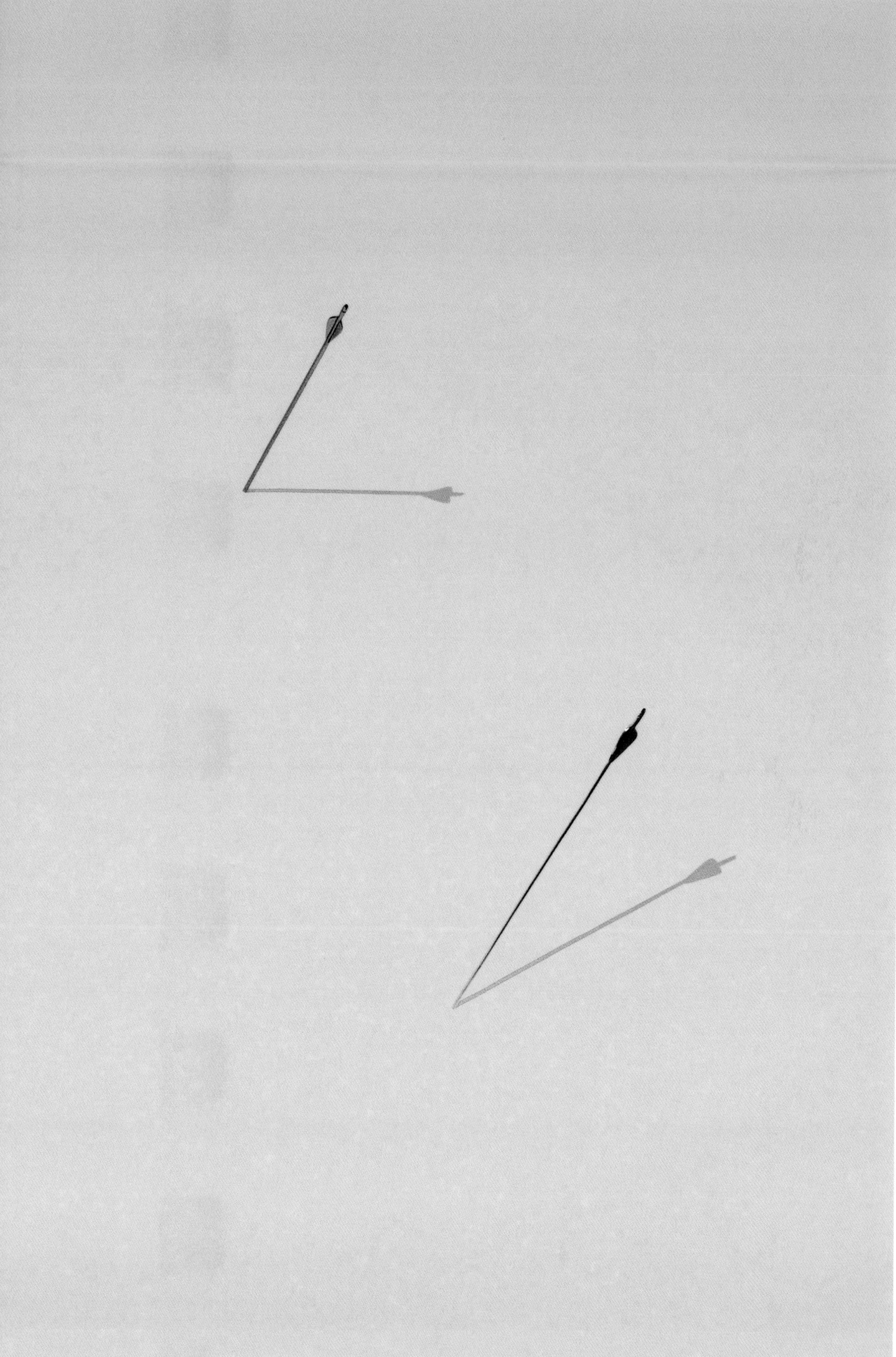

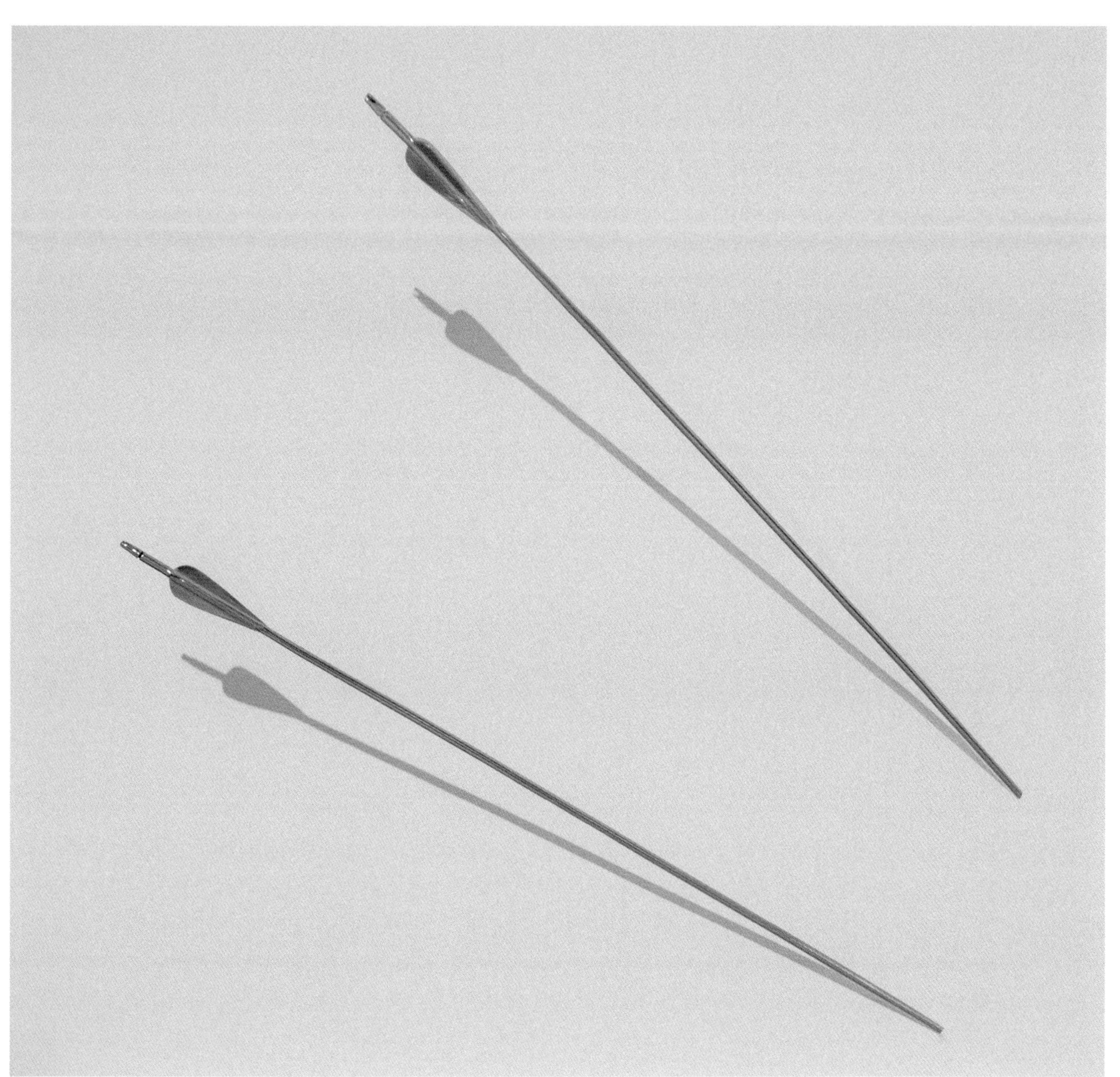

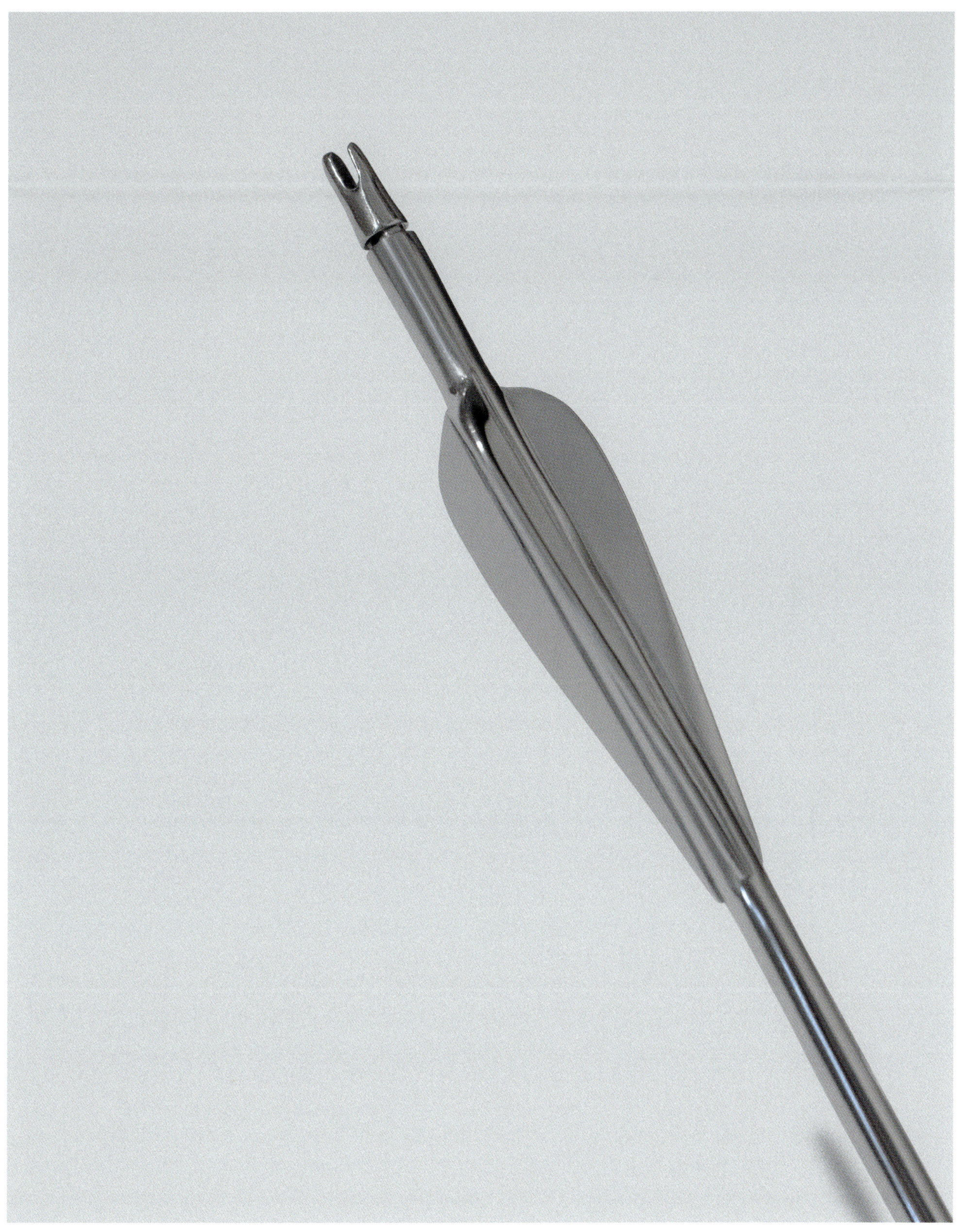

Afterword

With much excitement, Contemporary Arts Museum Houston (CAMH) presents *Olivia Erlanger: If Today Were Tomorrow*. This exhibition, curated by Patricia Restrepo and organized by CAMH, is Erlanger's first solo museum presentation in the United States. It culminates in newly commissioned work that brings together ten years of Erlanger's investigations into themes of domesticity, architectural interventions, and planetary life. We are honored to have Olivia Erlanger lead us into four newly built environments and sculptural landscapes in CAMH's subterranean Michael and Nina Zilkha gallery.

With this exhibition and catalogue, we are able to not only bring to fruition worlds imagined by Erlanger but also build connections through explorations of her work within this publication by acclaimed writer Chris Kraus, architect Lydia Kallipoliti, science fiction writer Mark von Schlegell, and CAMH Curator Patricia Restrepo. Each writer unpacks Erlanger's work from a different lens, adding more dimension to the exhibition.

CAMH is extremely grateful to our supporters, who have made this exhibition, catalogue, and related public programming possible. Presenting sponsorship has been generously provided by The Stolbun Family, whose support of CAMH and Olivia's work continues to enable artistic risk and discovery. The Andy Warhol Foundation for the Visual Arts provided additional and crucial support for the exhibition. This publication is supported by the William F. Stern Fund, which provides ongoing support to all CAMH publications.

CAMH exhibitions are made possible by the patrons, benefactors, and donors to CAMH's Major Exhibition Fund: Chinhui Juhn and Eddie Allen, Louise Jamail, Sissy and Denny Kempner, Dillon Kyle and Sam Lasseter, Cabrina and Steven Owsley, Elisa and Cris Pye, Beverly and Howard Robinson, Louisa Stude Sarofim, and Mary Ann and F. Carrington Weems Foundation.

CAMH is funded in part by the City of Houston through the Houston Arts Alliance and the Texas Commission on the Arts.

CAMH's exhibitions, catalogues, public programs and initiatives are above all team efforts, and this project could not have been realized without our remarkable staff: Lorielle Anderson, Sarah Atwood, Tim Barkley, Quincy Berry, Felice Cleveland, Naomi B. Crawford, Ryan N. Dennis, Kenya Evans, Marcelina Guerrero, Faye Hosein, Troy Jasmin, Autumn Johnson, Charonda Johnson, Kate Kendall, Melissa McDonnell Luján, Dawn J. Malone, Jack Morillo, Shavon Morris, Phillip Pyle, II, Joshua Pierre, Mike Reed, Michael Robinson, Jeff Shore, Mich Stevenson, and YET Torres, along with our Frequently Asked Questions and Visitor Engagement Teams.

Exhibitions and programs at CAMH would not be possible without our trustees' leadership, vision, and support, who enable us to bring extraordinary, thought-provoking art to Houston audiences and beyond.

I am exceptionally grateful to Patricia Restrepo for her advocacy for Erlanger's work and its timely signals. At a moment when it's increasingly difficult to feel grounded in place, Erlanger reframes our thinking of home and suburbia within a planetary context.

Most importantly, I extend a sincere thanks to Olivia Erlanger for entrusting us with bringing her otherworldly visions to fruition, for her infectious enthusiasm, and for her expansive ideas about how to share those visions with our audiences.

Hesse McGraw
Executive Director

List of Works

Appliance, 2024

HD video: color, sound; 17:01 minutes, courtesy the artist and Soft Opening, London.

Video credits

Writer and Director: Olivia Erlanger
Executive Producers: Jill Ferraro, Andrea Longacre-White, Seth Stolbun
Producers: Jill Ferraro, Ani Schroeter, a Paradise Production
Director of Photography: Mia Cioffi Henry
Production Design: Elysia Belilove
Makeup and Special Effects: Nina Carelli
Casting: Georgia Topley and Jo Harris
Costume Design: Natasha Hester
Editor: Anthony Miralles
Original Score: Alexis Georgopoulos

Starring
Sophie: Callie Hernandez
Crystal: Sasha Frolova

Featuring
Maya: Rose Mallick
Handyman: Jules Muir

Line Producer: Ani Schroeter
1st Assistant AD: Varya Rootwood
1st Assistant Camera: Summer Sierra
Gaffer: Ariel Horayoff
Grip: Steff Berek
Swing: Mad Collins
Sound Mixer: Ana Fernandez
Art Department Assistant: Lucy Krebsbach
Production Assistant: Charlotte Olver
Paradise Production Support: Mia Jarrett
Post Producer: Jill Ferraro
Post Production: Slip Studios
Visual Effects: Logan Triplett
Sound Design and Mix: Matthew Ericson
Slips Studios Post Producer: Helen Shope

Color: Company 3
Colorist: Kath Raisch
Colorist Producer: Jake Rioux

Titles and Graphics: Graphic Services
Storyboards: Thomas Slattery
Writing Support: Alex Butler
Story Support: Varya Rootwood

Special thanks:
Alexander Bondarenko, Jake Eleftheriou, Becky Elmquist, Crystal Fawn, Marko Gluhaich, Kat Herriman, Patricia Restrepo, and Carlos Valladares

Blue Sky, 2024

wire, flocking, foam, plaster, acrylic, aluminum, graphite, shoe polish, LED, and driver, courtesy the artist and Soft Opening, London.

Green Sky, 2024

balsa wood, resin, snow #15, plaster, foam, acrylic, aluminum, graphite, shoe polish, LED, and driver, courtesy the artist and Soft Opening, London.

Orange Sky, 2024

sand, flocking, foam, plaster, acrylic, aluminum, graphite, shoe polish, LED, and driver, courtesy the artist and Soft Opening, London.

Yellow Sky, 2024

rocks, flocking foam, plaster, courtesy the artist and Soft Opening, London.

Antimeridian, 2024

sand, aqua resin, aluminum, LEDs, drivers, and cord, courtesy the artist and Soft Opening, London.

Prime meridian, 2024

sand, aqua resin, aluminum, LEDs, drivers, and cord, courtesy the artist and Soft Opening, London.

Eros (When Night Was Last Dark), 2024

polished aluminum, courtesy the artist and Soft Opening, London.

Biographies

Olivia Erlanger (b. 1990, New York) works across sculpture, film, writing and performance to examine American dreams and delusions. Mining the myth of suburbia affords the artist a focus on the semiotics of the periphery, analyzing its architecture, infrastructures, and ecosystems. Erlanger was awarded the 2024 International Sculpture Prize by Fondazione Henraux. Selected recent exhibitions include *If Today Were Tomorrow* at Contemporary Arts Museum Houston, Texas (2024, solo); *Humour in the Water Coolant* at ICA London, UK (2024, performance); *Appliance* at Kunstverein Gartenhaus, Vienna (2022, solo); *Nonmemory* at Hauser Wirth, Los Angeles (2023), *Dream Journal* at Company Gallery, New York (2023); *On Failure*, at Soft Opening, London (2023) and *Shell* at Del Vaz Projects, Los Angeles (2022). Erlanger is the author of *Appliance* (Wild Seeds, 2022) and the co-author of *Garage* (MIT Press, 2018) with architect Luis Ortega Govela. Her writing has appeared in publications including *Tank Magazine*, *PIN UP*, *Flash Art*, and *Harvard Design Magazine*. Her work is in the collections of the Dallas Museum of Art, Texas; KADIST, San Francisco and X Museum, Shanghai. The artist lives and works in New York.

Lydia Kallipoliti is an architect, engineer, and scholar whose research focuses on the intersections between architecture, technology, and environmental politics. She is an associate professor at the Cooper Union in New York and the author of *The Architecture of Closed Worlds* (2018) and *Histories of Ecological Design* (2024). Her work has been awarded, published, and exhibited widely including at the Venice Biennale, the Istanbul Design Biennial, the Shenzhen Biennial, the Oslo Architecture Triennale, the Lisbon Triennale, the Royal Academy of British Architects, Storefront for Art and Architecture in New York, and the Design Museum, London. She is the principal of ANA*cycle* research think tank and head co-curator of the 2022 Tallinn Architecture Biennale. Kallipoliti holds a diploma in architecture and engineering from AUTh in Greece, a master of science in architecture studies (SMArchS) from MIT and a PhD from Princeton University.

Chris Kraus is a writer and critic. Her novels include *Torpor* (2006), *Summer of Hate* (2012), and the forthcoming *The Four Spent the Day Together*. She has written extensively about contemporary visual art and artists' projects in the US, Mexico, and Europe in her books *Social Practices* (2018), *Video Green* (2004), and *Where Art Belongs* (2011). A former Guggenheim fellow, Chris lives in Los Angeles and teaches writing at ArtCenter College. Alongside Hedi El Kholti she is a co-editor of the independent press Semiotext(e).

Patricia Restrepo is the curator at CAMH, where she has worked since 2014. Fostering exhibitions as laboratories, her curatorial work focuses on championing new commissions, the generative potential latent in archives, and interdisciplinary dialogue. Restrepo is co-curating a mid-career survey of Vincent Valdez with Denise Markonish at Massachusetts Museum of Contemporary Art (MASS MoCA). She co-curated *Slowed and Throwed: Records of the City through Mutated Lenses* (2020 and 2021), a transhistorical exhibition orbiting around DJ Screw's process of material manipulation and featuring artists including Jamal Cyrus, Shana Hoehn, Tomashi Jackson, and Sondra Perry. She curated *Will Boone: The Highway Hex* (2019–20), the artist's first solo museum exhibition. Restrepo explored CAMHs seventy-year history of championing performances by artists such as Laurie Anderson, James Lee Byars, Joan Jonas, Autumn Knight, and Robert Rauschenberg in *Stage Environment: You Didn't Have to Be There* (2018). She coordinated the museum's presentations of *Troy Montes Michie: Rock of Eye* (2022) and *The Dirty South: Contemporary Art, Material Culture, and the Sonic Impulse* (2021–22). Restrepo has managed CAMH's artist-centric publications and orchestrated their digitization to increase public accessibility. She previously worked at international art institutions including the Institute of Aesthetic Research (Instituto de Investigaciones Estéticas) of the Universidad Nacional Autónoma de México (UNAM). Restrepo is a PhD candidate in art history at Rice University and holds a master's degree from Katholieke Universiteit Leuven, Belgium and bachelor's degrees from Rice University.

Mark von Schlegell's science fiction has been crossing into art writing since the 1990s. Semiotext(e) has published the System Series novels since 2005 when *Venusia* (2005) was honor's-listed for the Otherwise Prize in science fiction. *Mercury Station* (2009) and *Sundogz* (2015) followed. *New Dystopia* (Sternberg Press, 2011) served as a catalogue for the large-scale exhibition *Dystopia* at CAPC, Bordeaux. Shorter fiction from art catalogues have been gathered in *Ickles, Etc.* (Sternberg Press, 2016) and *Ickles, Ad Infinitum* (Inpatient Press, 2019). He has taught literature and art in the US at NYU, CalArts, the San Francisco Art Institute, and in Germany at the Staedelschule, Frankfurt.

This book is published in conjunction with
the exhibition

Olivia Erlanger
If Today Were Tomorrow

Contemporary Arts Museum Houston (CAMH)
April 20–October 27, 2024

Presenting sponsorship for
Olivia Erlanger: If Today Were Tomorrow
is provided by The Stolbun Family and
The Andy Warhol Foundation for the Visual Arts.

CAMH exhibitions are made possible by the
patrons, benefactors, and donors to CAMH's Major
Exhibition Fund: Chinhui Juhn and Eddie Allen,
Louise Jamail, Sissy and Denny Kempner, Dillon
Kyle and Sam Lasseter, Cabrina and Steven
Owsley, Elisa and Cris Pye, Beverly and Howard
Robinson, Louisa Stude Sarofim, and Mary Ann and
F. Carrington Weems Foundation.

CAMH is funded in part by the City of Houston
through the Houston Arts Alliance and the Texas
Commission on the Arts.

Editor:
Patricia Restrepo

CAMH project management:
Marcelina Guerrero

Editorial management:
Kassandra Nakas

Copyediting:
Isabella Ritchie

Graphic design:
Kerstin Riedel, Berlin

Photography:
Sean Fleming: pp. 8–27, 66–71, 77–84, 87–88,
91–92, 95–96, 99, 107–113, 125–133
Daniel Terna: pp. 85, 89, 93, 97, 115, 117
Lucy Krebsbach: pp. 49–51

Production:
Alise Ausmane

Reproductions:
LONGO AG, Bozen / Bolzano

Printing and Binding:
Livonia Print, Riga

Paper:
Magno Satin, 150 g/m²

Published by
Hatje Cantz Verlag GmbH
Mommsenstraße 27
10629 Berlin
Germany
www.hatjecantz.com
A Ganske Publishing Group Company

ISBN 978-3-7757-5741-6

Printed in Latvia

Cover illustration:
Olivia Erlanger, *Appliance* (video still), 2024
HD video: color, sound, 17:01 mins
Courtesy the artist and Soft Opening, London

Frontispiece:
Olivia Erlanger, *Antimeridian*, 2024
Aquaresin, aluminum, LEDs, drivers, and cord,
dimensions variable
Courtesy the artist and Soft Opening, London
Photo: Daniel Terna

Back cover illustration:
Olivia Erlanger, *Yellow Sky*, 2024
Rocks, flocking foam, plaster
Courtesy the artist and Soft Opening, London
Photo: Daniel Terna

Produced in collaboration with

**Contemporary
Arts Museum
Houston**